Friedrich Dürrenmatt

Friedrich Dürrenmatt

Selected Writings

Volume 3 · Essays

Translated by Joel Agee

Edited by Kenneth J. Northcott

With an Introduction by Brian Evenson

THE UNIVERSITY OF CHICAGO PRESS *Chicago & London*

Publication of this work was made possible through the generous support of
Pro Helvetia, the Arts Council of Switzerland
www.prohelvetia.ch

Complete publication history appears on page 203.

The University of Chicago Press, Chicago 60637
The University of Chicago Press, Ltd., London
© 2006 by The University of Chicago
English language translation by Joel Agee © 2006 by Diogenes Verlag AG, Zürich
Der Winterkrieg in Tibet © 1981 and 1990 by Diogenes Verlag AG, Zürich. *Die Brücke, Auto—und
Eisenbahnstaaten, Das Hirn, Vinter* © 1990 by Diogenes Verlag AG, Zürich. *Die Schweiz—ein Gefängis*
© 1991 by Diogenes Verlag AG, Zürich. *Monstervortrag, Sätze aus Amerika, Nachwort zum Nachwort*
© 1986 by Diogenes Verlag AG, Zürich. *Theaterprobleme* © 1985 by Diogenes Verlag AG, Zürich.
Published 2006
Paperback edition 2024
Printed in the United States of America

33 32 31 30 29 28 27 26 25 24   1 2 3 4 5

ISBN-13: 978-0-226-17432-7 (cloth)
ISBN-13: 978-0-226-83832-8 (paper)
ISBN-13: 978-0-226-53121-2 (e-book)
DOI: https://doi.org/10.7208/chicago/9780226531212.001.0001

Library of Congress Cataloging-in-Publication Data

Dürrenmatt, Friedrich.
  [Selections. English 2006]
  Friedrich Dürrenmatt : selected writings / translated by Joel Agee.
    v. cm.
  Contents: v. 1. Plays / edited and with an introduction by Kenneth J. Northcott—v. 2. Fictions /
edited and with an introduction by Theodore Ziolkowski—v. 3. Essays / edited by Kenneth J.
Northcott ; with an introduction by Brian Evenson.
    ISBN 0-226-17426-3 (v. 1 : cloth : alk. paper)—ISBN 0-226-17429-8 (v. 2 : cloth : alk. paper)—
ISBN 0-226-17432-8 (v. 3 : cloth : alk. paper)
    1. Dürrenmatt, Friedrich—Translations into English.   I. Agee, Joel.   II. Northcott, Kenneth J.
III. Ziolkowski, Theodore.   IV. Evenson, Brian, 1966–   V. Title.
PT2607.U493A6 2006
832'.914—dc22

                                                                                                        2006013388

⊗ This paper meets the requirements of ANSI/NISO Z39.48-1992 (Permanence of Paper).

Contents

Introduction   vii
by Brian Evenson

The Winter War in Tibet   1

The Bridge   47

Switzerland—A Prison   63
A Speech for Václav Havel

Monster Lecture on Justice   73
and Law, with a Helvetian
Interlude
A Minor Dramaturgy of Politics

Sentences from America   115

Theater Problems   137

Automobile and Railroad   163
Nations

The Brain   171

Vinter   189

The Traveler's Standpoint   199

Introduction

Brian Evenson

In America, Swiss writer Friedrich Dürrenmatt is known primarily as a dramatist, as the author of plays such as *The Visit, The Physicists*, and *The Meteor*. His plays show him to have been influenced by, but not beholden to, Bertolt Brecht, Georg Büchner, August Strindberg, Thornton Wilder, expressionism, and absurdist drama, among other things. Indeed, Dürrenmatt's drama draws from a number of distinct traditions without ever committing fully to any given one.

Dürrenmatt is secondarily known as a writer of both serious and detective fiction, often producing work that combines generic and literary concerns. One of his novels that straddles the line between genre and serious fiction, *The Pledge* (1958), was recently made into a movie. *The Pledge* is perhaps Dürrenmatt's most impressive prose work. It has many of the satisfactions of a detective novel, but in addition it avoids the easy complacencies of the genre: in it, the detective figure concocts an impressive and clever scheme for trapping a child killer, but chance gets in the way, making a neat resolution impossible. Subtitled by Dürrenmatt "Requiem for the Detective Novel," *The Pledge* appropriates the form for literary effect. The result is a groundbreaking genre bender that puts Dürrenmatt on par with Alain Robbe-Grillet (*The Erasers*) and anticipates the work of Paul Auster (*The New York Trilogy*) as well as the neo-noir novels of writers such as Laird Hunt (*The Impossibly*), Marie Redonnet (*Nevermore*), and Jonathan Lethem (*Motherless Brooklyn*), not to mention David Lynch's and Dennis Potter's work in film.

I begin with Dürrenmatt's drama and fiction because the generic flexibility Dürrenmatt uses masterfully in both forms shapes his essays as well. Just as his drama and fiction resist generic strictures and structures, so too do his essays refuse to fit neatly into traditional essay forms. They draw on other forms, establishing an odd relationship to philosophy and fiction.

These are not the polite essays that fit snugly into the acceptable limitations of the form; instead, these are essays that refuse, in some very basic ways, to be treated as essays.

In America, Dürrenmatt is virtually unknown as an essayist. Only two of the ten essays gathered in this volume have had much circulation here. "Theater Problems" was initially published in America as "Problems of the Theater" in a volume of four Dürrenmatt plays by Grove Press in 1965; it was reprinted in 1982 in *Friedrich Dürrenmatt: Plays and Essays*. Perhaps not surprisingly, his most published essay is also the essay most focused on the theater, the essay most obviously subsidiary to his dramatic art. The other previously available essay, "Monster Lecture on Justice and Law," is a long meditation on the relation of justice and mercy. It is perhaps Dürrenmatt's most comprehensive attempt to work up a synthesis of political notions and philosophical ideas, but it has received a great deal less attention than "Theater Problems."

The essays gathered here span the majority of Dürrenmatt's writing life. "Theater Problems" is the oldest essay in the volume, written in 1954 and 1955, and the latest essays in the volume were published in 1990, the year of Dürrenmatt's death. Some of the essays are seemingly informal, as if transcribed versions of spoken lectures (which in fact several were), and come across as almost effortless meditations. Others, such as "The Winter War in Tibet," seem more akin to short stories than to essays, and recall some of Alexander Kluge's texts' ability to vacillate between the fictional and the real. Sometimes Dürrenmatt uses the essay to work through philosophical and poetic concerns that come to full fruition in his drama or his stories. Sometimes as well the political concerns that are submerged but always present in his drama are allowed to come to the fore. Even those essays that initially seem to be preceding in a straightforward fashion undergo odd and startling swerves as they approach their conclusion, with Dürrenmatt in their last few pages radically transforming our sense of the essay as a whole. For Dürrenmatt the essay form is much more fluid and open-ended than it is for most writers; indeed, he is one of the few real innovators of essayistic form.

Before speaking in some detail about the essays themselves it makes sense to speak of the original context from which half of these essays came. In 1981, Dürrenmatt published *Stoffe I–III* (translatable as "subject matter" or "material"), a single volume consisting of three sections: *The Winter War in Tibet* (*Der Winterkrieg in Tibet*), *Lunar Eclipse* (*Mondfinsternis*), and *The Rebel* (*Der Rebell*). Only the first of these is included here, and only part of that— "The Winter War in Tibet" is the longest and most extended narrative from a series of very different texts gathered in the section of the same name. Almost a decade later, in 1990, Dürrenmatt published a second *Stoffe* volume: *Turmbau: Stoffe IV–IX* (*Tower Building: Subject Matter IV–IX*; the tower in question is the Tower of Babel). This volume consists of six chapters, with portions of four of them reproduced here as "The Bridge," "Automobile and Railroad Nations," "The Brain," and "Vinter."

Initially this seems straightforward enough: essays and narratives taken from two volumes that gathered together essays and narratives. Where it becomes complicated is in Dürrenmatt's own sense of what *Stoffe* amounted to. Dürrenmatt considered *Stoffe* to be an autobiography of sorts, but an autobiography that has really very little interest in portraying Dürrenmatt's actual life. As Roger Crockett suggests, Dürrenmatt "considers his life as too privileged, measured against the fate of millions, to be worthy of narration. When he nevertheless writes about himself, it is not to give the history of his life, but rather the history of his subject matter—in particular that which he has never published. 'By outlining these especially, I am groping my way back in the development of my thought processes as though following an animal's track, and that which I scare up from the brush is my life.'"*

In other words, *Stoffe* is an autobiography that is hardly an autobiography at all. All the autobiographical elements of the two volumes are there not for their own sake, not as a record of Dürrenmatt's life, but as a provocation, as an attempt to use autobiography to get somewhere else, to understand the creative process. The narratives that are generated from this transformative process are thus sometimes quite a great distance from actual life; indeed, quite often they read like pieces of fiction.† But it is a fiction that, in the original German context, makes promises of connection between life and autobiography, which has been gathered together as a way of defining and presenting Dürrenmatt himself. It is this idiosyncrasy, above all, that helps to explain the oddness of many of these essays.

But, at the same time, it is hardly a satisfying explanation to state that the reason some of these essays read more like stories than essays is that they were originally part of an autobiography that didn't read like an

---

*Roger A. Crockett, *Understanding Friedrich Dürrenmatt* (Columbia: University of South Carolina Press, 1998). The quotation from Dürrenmatt at the end of the Crockett passage is from Dürrenmatt's *Gessamelte Werke in sieben Bänden*, volume 6, page 11. Crockett is the only Dürrenmatt critic writing in English to speak in any kind of detail about *Stoffe*.

†Moreover, in the table of contents of *Stoffe*, "The Winter War in Tibet" is referred to as an "Erzählung," the literary term for a story.

autobiography and wasn't exactly autobiographical in purpose. Such a statement makes it feel as if one is trapped in Dürrenmatt's play *The Physicists*, a play in which actual physicists are pretending to be madmen who are pretending to be historical physicists. Nothing is what it seems. You might say that these essays are pretending to be stories that are in turn pretending to be biography that are in turn pretending to be essays.

The choice of organization of the ten essays gathered in this volume in Joel Agee's masterful translation is somewhat eccentric, as is perhaps most appropriate to essays of this type, which are eccentrically composed as well. They are not arranged chronologically, or alphabetically, or even thematically; instead one moves from an essay that relies on fiction to a more philosophical essay to a speech to notes, and back and forth, the resulting order offering a quite satisfyingly varied read, which is perhaps best approached here in the specifics of individual essays rather than through generalities.

The Winter War in Tibet

The longest essay in the volume, "The Winter War in Tibet" is also the most complex. From the essay's beginning, which declares, "I am a soldier of fortune and I am proud of it," the reader is forced to ask, "To what extent can this really be classified as an essay?" The action is dramatic; the situation described is postapocalyptic and fictionalized. The piece is narrated by a soldier of fortune who first fights in the mountains of Tibet and then, after the destruction of the world by nuclear war, continues to fight in a labyrinth of tunnels found underneath the mountains. He fights "in the name of the Administration" against "the enemy." As the narrative progresses, neither he nor anyone else seems quite sure why they are still fighting or even who is fighting, and since both sides wear the same white uniforms anyone is a potential enemy. While belief in God or in an immortal soul is optional, "doubt in the existence of an enemy must never be allowed to arise in the mind of a mercenary, for the simple reason that it will kill him." One cannot ask who the enemy is, for to do so is to sow the seeds of doubt. As the war continues, its parameters become increasingly vague until all any mercenary has to hold on to is the hope that there might be some meaning behind the war. Mercenaries, to stay sane, begin to imagine what this meaning might be, and then begin to insist on the reality of their imaginings. Soon, in addition to fighting the enemy, the mercenaries are at odds with one another, at odds with those who see the war as having a different meaning.

Mercenaries form sects and murder other mercenaries. Even the mercenary who narrates this tale owes his rise in power to the killing of his own commander when the latter shows doubts about the existence of an actual enemy.

Soon, wounded, the narrator has been transformed into a sort of wheelchair-bound cyborg equipped with a prosthetic machine-gun arm. With a steel stylus on his other prosthetic arm he has been scratching his thoughts into the rock walls of the tunnels below the mountains. He writes, trying to describe the nature of the Administration. He quickly rejects, in his search for understanding, the laws of dialectical materialism and causality; he sees justice and injustice as "merely aesthetic concepts." Instead, he chooses to understand the state in terms of natural laws, comparing the life of the state to the stages of a sun's life.

As the piece reaches its end, the narrator finds himself alone in the dark, his wheelchair gone, dragging himself along the wall. It is only then that he can ask himself who the enemy is, and his imagination offers him an updated version of Plato's cave: the enemy are the shadows on a cave wall, and ricocheting bullets fired at them become their attacks. What has seemed throughout the narrative to be an exterior space is now revealed as potentially an interior or allegorical one.

The piece recalls two other German-language postapocalyptic works: Alexander Kluge's *Learning Process with a Deadly Outcome* and Arno Schmidt's *Afternoon of a Faun*. It is both a scathing indictment of the arms race and a strong statement about the meaninglessness of war, but the political opinions it offers are couched in fictionalized experience. In its exploration of tunnels, the narrative toys with the notion of the labyrinth that will surface in some of Dürrenmatt's other work. His reworking of Plato's notion of the cave is not dissimilar to José Saramago's reworking of Plato in *The Cave*. Indeed, Dürrenmatt's attitudes in general are not unlike Saramago's, with both writers setting themselves up in an adversarial relation to established orders—Saramago to Catholicism and the Portuguese government, Dürrenmatt to Switzerland and abstract systems.

At one point the narrator suggests, "no matter what a human being describes, he always describes himself." Perhaps this sentence can be seen as an indication of why Dürrenmatt included "The Winter War in Tibet" as part of his ostensible autobiography *Stoffe*: there is no writing, according to this rubric, that is not biographical. Certainly when taken in context of the other very different pieces that originally surrounded it in *Stoffe*, this appears to be the case. At the same time, the narrator also suggests that "Without taking the risk of fictions, the path to knowledge cannot be trodden."

Perhaps, then, "The Winter War in Tibet" can be read as an essay about fiction's importance to knowledge. At the end of "The Winter War in Tibet," Dürrenmatt allows a second narrative voice, sporadically present elsewhere in the text, to call into question all that has come before, suggesting the possibility that the narrative has not been entirely what it seems, and calling into question not only the narrative but, like Plato, what we ourselves perceive as the real world.

The Bridge

Taken from the second volume of *Stoffe*, "The Bridge" provides a series of permutations for a given situation involving a young student named F.D. (the initials obviously are Dürrenmatt's own) who staggers drunk across Kirchenfeld Bridge on October 15, 1943, as a meteor falls. Depending on minor changes and the role of chance, F.D. either is struck by the meteor, is narrowly missed by it, doesn't notice it at all, and so on. Indeed, Dürrenmatt offers thirteen different F.D.s, using the circumstances and development of each as a way of thinking not only about the relationship of chance to events but also about what he calls "the dialectic of belief," about the way in which reason and truth are connected to belief. The essay might be compared to Robert Coover's short fiction, particularly "The Elevator" and "The Babysitter," in which Coover offers several sometimes mutually exclusive versions of the same event.

However, what begins as an exercise in permutation becomes near the end something entirely different. In the last pages of the essay, Dürrenmatt works his way through possible F.D.s to a discussion of the arms race, its logic and illogic, sliding from the possibilities for a given individual to the fear that motivates armament and rearmament. By looking at thirteen versions of his fictionalized self, Dürrenmatt develops an interplay between reason and belief so as to apply this interplay to something completely separate from him. His conclusions come unexpectedly as he works through one seemingly theoretical problem only to arrive at a larger tangible one.

In a sense, then, the majority of the story is a setup for the last two pages. Yet, at the same time, that setup, because of the exuberance with which Dürrenmatt approaches it, becomes a good part of the point of the essay. On the one hand we are lulled by it, engaged in it in a way that allows his later argument to get beneath our defenses in a way it might not otherwise. On the other hand, the different permutations of F.D. are finally a great deal more memorable than the brief political comments that they spark.

Switzerland—A Prison: A Speech for Václav Havel

"Switzerland—A Prison" was a speech originally delivered in 1990 for Václav Havel, the absurdist dramatist who had become the president of Czechoslovakia. It is written directly to Havel, as if a letter, and in its salutation appeals to him first as "Dear Mr. President" and then as "Dear Václav Havel." Dürrenmatt used the occasion of Havel's visit to Switzerland to question the politics of his own nation. He quotes Havel's notions of what an ideal republic should be—"A republic of universally educated men and women"— and then goes on to suggest that many Swiss believe that Havel's dream republic is precisely the place where they live. Not surprisingly, considering the adversarial relation Dürrenmatt always had to his own country,* Dürrenmatt disagrees. As he says in his "Monster Lecture on Justice and Law," "I love the Swiss and I love having it out with them." For Dürrenmatt, the Swiss, through their neutrality, have taken refuge in a prison: "Because there was mayhem outside the prison and because only in prison can they be safe from attack, the Swiss feel free, freer than other people, free as prisoners in the prison of their neutrality. There is only one problem for this prison, namely that of proving that it is not a prison but a bulwark of freedom, since seen from outside, a prison is a prison."

A cross between a letter and a polemical address, "Switzerland—A Prison" was delivered in the year of Dürrenmatt's own death. Despite some of its rhetorical strengths, it is in some respects the most strident of Dürrenmatt's essays. It is less provocative and apropos for readers in America— whose foreign politics have tended toward overt meddling and control rather than neutrality—than for the Swiss.

Monster Lecture on Justice and Law, with a Helvetian Interlude

"Monster Lecture on Justice and Law, with a Helvetian Interlude," subtitled "A Minor Dramaturgy of Politics," was, like "Switzerland—A Prison," originally a spoken address that Dürrenmatt later expanded. It was first delivered

---

*Take, for instance, the cutting references to Swiss culture and bureaucracy in his play *Hercules and the Augean Stables*.

in 1968 at the invitation of members of the University of Mainz's law faculty, and was published in expanded form the following year. Dürrenmatt begins with a parable in which the Prophet Mohammad hides on a hill to observe what initially appears to be an amoral sequence of events, a sequence that, with Allah's guidance, he comes to realize is a moral sequence in which justice is meted out evenly and fairly. As Dürrenmatt continues, however, he begins to put pressure on the story, replacing certain elements, reconsidering how the story changes when, for instance, one replaces the Prophet Mohammad with a scientist. Indeed, as he tries to make the parable relevant to the contemporary world, more and more changes are needed; what seems relevant and even obvious to the Prophet simply won't fly in either a communist or a capitalist society.

Dürrenmatt goes on to critique both communism and capitalism as respectively a "good shepherd game" and a "wolf game." In the most basic version of the capitalist wolf game, people prey on other people just as wolves prey on lambs. As society develops and begins to enforce rules and codes of behavior, the game becomes more complex, with physical prey being replaced by potential profit and property. In the communist good shepherd game, on the other hand, the assumption is not that man is an "intelligent wolf" but rather an "intelligent lamb" and will act in harmony with other humans. Where it becomes complicated for Dürrenmatt is in the way both games eventually end up employing each other's moves, and in the way that "in both games the state has become too powerful." Dürrenmatt takes both communism and capitalism to task for what he sees as their institutionalized and ratified hypocrisy. Indeed, through either system individuals become paradoxical, strung between two conceptions of themselves that do not coincide, the first concept moving from society to the individual, the second from the individual to society. "Ideologies," suggests Dürrenmatt, "are the cosmetics of power," and desire for power is ultimately the basis of both games.

Sentences from America

"Sentences from America" was originally published in 1970 as a very short volume. It consists of ninety-one numbered sections that chronicle a trip Dürrenmatt took to this side of the Atlantic to accept an honorary doctorate at Temple University. It chronicles his travels in the continental United States, Puerto Rico, Mexico, and Jamaica.

About two-thirds of the way through, the essay undergoes a shift, largely forgoing local color and descriptions of the trip (including Dürrenmatt's loss of all his money in Puerto Rico) in favor of a comparison of the Soviet Union to the United States, in which he gives his impressions of both places. The United States, he suggests, "could be compared with imperial Rome when it had become a world power but found itself embroiled in increasingly difficult domestic problems, while the Soviet Union is looking more and more like the Eastern Roman Empire, which was a totalistic state and installed Christianity as an ideology." He speaks of America's glorification of the gangster, but suggests at the same time that America is "increasingly susceptible to every kind of fascism." At once a travel book and a political essay, "Sentences from America" weaves elements of both genres together to create an original and provocative whole.

Theater Problems

"Theater Problems" is based on a lecture Dürrenmatt first gave in 1954. In it, he talks quite candidly and openly about the role of the playwright, speaks about his method, critiques Bertolt Brecht (whose theory and plays, he feels, don't always correspond—and the plays are better for that), speaks of contemporary theater, and suggests that "art in our day consists of experiments, no more and no less, like today's world itself." Dürrenmatt defines himself as a playwright who is not a "representative of any particular movement in the theater, or any particular dramatic technique." He is not "an existentialist, a nihilist, an expressionist, or an ironist, or whatever labels get stuck on the jars in which literary critics keep their preserves." For Dürrenmatt, the stage is "not a field for theories" but rather "an instrument." On contemporary theatrical performance, Dürrenmatt is scathing. He criticizes it for being in large part a museum in which past plays are displayed, with actors functioning as "civil servants." He also speaks in passing about some of his own plays and the problems he saw them posing as they were being written, and speaks at some length about *An Angel Comes to Babylon*, his most recent stage play at the time.

The last few lines of the piece are unexpected, with Dürrenmatt coming down in praise of lightness and considering the possibility of making literature where it is least expected and least noticed, but apart from that "Theater Problems" is the most straightforward, academic, and traditional of the essays gathered in this volume. Though written before many of Dürrenmatt's most masterful plays, "Theater Problems" remains Dürrenmatt's most sustained and comprehensive statement on theater; it does a great deal to illuminate the drama collected in volume 1.

Automobile and Railroad Nations

"Automobile and Railroad Nations," like "The Winter War in Tibet," has the liveliness of a work of fiction. It functions as a carefully elaborated conceit. Beginning with the statement "Political systems differ primarily depending on whether they are subject to the patronage of freedom or of justice," the essay picks up some of the ideas of Dürrenmatt's "Monster Lecture," approaching capitalism and communism through a set of metaphors. For Dürrenmatt, a political system that holds freedom to be its central principle (capitalism) can be compared to a social order that opts for the automobile, while one that holds justice as its central principle (communism) is like a society that holds "that only the railroad is just." "Automobile and Railroad Nations" is a tale of two states, one of which allows only automobiles and the other only railroads. Through the story Dürrenmatt pursues the difficulty of having a society that enforces only one sort of transportation, in the end suggesting that automobiles and trains, like justice and freedom, function best together, not mutually exclusively.

Though there is a point to be made—namely, that "Freedom and justice are complementary concepts" infeasible without one another—the satisfactions of the essay come in Dürrenmatt's ability to pursue the metaphor in a lively and convincing fashion to its farthest possible extension, to create from that metaphor an absurd but fully rendered world.

The Brain

"The Brain" poses a problem: what can a pure brain without the stimulus of an external world teach itself to think? Like the end of "The Winter War in Tibet," which proposes a notion of the world analogous to Plato's cave, "The Brain" proposes an imagined world, one that, upon reflection, is meant to inform notions of our own world.

With great care, Dürrenmatt attempts to consider the way in which a brain under such conditions would develop, what it might, eventually, become capable of envisioning. At first the brain can only feel itself. Since it contains nothing, it will "feel that it feels nothing." "In the beginning," suggests Dürrenmatt, rewriting the opening lines of Genesis, "there will be dread, pure horror." But gradually, from this horror, thought itself will begin to develop and alongside it a notion of time. Very slowly, everything else will fall into place.

Nine-tenths of the piece focuses on this "everything else," offering a meticulous playing out of the details of the brain's imagining, with the brain finally envisioning all of human history up to the twentieth century. Indeed, the brain seems poised to reimagine all of human history, to be able to reproduce all that reality has given us. Yet, in the last few pages there is a sudden swerve, toward considering the unthinkable, toward what is unthinkable—the unthinkable in this case being very specific twentieth-century atrocities. "It is unthinkable," suggests Dürrenmatt, "and what is unthinkable is also not possible, because it makes no sense." He thus leaves the reader in a paradoxical dilemma; if "the foundation of [our world's] being as it is or as it could be, lies or would lie within us, regardless of whether we are real or imagined," then how can such things even exist?

Vinter

"Vinter" is a prose narrative very similar to a story, and indeed is often referred to in criticism as a work of fiction. It concerns a wanted man named Vinter who journeys to the capital of his country on assignment to kill the prime minister. Composed of short simple sentences, the piece resembles Dürrenmatt's early story "The Sausage." Although published late in Dürrenmatt's career it has the feel of his early fiction, and it was perhaps a reworking of a narrative that had been earlier abandoned.

After shooting the prime minister, Vinter hides out in a basement full of rats, escaping upstairs and lapsing into unconsciousness. When he awakens he finds himself in silk pajamas in a nice bed. Going onto the street he asks to be arrested for shooting the prime minister, but nobody will listen to him. Instead, he is treated as if he were a prince. What began for him as merely a "business arrangement" quickly becomes something else. Even though wanted posters with his picture are hanging everywhere and even though he confesses to the crime, he is allowed to go free. Eventually he learns that the population at large has paid for him to kill the prime minister. "Vinter" is absurd, with Vinter trapped in a world he struggles to understand, rewarded when he should be punished, trapped in the belief that everyone understands what is going on except for him. In the end, the frustration of the experience destroys him. As an absurdist work, of all the essays this one comes closest to capturing the feel of some of Dürrenmatt's drama.

The Traveler's Standpoint

The volume begins with the longest essay and ends with the shortest. The final essay gathered here is "The Traveler's Standpoint," a short essay that originally was included as a portion of an afterword to Dürrenmatt's late and not-yet-translated play *The Collaborator* (*Der Mitmacher*). The collaborator of the play is "Doc," a doctor who has invented a method of dissolving corpses so that they can be disposed of as sewage. He works for a syndicate of gangsters run by "Boss," and he is paid little: he does the job both for the pleasure he receives from his own invention and out of a kind of personal despair. He is in love with Ann, who turns out to be Boss's mistress. When "Cop" takes over the syndicate and gives Boss a raise, Boss gets jealous and kills Ann. By the end of the play Ann, Boss, and Cop are all dead, with Doc left alone with his machine and their bodies, doomed to work hopelessly on for the syndicate. While the play makes a strong statement against intellectuals' willingness to collaborate with the organizations that they should instead be actively working against, the play as a whole is stilted and cynical. It is far from being among Dürrenmatt's best, and seems in several important respects to recycle other plays, in particular *The Marriage of Mr. Mississippi*.

"The Traveler's Standpoint" does not deal with the specifics of the play. Instead, like "Theater Problems," "The Traveler's Standpoint" gives insight into Dürrenmatt's notions of himself as an artist and playwright. In the essay, Dürrenmatt describes his aesthetic position as "the traveler's standpoint" and suggests that "what I believe depends on the moment." He offers a hypothetical reader who keeps trying to question him, to pin him down about his beliefs, his political views and so on. But for Dürrenmatt the important thing seems to be to keep moving, to travel and see where traveling takes you. Indeed, one of the things that makes Dürrenmatt such an intriguing writer is his unwillingness to latch on to any one school, any one set of ideas.

All in all, this collection of essays is intriguing in that the essays shift, change, and experiment. Dürrenmatt speaks candidly, and sometimes bluntly, about politics and aesthetics, but he often gets caught up in the drama of the situations, which, in a lesser essayist, would serve only as illustrations. In addition, he demonstrates the way in which an essay can develop into a kind of hybrid form. Joel Agee's translations are respectful of both Dürrenmatt's intent and his syntax, and they show that Dürrenmatt has real strengths as a writer of imaginative nonfiction as well as of fiction and drama. He at once anticipates developments in current American creative nonfiction and surpasses them. With this final volume, American readers are finally given a full sense of Friedrich Dürrenmatt's inter-generic range.

The Winter War in Tibet

I am a soldier of fortune and I am proud of it. I fight against the enemy, not just in the name of the Administration, but also as an executive organ—with limited powers, to be sure—of its mission; that is, of that part of its mission that forces it to fight against its enemies, for the Administration is not only there to help the ordinary citizen but also to protect him. I am a combatant in the Winter War in Tibet. Winter War because on the slopes of Chomolungma, of Chooyu, of Makalu and Manasluit is always winter.* We fight the enemy at fantastic altitudes, on glaciers and bluffs, on rocky plains, in crevices, beneath overhanging boulders, in a labyrinth of trenches and bunkers, then again in the most glaring, blinding sunlight. And the struggle is all the more difficult as friend and enemy wear the same white uniforms. It is a war of cruel and unpredictable close-range combat. The cold on these eight-thousand-meter-high peaks and cliffs is inhuman, our noses and ears are frostbitten. The Administration's mercenary army is made up of all the races in the world: a huge black Congolese fights next to a Malay, a blond Scandinavian next to an Australian bushman, and not only former soldiers fight here but also members of former underground organizations, terrorists of all ideologies, as well as professional hitmen, mafiosi, and ordinary jailbirds. It is the same with the enemy. When we are not in combat, we crawl off into ice-holes and interconnected tunnels and ducts that have been blasted into the rock, a pattern of branching veins that is so confusing that here, too, members of the two armies occasionally run into each other and cut each other down. There is no safety anywhere. Not even in the brothel beneath the Kanchenjunga, the "five treasuries of the great snow," with prostitutes from

*Chomolungma, Chooyu, Makalu, Manaslu: Mountains in the Nepal-Tibet region. Chomolungma is also known as Mount Everest.

every corner of the world. The primitive establishment is frequented by the enemy as well, the whorehouse-officers of both sides have come to terms. I'm not blaming the Administration: sexual intercourse is a necessity that is hard to keep under control. But many of my comrades got knifed while lying on top of a whore—my Commander, for instance, who was already my Commander in the last war, and who already then preferred the rank-and-file brothels to the officers' bordellos. I still remember clearly the way I found him again.

Twenty, thirty years ago—but who still keeps track of time—I presented myself for active service in a small Nepalese town, identifying myself with a pass from the Administration. I was received and you might say processed by a female Army officer. By the time she unlocked a rusty iron door and slumped down again, I was as weak as a doddering old man. It had all happened in a bare room with a mattress alongside one of the walls. On the floor lay the woman's uniform and what shreds were left of my civilian clothes, the door was wide open, little brats everywhere. Scratched-up as I was and irritated by the mob of jeering children, I climbed over the mighty woman's huge naked body and staggered through the door, without noticing that behind it there was a steep stairway. I flew head over heels down those stairs, landed on a concrete floor and lay there, bleeding, not unconscious, but glad to be lying down. Then I looked around cautiously. I was in a rectangular room. On the wall hung white uniforms, submachine guns, and steel helmets covered with white fabric. Behind a desk sat a mercenary of indeterminable age, with a face that could have been modeled in clay, his mouth toothless. He was in a white uniform and was wearing a white helmet like those that were hanging on the wall. On his desk lay a submachine gun, next to it a pile of porn magazines. He was leafing through the magazines. Finally he took notice of me: "So there he is, the new one," he said. "Wiped out, as he should be." He opened a drawer, took out a printed form, closed the drawer, slowly, with fussy deliberation, sharpened a pencil stub effortfully with a penknife, cut himself, cursed, until finally he was able to write, smearing the form with blood in the process. "Get up," he said. I stood up. I was freezing. Only then did I realize again that I was naked. My nose and my hands were scraped, my forehead was bleeding. "Your number is FD 256323," he said without asking for my name. "Do you believe in God?" "No," I said. "Do you believe in an immortal soul?" he asked. "No," I said. "It's not mandatory," he said, "it just gets a little awkward when you believe in these things. Do you believe in an enemy?" "Yes," I said. "You see," he said, "that is mandatory. Put on a uniform, take a helmet and a submachine gun. They're loaded." I did as I was told. He put the printed form back into the drawer and shut it with the same fussy deliberation with which he had opened it, and stood up. "Do you know how to use a submachine gun?" he asked. "Stupid question," I replied. "Well," he said, "not everyone's an old trooper like you, twenty-three." "Why twenty-three?" "Because your number ends with twenty-three," he said, took his submachine gun off the table and opened a low, half-crumbled wooden gate. I followed him, limping. We entered a narrow wet tunnel that was dug into the bare rock. It was dimly lit by small, red electric light bulbs whose cords were loosely strung along the walls. Somewhere a waterfall was roaring. Somewhere shots were fired, then a dull detonation. The mercenary stopped. "If someone approaches us, just shoot," he said. "It could be an enemy, and if it isn't, that's all right, too." The tunnel appeared to be descending, but I wasn't sure, since often it rose so steeply that we had to climb, and then again we would lower ourselves with ropes into uncertain depths. At times the underground veins and arteries were timbered and we were conveyed from one tunnel to the next by an intricate system of elevators, then again everything was unspeakably primitive, as if built in some prehistoric age, close to collapse: probably it will never be possible to make a "geographic" representation—not even a roughly approximate map—of the labyrinth we soldiers of fortune live in. My hands were bleeding profusely. Like beasts, we crawled into a cave to sleep for a few hours. The labyrinth seemed to be getting simpler. The tunnel ran straight as an arrow, but it was impossible to tell its direction. Sometimes we walked for miles through ice-cold water that reached up to our knees. On our right and left, other passages branched off from ours. Water was dripping everywhere, but sometimes it was deadly quiet, and all we could hear was our steps. Suddenly the mercenary was advancing more cautiously, holding his submachine gun at the ready, and at the mouth of another tunnel some bullets went whistling past us: I was back in World War Three. Ducking, we ran to a sort of winding staircase made of rotting wood, from where the mercenary senselessly—there was no one to be seen—fired into the tunnel until his submachine gun was empty. After a brief descent we reached a slightly better lit cave into which other winding stairs led, some of them from above, like the one we had come down on, and some from below. From the cave, a wide tunnel led to an elevator door. The mercenary pressed a button. We waited. About a quarter of an hour. "When we step out," the mercenary said, "throw your gun out right away and raise your hands." The door opened, we stepped into the elevator. It was small and narrow, and strangely, its walls were tapestried with torn sheets of claret-red brocade. I no longer know whether the elevator went up or down. It had two doors. I didn't notice this until about fifteen minutes later, when the door behind my back opened.

The mercenary threw out his submachine gun, I did likewise. I stepped out with my hands raised; the mercenary, too, had thrown up his hands. I froze, horrified: sitting before me on a wheelchair was a legless mercenary. He had prostheses instead of arms. The left one was a construction of steel rods that merged into a submachine gun. The right one ended in an artificial hand consisting of pliers, screwdrivers, knives, and a steel stylus. The lower part of the face was also made of steel, with a tube instead of a mouth. The creature rolled away from us, signalling us with his gun to come closer. We lowered our arms. In the middle of the cave, a naked bearded man hung suspended by his hands. A heavy stone was tied to his feet. The man hung motionless; once in a while a rasping gasp passed his lips. In the background, right next to the rocky wall of the cave, on a primitive plank-bed, in the midst of a heap of weapons and caissons, surrounded by cognac bottles, sat a gigantic, aged officer, his hairy white chest shimmering under an open tunic, bathed in sweat. I knew that uniform, I remembered it from the war: the officer was my old Commander. He raised a bottle to his mouth and drank. "Jonathan, roll to the corner," he said, thick-tongued. The creature rolled to the wall of the cave and started scribbling something on the rock. "Jonathan is a thinker," the Commander explained, fixing his gaze on me. Suddenly it dawned on him: "My Hansie," he laughed hoarsely, "don't you recognize me? It's me, your old Commander." He beamed. "I fought my way through to Bregenz.* Come here." "Your Excellency," I stammered. I went up to him, he cradled my head against his moist chest. "So you're back," the hoarse voice above me continued, "you're back again, you little bastard." He gripped my hair and shook my head back and forth. "I would have been very surprised if the Administration had managed to tame my Hansie. Once a soldier, always a soldier." And then, letting go of me and raising his right knee at the same time, he dealt me such a blow that I lurched into the hanging man, who groaned loudly and swung back and forth like the tongue of a giant bell. I rose to my feet again. The Commander laughed. "A stogy, you son of a bitch!" he yelled in the direction of the mercenary who had brought me there. "I've already used up my share." The mercenary silently handed him a cigar, pulled out a notebook, and said, as he made his entry: "You already owe me seven, Commander." "Fine, fine," the Commander muttered, lighting his cigar with a golden lighter that strangely contrasted with his disheveled

*Capital of the Austrian province of Vorarlberg.

uniform and the barrenness of the cave. I remembered seeing him with this lighter back in the spa hotel in the lower Engadine.* This memory filled me with satisfaction: the good old days weren't over yet. "Get out of here," the Commander said to the mercenary, who saluted, turned around, and bent down to pick up his submachine gun. At that moment the Commander riddled him with bullets. Satisfied, the Commander put his submachine gun back on the plank-bed. Jonathan rolled over to the corpse and examined it with his right arm prosthesis. "Doesn't he have any more cigars?" the Commander wanted to know. Jonathan shook his head. "No skin magazines either?" Jonathan shook his head again, attached the body to a hook on his wheelchair, and dragged it away. "Now no one knows how to find me," the Commander said. "Outposts are dangerous. They like to switch sides. That bastard was a deserter too, he used to always bring me skin magazines." Then he stared at the hanging naked man. "Hansie," he said, puffing a cloud of smoke into the air, "Hansie, you seem surprised to see a guy hanging like that here, among us. The army—I hope you haven't forgotten this—the army doesn't care for bullies, and I'm sure you remember that your old Commander is not a bully. I loved my soldiers as if they were my own children, and I love my mercenaries like my own children as well." "Yes, sir, your Excellency," I said. He gave me a nod, stood up, tottered over to the wall of the cave next to Jonathan, who had rolled out again and had resumed his scribbling on the rock. The Commander pissed. "When you see a guy dangling from a rope," he said, still pissing, "that would go against my sentimentality, right, Hansie? You're a decent guy, you know I feel sorry for the son of a bitch. Out of sentimentality. And sentimentality is human. Animals aren't sentimental. Stand at attention when I'm talking to you." I stood at attention: "Yes, sir, your Excellency." The old man turned around, buttoned his pants, and looked at me through narrowed eyes. "Hansie," he asked, "What's up with this swine, what do you think?" I thought about it. "He is a prisoner, your Excellency," I replied, still standing at attention, "an enemy." The Commander stamped on the ground. "He's from my company," he said, "a mercenary. Isn't that what you want to become, Colonel?" He scrutinized me silently, with an intensity that was almost hostile, and I replied, without moving: "That is my firm intention." The Commander nodded. "I can see you're still the same good old reliable scumbag," he said, "up for anything, just like in the spa hotel. Now take a good look, sonny-boy, and watch what I'm doing." Swaying on his feet, he slowly walked to the middle of the cave and extinguished the burning cigar on the hanging man's stomach. "All right,

Engadine: District in eastern Switzerland.

now you're allowed to piss, too," the Commander said. The soldier just groaned. "The poor guy can't piss any more," the Commander said, "it's a crying shame," and he set the mercenary swinging. "Hansie," the Commander asked. "Your Excellency?" "This dog has been dangling for twelve hours," he said, still swinging the hanging man. "And he is a good dog, a good mercenary, a dear little son whom I love." He planted himself in front of me. The aged giant towered over me by a head. "Do you know who ordered this outrage, Hansie?" he asked menacingly. "No, your Excellency," I replied, clicking my heels. For a few moments, the Commander said nothing. Then, sadly, he said: "I did, Hansie. And do you know why? Because my sonny-boy imagined there are no enemies. Take your submachine gun, Hansie. It's the best thing for my sonny-boy." I fired the gun at the hanging man until the magazine was empty. All that was left was a mass of bloody meat dangling from the center of the cave. "Hansie," the Commander said tenderly, "let's go to the elevator. I'm suffocating down here. I have to go back to the front." We used more than one elevator. The first one was magnificent. We sprawled and stretched our limbs on a chaise longue; on the opposite wall, a picture of a naked girl, lying on her stomach on a chaise longue. "I got this Boucher from the Alte Pinakothek," the Commander explained.★ "All of Munich was one big slag heap. A looter's paradise. But after that, the elevators got more and more shabby—after a while their walls were just papered with pages from porn magazines, with graffiti scribbled all over them—until there were no more elevators." Wearing masks, with the heavy oxygen cylinders on our backs, we climbed up steep tunnels, but the Commander did not get tired, the giant was getting more and more vigorous, and since he knew countless hiding places where cognac was stored, he was getting more lively as well: when the climbing got hard, he would holler and yodel with pleasure. We crawled onward and upward through narrow ducts; then again we were hoisted up in cages, until, just a few meters below Gosainthan, we encamped in the Commander's bunker.†

I slept a long, dreamless sleep. By riddling the mercenary's body with bullets, I had become a mercenary myself: it was my first act of duty in the service of the Administration. Doubt in the existence of an enemy must never be al-

---

★*Alte Pinakothek:* Art museum in Munich containing an important collection of European paintings from the fourteenth to the eighteenth centuries. François Boucher (1703–1770) was a French artist famous for his sensuous rococo paintings.

†*Gosainthan:* Mountain in Tibet.

lowed to arise in the mind of a mercenary, for the simple reason that it will kill him. If he questions the existence of the enemy—even unconsciously—he cannot fight. If the question has driven him to the point of actually voicing his doubt, he is beyond help; then the only issue for the Commander and the other mercenaries is how to help everyone else. That is why I am proud of having shot him; I did it in the name of all of us. The question of the enemy has never been raised since. Unanswerable questions are part of a mercenary's training in the Winter War, but these questions have a meaning. A mercenary is not interested in knowing who the enemy is, what interests him is what he is fighting for and who is giving him his orders. These questions are meaningful, while questions concerning the enemy tempt us to deny the existence of the enemy, even though we fight him every day, knowing that he exists because we kill him. A war without an enemy would be absurd, it would be absurdity itself, which is why a mercenary does not ask this question, or he might as well set himself up as a target for the nearest submachine gun: the only certainty he has left, there is no other. Fantastic victories are reported, final victory is always imminent if not already won, but nevertheless the Winter War continues. The mercenaries don't know what they're fighting for, why they're dying, getting amputated in primitive hospitals, sent back to the front with crude artificial limbs, some of them with hooks and screws in place of hands, some of them blind, their face just a crude mass of flesh, to a front that is everywhere. All they know is that they are fighting the enemy. They commit inhuman and senseless heroic deeds without knowing why; they have long since forgotten that they volunteered to fight in this war; they start looking for a meaning of the Winter War, they develop fantastic systems in their minds—why this war is necessary, why the fate of humanity may depend on it—because these questions are the only meaning they have left. This hope for a meaning gives them the strength they need, it is the process that makes the slaughter possible and bearable. Understandably, therefore, the mercenary fights not only the enemy but also the mercenaries in his own ranks. Thus the mercenary is not only acquainted with an enemy but also with an opponent, namely the mercenary who sees a different meaning in the Winter War than his own; this opponent he hates, while the enemy leaves him indifferent; he is cruel to his opponent, he murders him, while he merely kills the enemy. Therefore the mercenaries form sects, and defect to what they may consider an opposing sect but still a more bearable one than the sect they agree with in principle but whose perhaps quite unimportant secondary opinion or variation on a secondary opinion they cannot agree with: nuances that suddenly seem more important to them than the main principle. Some sects develop the strangest theories about who is leading these struggles, in what mountain ranges the enemy's general staff lies hidden, under Changtse or Lhotse, while their own is presumed to be positioned beneath Anapurna or Dhalaugiri.* One small sect that is hunted by everyone, including the enemy, believes there is only *one* general staff, and that it is hidden inside the far-away Broad Peak; in fact, there is supposed to have been a sect—it was exterminated—that declared there was only one Supreme Commander, an ancient, blind Field Marshall beneath the mighty KZ, waging war against himself, as it were, because the two great Powers had bribed him at the same time; and there is also supposed to be a sect that believes that this Field Marshal is also insane. These various sects form military fronts that battle each other, and these fronts themselves disintegrate into further fronts and counter-fronts. Thus the mercenaries' discipline is not the greatest; all too frequently, during the carnage, they regroup and mow each other down instead of the enemy; their own shrapnel tears them to shreds, they are riddled by volleys from their own machine guns, are incinerated by their own flamethrowers, they freeze to death in ice gorges, die of oxygen deprivation on the fantastic heights where they have dug themselves in because they no longer dare to return to their own camp, where new groups may have formed, while more and more reinforcements from every country and every race throw themselves into the maelstrom of the massacre. But it's probably no different on the enemy's side, presuming this enemy actually exists—that is a question I am permitted to ask myself now: I have been the Commander for quite a while now.

When they lifted his huge naked body off the whore, when they put away his corpse, I put on his uniform and was respected by the soldiers. I know that the mercenaries know that I knifed him: they don't need to know that it was his wish. "Hansie," he laughed before we went to the whorehouse, leaning against the wall of his old cave where the mercenary had hung two years earlier, "Hansie, why don't you blast me away. There is no enemy: it's idiotic to think so. Go ahead, sonny-boy." I didn't say anything and pretended I hadn't understood him, while Jonathan in his wheelchair scraped something into the wall of the main tunnel. Then we set out through the endless system of caves and tunnels, to the whorehouses. As he let out a moan on top of his whore, I stabbed him—my Commander had deserved a good death. The whore screamed, other whores put him on the ground and stood naked and

Changtse, Lhotse, Anapurna, Dhalaugiri, Broad Peak: More Nepalese and Tibetan peaks.

heavy around him. I wiped the dagger on a sheet. I saw that the Commander was observing me. "Hansie," he whispered, and I had to kneel down to make out his words, "Hansie, did you go to college?" "Yes," I said. "Your major?" "Philosophy," I replied, "with a specialization in Plato. Just before my orals, World War Three broke out." The Commander was gasping hoarsely. It took me a while to realize that he was laughing. "I studied literature, Hansie— Hofmannsthal."* I stood up. "He's dead," a whore said. The Commander had been a great Commander. Today, he would be doubly grateful to me for killing him: the whorehouses have long since disappeared, they were his only passion, cognac was just one of his habits. Instead, female mercenaries have gotten involved in the fighting. I admit that often they are greater dare-devils than the men, and sex has now made the front lines even more hellish: people are trying to outdo each other in killing and fucking, streams of blood, sperm, intestines, amniotic fluids, hearts and lungs, embryos, vomit, screaming newborn babies, brains, eyes, placentas are shooting down the huge glaciers and trickling away through bottomless crevices.

This no longer disturbs me. I am sitting legless in a wheelchair in the old cave, my hands are gone, too, my left arm is merged with a submachine gun. I shoot at anyone who shows up, the tunnels are littered with corpses; fortunately there are rats. My right hand is an assortment of diverse tools: pliers, ham-mers, a screwdriver, scissors, a stylus, and so on, everything made of steel. In one of the neighboring caves there is a huge store of provisions and first-rate cognac—my predecessor took care of that. True, it has gotten quiet, I no longer need my left submachine gun arm; years ago, everything shook, maybe the Administration had dropped a bomb. Whatever. I have time to reflect and time to scratch my thoughts into the walls of rock with the steel stylus on my right arm prosthesis. It was Jonathan who gave me the idea, and also the method. There are plenty of walls, hundreds of miles of them, and parts of them are still lit, even though burned-out light bulbs aren't being replaced. But I can—if I have to—write in the dark as well: I have already described the Winter War and how I signed up for it, and my meeting with my Commander and his death; the walls of the cave are covered with my handwriting; now I am covering the walls of the large main tunnel that led to the whorehouses, one line is two hundred meters long; then I roll back and write another two-hundred-meter line—until I've written seven

---

*Hugo von Hofmannsthal (1874–1926), Austrian poet and dramatist, best known for his libretti for the operas of Richard Strauss.

two-hundred-meter lines, one beneath the other. When I'm done, I start inscribing the opposite wall of the tunnel; after covering these for two hundred meters, I continue writing where I stopped on the first wall, another two hundred meters, and so on; each wall gets seven two-hundred-meter inscriptions. In the long run it makes you a stylist.

[*A long, illegible passage, due to the writer's overlooking, or not being able to see, that he was scratching his message into a wall that was already covered with writing, with the result that it is no longer possible to read either inscription. After a few meters of unmarked rock, the writing continues.*] . . . that what I am writing here is not some kind of mystical parable, nor am I describing the mad dreams of a painstakingly reconstructed, disabled soldier of fortune—after all, even my cranium is made of chrome steel. All I am trying to do is describe the nature of the Administration. Of course one could object that I lack the distance we all need to form judgments about reality; that in the caves and tunnels of these immense massifs I couldn't possibly have any kind of distance. This objection cannot be refuted. It would be ridiculous to try to do so, unless allowance were made for the fact that all I have left in my wheelchair are my thoughts, my artificial hand of steel, and endless walls of rock: I am forced to think in a priori terms. It was unavoidable that the Administration would emerge from World War Three. I cannot conceive of the laws governing human society as anything other than natural laws. To my understanding, the laws that dialectical materialism claims to have discovered are nonsense: as if it were possible to describe any natural law with Hegel's logic.* The idea of causation, the notion that the totality of events can be arranged in pairs that are in a cause and effect relationship, is not defensible either; the principle of sufficient reason, according to which nothing exists without a cause, is a platitude, any occurrence has not just *one* cause but an infinite number of causes; for the occurrence does not just imply *one* other occurrence as its cause, it is "causally" connected to all causes, to the entire past of the world. But the thesis I found in a book by an old, forgotten writer, that the Law of Large Numbers presupposes the primacy of Justice, is also wrong: one cannot draw inferences about ethics from a mathematical concept. Besides, I consider justice and injustice to be merely aesthetic concepts—it makes no difference whether my rolling about legless, equipped with two artificial arms, and scribbling all over the walls of my labyrinth is just or unjust, because neither justice nor injustice can change my situation; at

---

*George Wilhelm Friedrich Hegel (1770–1831), German philosopher best known for his development of dialectical reasoning.

the most, the question amuses me—from a mathematical concept, one can only draw inferences about physics or, in the human sphere, about an institution: only here does the Law of Large Numbers play a role. Just as the laws of thermodynamics don't arise until "very many" molecules are involved, so the institutional laws of nature, whether in the economy or in the state, arise only when "very many" people are present, independent of the values or ideologies these people believe in: the laws of institutions correspond to the laws of thermodynamics. A cruel sentence. It is permissible to scratch it into a wall thousands of meters beneath Gosainthan. Of my university studies—World War Three put an end to them—all I remember is Loschmidt's constant, even though it had nothing to do with my field of study; I don't even recall where I picked it up: at zero degrees centigrade and a pressure of one atmosphere, $22,415 \text{ cm}^3$ of an ideal gas contain 6.023×10^{23} molecules. In other words, Loschmidt's constant expresses precisely the ratio of volume, mass, pressure, and temperature in a gas: if the mass increases and the volume remains constant, then pressure and temperature increase, and if the volume expands and the mass remains constant, then pressure and temperature are lowered. 6.023×10^{23} is a "large number." But it is small compared to the number of atoms involved in a star; I estimate that number at 10^{53}. The movement of a single atom is impossible to determine, but stars can be calculated, they are institutions of atoms. These institutions are subject to laws that of necessity deform the atoms. The institutions of men deform man by a no less imperative necessity. An institution of men is the state. Therefore, when I, inside the Himalayas, think about the stars, I am thinking about political states. In my situation, that is the only way I can still think about man. For me, there is no other point of departure for thought than the one I salvaged from the time before World War Three and brought with me into my cave, even though what remains of my knowledge is just an approximate memory of an approximate hypothesis. What I want to refute is the view that World War Three broke out because there was no Administration that might have prevented it. In reality it broke out because no Administration was possible yet. A primitive sun, a protostar, evolved by gradual condensation from a chaotic cloud of gas—like the one in Orion—is of enormous extent, its diameter amounts to a light-year, its density is ridiculous (but already decisive for its ultimate fate), almost a vacuum, the composition of the gases: 80 percent hydrogen, 2 percent heavy elements, projected into it by a supernova explosion (without the heavy elements, no planets can develop), 1 percent carbon, nitrogen, oxygen, neon, the rest is helium; the rotation impulse is barely ten centimeters a second, the temperature is low; the gas is a mixture of cosmic dust, even "organic" molecules made of carbon compounds occur. Gravitation makes this enormous primitive sun shrink, it becomes a red supergiant, it is now a light-hour in diameter, its rotation impulse is constantly increasing. When it has contracted to the approximate size of Mercury's orbit, with a diameter of three light-minutes, the sun, flattened into a disc by its equatorial rotation speed of one hundred kilometers per second, hurls matter out into space. The larger part of this hurled-out matter, especially the hydrogen, escapes the sun's gravitational pull forever; carbon, nitrogen, oxygen, and neon form the large outer planets; iron, magnesium, and silicon the smaller inner ones; the sun has contracted to the ten-billionth part of its original size, it has become a yellow dwarf, with a diameter of a million kilometers; its equatorial rotation speed, retarded by the hurling forth of matter, is two kilometers an hour, its state has become stable. Now the pressure in the sun's interior has grown to about one hundred billion kilos per cubic centimeter—it ought to collapse under this weight—but the temperature of the sun's interior is thirteen million degrees centigrade, resulting in a pressure equilibrium. The enormous internal temperature starts a nuclear process that transforms hydrogen into helium; the resultant energy is radiated away by emissions of light quanta, but the interior of the sun is completely dark. Because of the enormous temperature of the sun's interior, the light is absorbed after fractions of centimeters; the result is a steady process of emission and absorption in which the light quanta convey the energy into the cooler convection zone that encloses the sun's interior like a coat; this transportation lasts ten million years. In the convection zone, hot masses of gas are mixed with cooler ones, but most of the light quanta do not succeed in shooting through the convection zone; a part of the energy radiates back to the center, but the energy that has made its way into the convection zone sets it into seething motion: the outer convection zones become unstable, sunspots develop, protuberances arise in the sun's atmosphere, fall back to the surface, the light quanta are finally released and pass through the photosphere, the chronosphere, and the corona out into space. Surface equilibrium and energy equilibrium have been added to the pressure equilibrium in the interior, the photosphere is emitting as much energy into space as it is receiving from the convection zone: the sun's energetic processes are now regulated—even though the sun is losing 360 billion tons of matter a day, a paltry amount for a body of its size. However, this ideal condition cannot last forever; the nuclear process in the sun's interior penetrates into the convection zone, the surface of the sun heats up: life on Earth is scarcely sustainable. The sun begins to bloat, until it reaches Mercury's orbit again: life on earth is extinguished, the atmosphere, the seas evaporate. The sun's surface begins to cool off, the sun shrinks; this raises its surface temperature once again. The sun returns to its present size, but it is incomparably brighter and hotter; it becomes a blue star. The pressure equilibrium has been restored, but the sun is already burning the helium in its core and heating up the hydrogen surrounding the core. The heated hydrogen expands, but it is not fast enough to escape the sun; only a hundredth of 1 percent of the total mass of the sun escapes. For weeks during this phase of expansion, the sun shines a hundred thousand times more brightly than today's sun, it has become a nova. After a thousand such expansions, the sun is relieved of its hydrogen and is now a white dwarf, no larger than the earth; the gas is degraded, only a few electrons are still moving freely; the sun has exhausted its supply of nuclear energy, it has become a molecule. Gravity has vanquished expansion, the sun grows cold, it turns into a crystal the size of the earth, and finally into an invisible black dwarf, even though the time this takes is longer than it took our Milky Way system to develop. But not all suns come to this end. Stars whose mass is smaller than that of the sun, the red dwarfs, were probably never able to develop a convection zone worthy of the name; they prematurely became small novas, but the remaining core did not have enough mass to collapse into a white dwarf. As for stars whose mass exceeds that of the sun by a factor of 1.44, the heavier they are, the more quickly they become unstable; it is rare for them to attain any kind of equilibrium—whether of pressure, surface tension, or energy—for more than a brief period of time; they are too wasteful of their energies, like the blue giants, for instance: the immense interior pressure produces temperatures of more than three billion degrees at the core; in this hell, all elements are converted into helium. The more excessive a sun's mass is, the greater the danger of its becoming a supernova: a colossal explosion sweeps the sun's convection zone into space, emitting more light than a galactic system with its hundred billion suns, while the core, if its mass is 1.44 times that of our sun—the notorious Chandrasekhar limit— is no longer able to attain the equilibrium of a white star;* it collapses under its own weight and becomes a tiny sun of grotesque density, with a diameter of ten kilometers, revolving around itself thirty times a second. This neutron star is no longer able to explode, its atoms have broken down; due to the compaction of electrons and protons the atomic nuclei have disintegrated into neutrons, forming a degraded neutron gas. If the core is even heavier, the gravitational collapse is complete: a star that attains such extraordinary

---

*Chandrasekhar limit: The theoretical upper limit to the mass of a white dwarf (the remains of a star like the sun when it has exhausted its nuclear fuel). Named for Subrahmanyan Chandrasekhar (1910–1995), Nobel Prize–winning astronomer.

density stands outside space and time, it becomes a black hole whose gravitational field sucks in everything in its vicinity. Here I am, scratching this solar death into the wall of a pitch-dark tunnel: in this there is an undeniable irony. [*The inscription breaks off and is continued in another tunnel.*]

I couldn't find my way back to the main cave. I didn't know through which tunnels I was rolling, into which wall I was scratching my inscription. The food I accidentally discovered in the dark—tin cans filled with a cheap broth—came from the supplies of a cave that was much smaller than my Commander's. I found an elevator, it doesn't work any longer, the walls are bare, no Boucher. Using my right arm prosthesis, I attached the box full of soup cans to my wheelchair. I worked at this for an entire day: it's hard looking for something in the dark with a mechanical hand, and my left submachine gun arm has become meaningless. I've tried to dismantle it again and again—in vain, so far. I dragged the box with the soup cans behind me, I didn't know in which direction, stopping occasionally to scratch notes for my inscription into the wall, notes that I couldn't read, but which had to be inscribed there nonetheless: I am neither an astronomer nor a physicist, my knowledge of the stars is merely approximate. Before World War Three I read up on this subject in some books that must be obsolete now. I have tried to remember them and to reconstruct the evolution of stars. That is why I have made three versions of this inscription. [*To date, only one version has been found. It is made up of inscriptions in many tunnels. However, it is possible that it is a composite of all three versions.*] In the course of writing the last version I must have lost my way completely. I didn't find the way back to the second cave either. Others will turn up. So I'm just rolling along. I assume I'm still in a tunnel beneath Chomo-Lungma. The rock is smooth here, I always work on my inscriptions as carefully as possible. It isn't just the thought of a black hole that cheers me up: Chomo-Lungma used to be called Gaurisankar, so it is underneath Gaurisankar that I am thinking about Chandrasekhar's law. Maybe this is the reason why I had to end up in the Winter War: I was seduced by a name. In retrospect, every fate is logical. The iron in the prosthetic parts of my patched-up torso and the giant mountain Gaurisankar both come from that sun that ignored Chandrasekhar's limit and became the supernova that polluted a protosun, enabling it thereby to give birth to our planet: the greater part of me is older than the earth. It is with awe that I scratch the name "Chandrasekhar" into the rock. Some observations suggest that changes have occurred in the sun's interior, which in the course of the next ten million years will make the earth forever uninhabitable, but there is a chance that the Himalayas will be preserved on the moon-like earth, just as there are mountain ranges on the moon. And there is a chance, admittedly a ridiculously small one, that in the course of the many billions of years during which the burned-out earth will revolve around the white dwarf we now call our sun, and the countless billions of years the earth will revolve around the black dwarf that will have become the sun, space travelers of another, future world will set foot on the earth. And there is another, inexpressibly smaller chance, a chance that is actually improbable, that these alien beings will discover and explore the system of caves beneath the Himalayas. My inscription will be their only source of knowledge about humanity. It is with this improbable prospect in mind that I have committed my thoughts to writing. In my situation, this is the only task that is left to me. I had to come up with an inscription from which the fate of humanity can be read: this inscription cannot be something private, something of interest only to me, even though I am part of humanity; indeed, it should not have anything to do with humanity. The alien beings who will read the inscription some day, in countless billions of years, would not understand anything, for in the improbable event that this inscription gets read, surely those who will read it will not be human beings: Nature, stubborn though she is, is not likely to repeat the stupid mistake of creating primates; the accident that eventually created us as a species will almost certainly not recur. Communication with these beings cannot be about ourselves, but only about something that concerns both them and us: the stars. While they will not learn anything from my inscriptions about our religions, ideologies, cultures, arts, feelings, and so on, and nothing about how we nourish ourselves and reproduce, they will conclude from my three inscriptions that we were thinking beings, however inept some of my expositions may be. They will be able to guess at our degree of knowledge, but they will also infer that we had atomic and hydrogen bombs and that World War Three was inevitable. They will unravel the code of my inscriptions, for no matter what a human being describes, he always describes himself. The alien beings will conclude from my inscriptions that on the naked, charred, stony planet they have landed on, creatures endowed with intelligence once existed, and that these creatures in their totality crossed the Chandrasekhar limit. Just as the sun is an accumulation of hydrogen, the state is an accumulation of people. Both are subject to the same laws. Both are stable when there is an equilibrium of pressure, energy, and surface tensions. Both are effects of gravity. In both, gravity starts to form a core with a convection zone around it. Imperceptibly at first: the core and the convection zone of a protosun are still latent, rudimentary versions of what they will become. Applied to the state: the convection zone represents the government, the core stands for the people. There once was an emperor who drove in an oxcart, accompanied by his chancellor, from monastery to monastery and from city to city, to receive food and lodging. The emperor and his chancellor were the government: their Holy Roman Empire of the German Nation was comparable to a protosun. Barely five hundred years later this protosun had become an unstable sun: the Third Reich. But there is no need to adduce any further historical and therefore incomprehensible examples. The function of the state originally consisted in providing protection against threats from without, against threats from within, and protection against the protectors for whose sake the individual surrendered his power to the state. If this function is equated with the equilibrium of pressure, energy, and surface tension in a stable sun, the resulting image describes the relationship of the state with each individual as well as the relationship of the individuals among each other. In a stable state, pressure equilibrium consists in the individual's being able to move as freely as possible, which is to say, as freely as is possible with regard to the other individuals; the larger mass of those others, the more limited is the freedom of the individual: the pressure on the individual has risen and with it the temperature within the masses; they begin to feel the state, emotions against the state are released, and so on. Energy equilibrium, in a sun, means that no greater amount of matter is transformed into energy than the sun is able to emit; in political terms, it means that the state does not produce more than it can deliver. The balance of energy collapses when pressure declines or increases. In the case of a blue giant like S-Doradus, eighty thousand times brighter than the sun, the convection zone is weak; therefore the pressure toward the inside becomes insufficient, there is nothing to inhibit the conversion of matter at its core into energy, the star overproduces, it burns up. There used to be nations like that as well. In most cases, however, before World War Three, the convection zone—that is, the government—prevailed. The power of the state grew. Especially the superheavy states began to emit less energy than they were generating. They became the prisoners of their own bureaucracies. An energy equilibrium takes place when the supply side takes its bearings from the demand. In the case of a blue giant, a sun with a weak convection zone—even though it is many times more powerful than our sun's convection zone—the supply exceeds the demand, and a tremendous competition takes place within such a star. For a while, the same could be observed in the industrial states before World War Three. But in the case of a superheavy sun, the demand begins to exceed the supply; although matter is being converted into energy, that energy is absorbed by the convection zone. A state of this kind is abused by its government agencies. The government needs weapons to protect itself against threats from without and from within. And not only weapons, it also needs an ideology: it sets up a mighty force field of ideas. The convection zone cannot suffer any ideologies beside its own; anyone who thinks differently is declared to be antisocial or insane or even a traitor. The state's density grows, its inward-directed pressure increases. The nuclear process taking place in the greater part of the population is of benefit only to the state, or more precisely: to its bureaucratic agencies, whose power potential increases steadily, not out of malice but out of helplessness. Superheavy states are planned from top to bottom. Intrinsically, therefore, they are incapable of an energy equilibrium, for their pressure can only increase and cannot decrease; the end result is a gravitational collapse. Such were the conditions of political life before World War Three. The superheavy stars did not want to conquer the world, but thanks to their weight, they blackmailed the world. One could say that their gravity absorbed all the energy released by the conversion of matter in the blue giants. As a result, the blue giants shrank, and now their pressure increased as well; having lost their economic equilibrium, they "socialized" their economy and now themselves became superheavy suns—irrespective of their economic, social, and ideological structure—for even "free" nations began to exert pressure on their own interior by issuing decrees against dissidents. The process was irreversible. An arms race began. Every state was now producing more energy than it was expending. In every country, the inward pressure mounted to an unbearable degree. Under the enormous pressure, a deterioration took place in the suns' interior of every society: extended families broke down into nuclear families, and even these became unstable, and clumped together as rural and urban communes that flared up and dispersed again; everything moved at a hectic, insanely industrious pace, a merciless struggle for existence, combined with an insatiable hunger for life. More and more, society divided into two classes: those who resided in the convection zone and had secured a livelihood there, and those who were helplessly exposed to the pressure and the equally enormous temperature in the sun's interior. But here, too, the tremendous energy generated by the hectic commotion within the sun's interior was absorbed by the convection zone, by the government agencies, which needed more and more taxes to resist the forces in the sun's interior. More and more, politics became an activity that took place on the surface of the sun, unable to exert any influence on the nuclear processes in the sun's interior, a ritual of hollow phrases without conviction, and now there was nothing to contain the developments in the sun's interior: the pressure became too great, erupting through the convection zone more and more frequently; mighty industrial empires rose up and collapsed again, violent crises broke out, inflations, fantastic scams, mad acts of terrorism, an explosive increase of crimes and catastrophes—the nations became unstable. Helpless in the face of these tremendous eruptions, political practice became cynical and, like a dead church, cultic, and finally occult. Some preached class struggle, others liberalism, neither side being aware that everything depends on how mass is transformed into energy, neither side considering how a people behaves when it becomes a mass: unpredictably. All sorts of states were being propagated: the socialist state, the liberal state, the welfare state, the Christian, Jewish, Moslem, Buddhist, Communist, Maoist state, and so on, without the slightest suspicion that an overloaded state could become as dangerous a formation as an overly heavy star. And that is precisely what happened: World War Three broke out. The effect of hydrogen bombs on oil fields, a factor no one had anticipated, was just a symbolic indication, as it were, that the sun had become a supernova, to say nothing of the effects of the other bombs. The internal pressure and with it the internal temperature had become too powerful, the surface equilibrium gave way, the enormous convection zones—the armed forces, equipped with monstrous weaponry by an establishment of which they were a part and over which they had long since assumed control—swept out into space: the effect was all the more catastrophic, as our suns were close neighbors, while in space an average distance of three and a half light years separates the stars. After the supernova, the final stage: the human race as a neutron star. The remnants of humanity crowded together on the few strips of land that were still habitable or had been made habitable—impossible to estimate the number of people who perished in the Sahara Project alone—became a single convection zone, astronomically comparable to a "degraded neutron gas," a totalistically administered mass, in short the "Administration," in which the administrators and the administrated have become indistinguishable. Of course, like a neutron star, the human race retained its old rotational impulse, its aggressiveness, for the time being. In the case of a neutron star, that impulse wears down by itself in the course of time; in the case of humanity, it was the Winter War in Gaurisankar that wore it down: the mutual slaughter of those whose aggressiveness needs the foil of an enemy, no matter under what pretext. (The pretexts of the terrorists were at their most grotesque before World War Three, a kind of self-hypnosis. They actually imagined that they were fighting for a worldwide brotherhood of man: if they had been transplanted into such a world order, they would have died of boredom.) Chandrasekhar's calculation had worked out exactly.

But at this point, before I go on, I must meet an objection that might be made by the alien beings, should they read my inscriptions some day: matter is subject to entropy and tends toward its most probable state. Its beginning, the conglomeration of matter in a space the size of the orbit of Neptune: that is the amount of space occupied by the elementary particles of the universe when they were still pressed together. This was the most improbable state that matter could assume. Its most probable state is its end: 95 percent of matter radiated away, the ruins of the stars as black red dwarfs, black white dwarfs, black holes, heaps of dead planets, asteroids, meteors, and so forth. Inversely, life: the conditions under which it arose were also improbable, but this improbability produced its most probable sequel, the virus, followed by the protozoan. From its point of view, life becomes more and more improbable: a thinking being is the most improbable, because the most complex, being in the universe. This being seems to resist cosmic law, the law of entropy, especially in view of the fact that, over the course of three million years, it has evolved from a rare species into a mass of six billion. But appearances are deceptive: the more improbable life is, the more probable is its terminal state: death. A virus, even a protozoan, can live "forever"; animals die, but have no knowledge of death. But since man knows that he must die, his death becomes something more than his most probable terminal state, it becomes his certain terminal state. Death and entropy are the same cosmic law, they are identical; and this in turn establishes the identity of us "human beings" (a term that will mean nothing to you) and you who will read these inscriptions: for you, too, will die.

[*The following inscription was found in another tunnel.*] The Administration is grounded in the law of *homo homini lupus:* man is a wolf to man. Curiously, I thought of the deaf-mute as I scraped this sentence into the rock, and the thought shot through my head that the deaf-mute could have been Jonathan. An absurd suspicion, which probably arose because I did not remember Jonathan until I thought of the deaf-mute: Jonathan was gone when I rolled into the commander's cave. Maybe somewhere he is scratching messages into the tunnel walls just like me.

I met the deaf-mute after World War Three in my old native city: already, before the outbreak of the war, the government with all its officialdom had withdrawn into the big bunkers beneath the Blümlisalp along with the two parliaments,* for it seemed that a prerequisite for any national defense was a legislative and an executive that were safe from any attack. The parliament building in the capital had been precisely recreated underneath the

---

Blümlisalp: Mountain group near Kandersteg in the south of Switzerland.

Blümlisalp, along with the radio station and secret communications bureau beneath the building. It even had the same view: set designers from the municipal theater had installed it by means of enlarged photographs and flood lights. All around the building, the residences, the movie theaters, the bars, the bowling alleys, the hospital, and the fitness center had been installed inside the Blümlisalp. Ranged around these in concentric circles were the three "rings": the supply ring where food and wine (especially from the Vaud region*) were stored, and the inner and outer defense rings. Beneath this enormous complex lay the treasury vaults with the hoarded bullion of half the world, and beneath these, a nuclear power plant. The government and the parliament were in permanent session. The bureaucracy was working at its highest capacity. When I had received my secret assignment and reported for leave in order officially to assume my function as liaison officer with the Commander, they had just passed a new national defense plan and decided to acquire a hundred Gepard 9 tanks and fifty Vampire 3 bombers over the next ten years. I saluted, the government and the two parliaments rose and sang our anthem: "When the morning skies turn red." The mood was depressed. No one really believed that World War Three would break out, despite the mobilization; everyone hoped that the bombs would prevent it, for after all, everyone had them, including us. Despite the bitter resistance of the progressives, antinuclear activists, conscientious objectors, priests, and other defeatist circles, we had built the bomb—after the principality of Liechtenstein—every African country had it already! So we were convinced that if there were to be a war, it could only be a conventional war, a possibility we didn't believe in, however, because on the one hand the production of bombs had cost us so much that we were underequipped for conventional war, and because on the other hand we had built the bomb precisely in order to prevent a conventional war. What depressed us was the miserable state of our foreign policy. Over and over, we solemnly affirmed our position of political armed neutrality, but more and more menacingly, a creeping suspicion came over us that neither side believed in our sacred political creed. One side considered us part of its political and therefore military camp, while the other side regarded us as a potential military enemy. Thus we were forced to transfer our mobilized army—a not inconsiderable force of eight hundred thousand men—to the eastern border; otherwise, the western powers would have become too unpredictable, they would have suspected a weak spot in their own front lines. Also, it is undeniable that the population mistrusted the government and that the soldiers were only cooperating because they had

*Region bordering on Lake Geneva famous for its wine and gastronomical delights.

to: for some time, we had been forced to give life sentences to conscientious objectors; it was only by acts of clemency that they escaped the death penalty demanded by the military department. The population was downright hostile to the government. They knew that the government, the parliament, and the bureaucracy—five thousand people—were safe beneath the Blümlisalp while they themselves were in danger; fortunately we had been able to mobilize before the general elections. The first two days of World War Three began conventionally and brought considerable glory to our army, for the first time since 1512, when we conquered Milan:* when the big bomb fell on the Blümlisalp and the other big bombs fell on the government bunkers of the other countries—a single chain reaction of blows and counterblows—we had detained the Russians at Landeck as they invaded Northern Italy.† News reached the Commander in a spa hotel in the Lower Engadine that the allied and enemy armies had capitulated. We were sitting in comfortable, high-backed armchairs in the spacious lounge, surrounded by the staff. There was still plenty of liquor there. One hell of a mood. The Commander was indulging his artistic leanings. A quartet was playing Schubert: "Death and the Maiden." The adjutant handed him the telegram. "There, Hansie, take this rag and read it," the Commander grinned after scanning it briefly. Shouts of joy outside, the radio officer had already announced the telegram's content. The Commander seized his submachine gun. I stood up. The quartet stopped playing. I read the telegram out loud. The effect was tremendous. The quartet fiddled a Hungarian Rhapsody by Liszt. The officers cheered and hugged. The Commander's submachine gun mowed them down. He emptied out three magazines. The lounge presented an indescribable mess of corpses, torn armchairs, shards of glass, shattered champagne, whisky, cognac, gin, and wine bottles; the four musicians were playing for their lives. It was the *andante con moto* of the Schubert quartet, the variations on Death's reply to the maiden: "Be of good cheer. I am not wild, thou shalt sleep gently in my arms." In the jeep, the Commander said: "Bunch of chickenshits and traitors." Then he turned around again and mowed down the quartet. We parted in Scuol.‡ The Commander took off in the direction of Innsbruck, I drove to the Upper Engadine. Outside Zernez I counted more than three hundred bodies neatly lined up by the side of the road, all of them officers, from a corps commander down to a lieutenant, shot by their soldiers. I saluted them as I drove past. In St. Moritz, the looters were hard at work, the luxury hotels

---

*Milan was held by the French until it was stormed and captured by the Swiss in 1512.

†*Landeck:* Austrian town on the border of eastern Switzerland.

‡*Scuol, Zernez, St. Moritz, Maloja Pass:* Places in the Engadine.

were burning sky-high, the famous movie director's chalet went off like a rocket. I changed into civilian clothes, in a stylish men's boutique for the jet set. I picked a denim suit, the price tag was still on it: 3,000; in a discount store it would have cost 300 or less. All the sales personnel were gone. There was no gasoline to be found anywhere. I left my jeep standing where it was, with my two submachine guns lying inside it; loaded my revolver, found a bicycle, and drove it across the Maloja Pass. After the head of the pass, the first clear night, the dark side of the half moon set against a malevolent red, the refraction of boundless fires raging on the earth. I sought shelter in a little village near the former border. The village was steeped in twilight, the opposite side of the valley shone like vermilion. I crept up to what I presumed was an uninhabited barn. Behind it, I found a flight of stairs leading up into the building. The door opened easily. The interior was dark, so I scanned my surroundings with the beam of my flashlight. I was in a painter's studio. There was a picture leaning against a wall: several human figures, all of them looking as if they had been thrown there. The emptiness of the picture was eerie; the loosely mounted, virtually unprimed canvas gave the impression of a net in which people were caught. The picture on the other wall represented a cemetery, with the larger-than-life portrait of a person slashed across the white grave stones, senselessly, as if in an inexplicable act of protest the painter had intentionally set out to destroy his painting: the end of the world seemed to have already taken place in this artist's studio. In the middle of the studio stood a hideous iron bed, on top of it a striped mattress with mounds of horse hair bursting from it on all sides. Next to the bed stood an ancient, torn leather chair, caked with daubs of paint. In the background, under a window, stood a picture of a dying dog, a bitch, lost in an infinity of ochre. Then a portrait appeared: a man who looked like the Commander. He was lying naked and fat on a bed, his beard spread wildly across his chest, which was raised toward the chin by the bloated belly, his liver swollen, his legs spread apart, his gaze proud and deranged. I felt cold. I cut the picture out of the frame, lay down on the bed, and used the canvas, which still stank of oil paint, as a blanket. In the dirty light of morning I awoke. I reached for my revolver. In front of the empty wooden frame from which I had cut the canvas stood an old woman in heavy shoes, dressed in black, with a pointy nose, her white hair knotted in the back. She was holding a large, wide-bellied cup in both hands. She looked at me with motionless, bloodshot eyes. "Who are you?" I asked. She didn't respond. "Chi sei?" I asked in Italian.* "Antonia," the old woman replied. She approached me solemnly and offered me the cup. It was

Chi sei? "Who are you?"

filled with milk. I drank and rolled out from under the canvas. She stared at it and laughed, "l'attore," and as I passed her, she solemnly said: "Non andare nelle montagne. Tu sei il nemico."* Like many, she had gone crazy. I walked out of the studio. My bicycle had been stolen, the village was abandoned, the border was unguarded. The small town of Chiavenna had been plundered by Turkish officers trying to escape their own troops.† In a garage I took a motorcycle; the owner watched me indifferently, his wife and two daughters had been raped and killed. On the Splügen, I threw a Russian officer into the reservoir, the motorcycle sank as well. He had attacked me when I stopped to admire the atomic mushroom cloud standing in the western sky. I saw the mushroom for the first time. A little later I came across a crashed helicopter. I searched it and found papers that had belonged to the officer. I have forgotten his name, all I remember is that he came from Irkutsk. Thusis was devastated. I began to grasp what was happening in our country. The fact that it took me two years to reach my goal says everything. So my wanderings through the inferno of this age need no more than a few sparse indications: the people who had survived the Bomb—if one can call that survival—held all technology and all education responsible for World War Three. Not just the nuclear power plants, but also the irrigation dams and electric power plants were destroyed, countless hundreds of thousands perished in the floods and in the clouds of poison gas released from chemical plants that were set on fire by the enraged population. Gas stations and burning cars were exploding everywhere; the now meaningless radios and TV sets, the record players, the washing machines, the typewriters, the computers were smashed to pieces; the museums, the libraries, the hospitals were demolished. It was as if a whole country were committing suicide. Chur, for example, was a madhouse. In Glarus, "witches" were burned: stenographers and laboratory assistants. In Appenzell, people destroyed the St. Gallen monastery under the pretext that Christianity had given birth to science. The precious library with the *Song of the Nibelungen* went up in flames. In the huge slag heap that had once been Zürich, the motorcycle gangs took over. They drowned the progressives and the socialists as well as the professors and assistant professors of both universities. A sect was holding a

---

*"Don't go to the mountains. You are the enemy."

†*Chiavenna:* Small Italian town near the southeastern border of Switzerland. Splügen and the other towns mentioned later in this paragraph are all towns in Switzerland. St. Gallen is the most notable, with its monastery dating to the seventh century. Manuscript B of the *Nibelungenlied,* the famous thirteenth-century German epic, is held in the Abbey Library of St. Gallen.

convention in the ruins of the Schauspielhaus.* They believed in the Hollow Earth theory. Their priestesses were pregnant. They gave birth to hideous monstrosities. In Olten, thousands of primary and secondary school teachers had been hanged from large scaffolds. They had been herded together from all over the country. In Graubünden, on the other hand, the "great dying" had already begun. Where at first the people had let themselves go in acts of indescribable excess, plundering, smashing, destroying everything they could get their hands on, setting enormous fires, and paralyzing all traffic, eventually they became apathetic. A leaden weariness overcame them. They sat in front of the ruins of their houses, which they themselves had destroyed, staring into space, or lay stretched out somewhere and died. Gradually the destructions abated. There were no longer any cars, any trains, just ruins, enormous accumulations of food, intended for a population of eight million that was now reduced to no more than a hundred thousand. Along with the people, the animals were dying. The fields were densely covered with cadavers. Only the birds had multiplied astronomically. The human dead were given ceremonious burials. Coffins were built, but still there were never enough, so people plundered the old graveyards for coffins, or else buried the bodies in cupboards and wardrobes. Endless solemn funeral processions; in the enormous heat, which did not diminish in the fall, people followed the coffins, everyone dressed in black; or else, pulling on long ropes, they would drag carts laden with stacks of coffins behind them. Huge burial feasts were given; for many, this was their last meal before they, too, were buried, and the funeral processions, smaller by now, went out once again to the graveyards. It was as if the nation were burying itself. Then our N-bomb depot in Schratten-Ruh must have ignited by itself. In the Emmental I walked through a village with a large milk processing plant. It was clean and well tended, with fiery-red geraniums in front of the windows, but the streets were vacant. I was hungry. I entered an inn called "The Holy Cross." There was no one in the taproom. I found the dead innkeeper in the kitchen, a peaceful colossus, with his face in an ice cream sundae. I entered the dining room. About a hundred people were sitting at festively decked tables—men, women of all ages, also girls and boys. At the long table in the middle sat a bride and a bridegroom. The bride in a white bridal dress, next to the groom a powerful woman in traditional Bernese garb. They were all dead and utterly peaceful in their Sunday garments. Their plates were half emptied; no doubt it was their second helping. Between the tables lay the bodies of the waitresses. On the tables stood mighty "*Bernerplatten*": cutting boards laden with

*Theater.

country ham, pork ribs, broiled meat, bacon, tongue sausage, beans, sauer-kraut, boiled potatoes. Next to the bride, a chair had been shoved aside, and on the floor lay an elderly man, his mighty beard spread across his chest like a veil. In his right hand he was holding a sheet of paper, I looked at it, a poem. I took his chair, sat down next to the bride, heaped some of her *Bernerplatte* onto my plate, the food was still warm.

But I am scratching these memories into the tunnel walls with some hesitation: in many ways they have become unbelievable to me. Especially this: it seems to me that the heat persisted through the entire winter: when I think back, I keep seeing enormous floods. I reached my native city by foot on the empty highway. The closer I came, the emptier the landscape became. For miles on end, the highway was already overgrown—the grass had cracked the pavement. I also passed long rows of cars that were overgrown with ivy. At one point I thought I spotted a plane in the sky; it was flying so high that it couldn't be heard. When I reached the city, the suburbs were ruins: shopping malls that had turned into absurdities, the burned-out shells of sky-scrapers. I left the highway. In the evening sun, then, I saw the old part of the city before me. It lay seemingly untouched on the boulder above the river. The light pierced its walls like warm gold. The town seemed so marvelously beautiful that in my memory even the sight of Makalu and Chomolungma pales by comparison. But the bridges leading to it were destroyed. I returned to the highway; on its ruins one could cross the river. The mushroom cloud now stood in the south. It turned into a radiant bell, cupping the Alps and brightening the night sky as I entered the forest. The bunkers were untouched, the beds were neatly made. I waited. Bürki did not come. I fell asleep. In the morning I set out for the center of town. The university was a ruin, the room where the philosophical seminars took place was blackened, the wall where the windows had been had caved in, the books of the library were a black, pulpy mass. The table we had sat around had collapsed. Only the blackboard was undamaged. In front of it stood a man. He turned his back to me and had buried his hands in a ragged army coat. "Hello," I said. The man did not move. I raised my voice: "Hey!" The man did not seem to hear me. I went up to him and touched his shoulder. He turned his face to me. His face was seared by radiation and completely expressionless. He took a piece of chalk that was lying under the blackboard and wrote: "Head shot. Deaf-mute. Lip-read. Speak slowly." Then he turned to me. "Who are you?" I asked, slowly. He shrugged. "Where is the Veterans' Welfare Center?" I asked. He took the chalk and wrote on the blackboard. "Tibet. War." He looked at me. "Veteran's Administration," I said slowly, emphasizing each syllable, "where is it?" He wrote 60231023, a meaningless number that I have only retained because as an officer I am used to memorizing numbers: sixty, twenty-three, ten, twenty-three. He looked at me. His burned mouth grimaced. I couldn't tell whether he was smiling or grinning. I tapped my forehead. The deaf-mute wrote: "Thought is enough," and watched me again. I took the chalk from his hand, crossed out what he had written, wrote "nonsense" underneath it, threw the chalk on the floor, crushed it with my foot, and left the ruin of the university. Outside the burned-out students' lounge, a little man approached me. On his right cheek was a large black ulcer. He was trundling a handcart filled with books. He was coming from the German department, he said, pointing toward the field of ruins behind the university. He hadn't found the books yet, he said. I picked up a book from his handcart: Lessing's *Emilia Galotti*.* "I am a bookbinder," the man explained. "And there's a printer, well, he works with me. We're publishing a book, a hundred copies and then another hundred copies. People are reading again, they'll turn into regular bookworms yet. You'll see, it'll sell like hotcakes." He was beaming. "You see, I'm not dying. I survived. What you see on my cheek is just a melanoma." I replied that Lessing wasn't the easiest thing to read. The man asked who Lessing was. I showed him the book. "That?" the man asked, surprised. "That's not for reading, that's for burning. I'm printing *Heidi*.† By Johanna Spyri. Remember that name: Johanna Spyri. A classic." Then he became suspicious. "Were you a soldier?" I nodded. "An officer?" His voice sounded threatening. I shook my head. "And before that?" he asked. "Student," I said. He glanced at his handcart. "Ever read books like these?" "Like these, and others, too," I said. "You all made one hell of a mess with your education," he grumbled. "You and your crappy books." I asked him where the Veterans' Welfare Center was. "By the town hall," he replied. "Maybe you *were* an officer." He trotted off with his handcart.

I went back to the ruins. They were overgrown. The woods by the north of the city had advanced into their midst. All I could find in the destroyed German department were parts of a *History of Tragic Literature* and some pages of an introduction dealing with the *Principles of Poetic Theory*. The railroad station below the university was one big heap of rubble. The houses, the Spitalgasse and the Marktgasse, once thriving commercial streets, were derelict, the

---

*This play by the German dramatist Gotthold Ephraim Lessing (1729–1781) is an early example of the bourgeois tragedy (i.e., one in which the hero or heroine was not of noble birth). It tells the story of a father who murders his daughter to save her from a prince's seduction.

†Well-known children's book by the Swiss author Johanna Spyri (1827–1901).

windows of the empty shops broken. The Münster was still standing. I went to the main portal; the *Last Judgment* was smashed to pieces. As I passed the nave, a gargoyle crashed to the ground behind me. At the entrance to the Kreuzgasse a man in rags was leaning against the wall of a house. "You enjoy risking your life?" he asked. I asked him who had demolished the *Last Judgment*. "I did," the man said. "We no longer need a 'Last Judgment.'" The Veterans' Welfare Center was near the town hall, a former chapel, as I seemed to remember. Alongside the walls lay some mattresses and a heap of woolen blankets. Around the font, three chairs, and on top of it, a dish with a slice of cake. On the walls were the pallid remnants of a fresco, but the images were impossible to make out. The chapel was empty. I walked back and forth several times. No one came. I opened a door to the south of the font. I entered the sacristy. Behind a table sat a fat old woman with nickel eyeglasses, eating cake. When I asked if this was the Veterans' Welfare Center, the woman replied, munching: "I am the Veterans' Welfare Center," and after gulping down her mouthful, she asked: "Who are you?" I gave her my code name: "Rückhart." The fat woman pondered. "My father had a book by someone named Rückhart," she said then: "The Wise Sayings of Brahm." "*The Brahman's Wisdom* by Friedrich Rückert," I corrected her.* "Could be," the fat woman said, cutting herself another slice. "Carrot cake," she explained. "Where is the Commander in charge of the city?" I asked. She ate. "The army has capitulated," she said. "There's no Commander any more. There's only the Administration." That was the first time I heard of it. "What do you mean?" I asked. The woman licked her fingers. "By what?" she asked. "By administration," I said. "Administration is administration," she explained. I watched her devouring the carrot cake. When I asked her how many soldiers were in her care, she replied: "A blind man." "Bürki?" I cautiously asked. The woman ate and ate. "Stauffer," she finally said. "The blind man's name is Stauffer. Before that I had several soldiers. They all died. They were all blind. You can live here, too. After all, you were a soldier too, otherwise you wouldn't have come here." "I live elsewhere," I said. "It's up to you," she replied, and shoved the rest of the pie into her mouth. "We eat carrot cake exactly at noon and at eight o'clock sharp in the evening." I left. In the chapel, an old man was sitting by the font. I sat down across from him. "I'm blind," he said. "How did it happen?" I asked. "I saw the flash," he said. "The others saw the

*German poet and scholar Friedrich Rückert (1786–1866) is now almost forgotten except for the musical setting of his *Kindertotenlieder* by Gustav Mahler. *The Brahman's Wisdom* is a long didactic poem incorporating "wisdom" from Hindu, Islamic, and Christian sources.

flash, too. They're all dead." He shoved the plate away. "I don't like carrot cake. The only one who likes it is the old lady." "Stauffer?" I asked. "No," he replied, "Hadorn. My name is Hadorn. Stauffer is dead. Is your name Rüeger?" "My name is Rückhardt," I said. "Too bad," he said, "if you were Rüeger, I would have something for you." "What?" "Something from Stauffer." "But he's dead." "He got it from a dead man too." "From which dead man?" "From Zaugg." "Don't know him." "He got it from still another dead man." I weighed my options. "From Bürki?" He thought about it again. "I have a bad memory for names," he said then. "Because my name really is Rüeger," I said. "Then you have a bad memory for names too," he said, "because earlier you said you were not Rüeger. But I don't care who you are." He shoved something in my direction. It was Bürki's key. "Who is the Administration?" I asked. "I don't know," the blind man replied. I stood up and put the key in my coat pocket. "I'm leaving," I said. "I'm staying," he said, "I have to die soon anyhow." The Metzgergasse was a heap of rubble, the Zyttglogge Tower had collapsed.* It was night when I reached the government building, but as bright as if a full moon were shining. The two statues next to the main entrance had lost their heads. The dome had caved in, crossing the big entrance-hall was a dangerous undertaking, but the hall of the Great Chamber was surprisingly undamaged, even the huge hideous fresco was still intact; the deputes' benches, on the other hand, were gone. The hall had instead been furnished with tattered sofas, on which women in equally tattered dressing gowns were seated, some of them bare-breasted, all of them only sparsely lit by a few kerosene lamps. The spectators' booths had been covered with curtains. The tribune had been preserved. A woman with a round, energetic face was sitting on the Speaker's chair. She was wearing the uniform of a Salvation Army officer. The place smelled of onions. I stood hesitantly in the doorway. "Come here," the Salvationist commanded, "and take your pick." "I don't have any money," I replied. The woman stared at me. "My son," she said, "where are you coming from?" "From the front." She was amazed. "Then you've been on the road an awfully long time. Do you have an eraser?" "What for?" "For a girl, of course," she said. "We take what we need. A pencil sharpener would be even better." "All I have is a revolver," I said. "My son," the woman said, "hand it over, otherwise I'll have to report you to the Administration." "To Edinger?" I asked. "Who else?" the woman replied. "Where is the Administration?" I asked. "On the Eigerplatz," the woman replied. "Was this whorehouse—" "This establishment, my son!" "—this establishment, was it Edinger's idea?" "Of course," she replied. "We've been polluted by the Bomb,

---

Zyttglogge: Clock tower in Bern.

my son. We have to die. Any pleasure one person can give to another is a to-ken of divine love. I am a Major. I am proud that my brigade has understood this." She pointed at the women on the tattered sofas. "Consecrated to death, dedicated to love." "I am looking for Nora," I said. The Major seized the bell and rang it. "Nora," she called. In the diplomats' booth above us a curtain opened and Nora's head appeared. "What?" Nora asked. "A customer," the Major said. "I'm still busy," Nora replied, and disappeared again. "She's still on duty," the Major noted. "I'll wait," I said. The Major named her price: "For the gun." I gave her the revolver. "Sit down, my son," she said, "and wait." I sat down between two women on one of the tattered sofas. The Major pulled out a guitar from behind her Speaker's chair, tuned it, and all the women sang:

> "Nothing can defile our virtue
> When love dwells within the heart.
> All our torments are but specters
> When death's blade cleaves us apart.
> God did not have such a hard time,
> Crucified on Calvary.
> Ever since the Bomb exploded
> We are much worse off than he."

Nora came down. At first I thought she was carrying a boy, but it was a legless sixteen-year-old with a wrinkled child's face. "All right, my little hopper," Nora said, setting him down on a sofa, "now your soul's in better shape." "Nora," the Major said, "your next customer." Nora looked at me and pre-tended not to know me. She was naked beneath her dressing gown. "Well, let's get up there, my friend," she said and went through the door that led to the lobby. I followed her. The Major started playing the guitar again, and the brigade sang:

> "Sisters, open up your blouses,
> Give yourselves in charity.
> Fallen low, we lie down gladly,
> Lusting for eternity."

"Do you have the key?" Nora asked. I nodded. "Let's go," she said. We cau-tiously went through the ruined arcade and through the passageway to the east wing. We entered the corridor and inadvertently stopped. "I can't see anything," I said. "We have to get used to the dark," she replied, "something's always visible." We stood motionless. "How could you!" I said. "What?" she asked. "You know what I mean," I said. She fell silent. The darkness before us was impenetrable. "I had to maintain my position here," she replied. "Did Edinger force you?" She laughed. "Oh, no! But there wouldn't have been any reason for me to stay here otherwise. Can you see something now?" I lied: "Something." "Let's go." Cautiously we walked further into the corridor. I felt like a blind man. "Why were you so angry before?" Nora asked. "I used to carry on with all of you guys, too." I groped my way further into the darkness. "Yes, but that was with us," I said angrily. "My dear," Nora said, "I think your time is pretty much over." We climbed down into the basement. "Here," she said, "watch the stairs, there are twenty-two of them." I counted them as we walked down. She stopped. I heard her breathing. "To the right now," she said, "in this wall." I tapped the paneled wall with my hands, found the spot, it clicked open. I found the keyhole with my fingers, the key fit. "Close your eyes," I said. The door of the bunker opened. We sensed the light around us. We groped our way in, the door closed behind us. We opened our eyes; we were standing in the computer room. Nora examined the instruments. "The generators are working," she said. We went to the radio transmitter. Nora switched it on, and to our surprise "When the Morning Skies Turn Red" blasted out with such force that we jumped. "The Blümlisalp!" Nora cried. "It's the automatic transmitter," I reassured her, "there's no way anyone could still be alive down there." But then we heard a voice. It was Hosmann, the popular host of the night program with light music, anecdotes, and interviews: "Hosanna, here is Hosmann." "Dear listeners," said the voice, "It is now ten p.m." Then Hosmann gave the date and announced a repeat of a patriotic program. "They're still alive!" Nora cried, "They're still alive! That was today's date!" And then the voice of the Chief of the Military Department rang out through the loudspeaker. "My Chief!" Nora was beside herself. The Chief was addressing the nation with his sonorous voice. He explained that all of them, the government and the parliament and the bureaucracy, four thousand people altogether, women and men, mainly men of course, along with a thousand stenographers, had survived beneath the Blümlisalp, without radiation damage, with provisions that would last another two or three generations; that the nuclear plant was still operating, providing them with light and air—which surely ought to put the arguments of the antinuclear crowd to rest; that the government, the parliament, and the bureaucracy were therefore capable of continuing to govern the country and continuing to serve the people, even though it had become impossible for them to leave the Blümlisalp, since the enemy had been so cowardly as to drop a bomb precisely on top of the Blümlisalp; but beyond that, he said, they, the government, had nothing to complain about: it was up to the executive and the legislative branches and their agencies to sacrifice themselves and not the people, and that was what they had done. As the Chief of the Military Department continued with his speech, I stared at Nora. She stood there, her dressing gown had opened, and she was listening to her Chief with bated breath. I pounced on her, dragged her to the floor, yanked her thighs apart; I hadn't had a woman for ages. And the Chief spoke on, saying that it was with great joy that he had learned of our craven enemy's defeat at Landeck, and that he was convinced that the army and its courageous allies were already advancing toward final victory deep in the steppes of Asia, indeed that victory was probably already at hand, but that he along with the rest of the government had not yet heard anything from the outer world because the extremely intense radioactive field on the Blümlisalp was apparently interfering with the reception of wireless transmissions. He talked and talked. Nora was still listening to him. I gasped, groaned, she pressed her right hand over my mouth so that she could hear her boss, so that she wouldn't miss a single word of his. I was on top of her, frantic, and all the more insatiable as she would listen only to this voice from the loudspeaker, while her body gave itself over to me without the slightest welcome or resistance. Of course it was possible, the boss explained with noticeable apprehension, of course it was not entirely out of the question, although quite unlikely, that the war had taken a different course than the one our generals had anticipated; that given the enemy's numerical and in terms of conventional weaponry downright gigantic superiority, the victors might turn out to be those who could claim territorial conquest, that is to say conquest of land alone, not of the people, who were as unconquerable now as they had been back in the days of Morgarten, Sempach, and Murten.* I was in a frenzy on top of Nora, working myself into a rage, because she was still listening, because she was still indifferent to me. Precisely this fact, the chief continued, must be dawning on the enemy by now, not only as a result of the people's heroic resistance, which continues unabated—how could anyone doubt that—but especially because the legitimate government, the parliament, and the bureaucratic organs elected by the people were freely discharging their obligations beneath the Blümlisalp by day and by night, governing, passing decrees, issuing laws; indeed, they and no one else *were* the people, properly speaking; therefore they alone were entitled to negotiate

*Morgarten, Sempach, and Murten: Morgarten, a town south of Zürich, was the scene of a battle in 1314 that was the first victory of the Swiss confederation over the Hapsburgs. Sempach, a town near Lucerne, was the scene of a further defeat of the Hapsburgs in 1386. Murten (in French, Morat), a town about 30 kilometers from Bern, was the scene of a bloody battle in 1467 that ended in the defeat, by the Swiss, of the Duke of Burgundy and in his death.

with the enemy, not as a vanquished nation but as the true victor. For no matter how devastated the country was—assuming, for the moment, that this unlikely event had actually occurred—indeed, even if the country had ceased to offer any resistance, or—this, too, was unfortunately conceivable—that it no longer existed, its functioning government, its freely elected parliament and perfect bureaucracy certainly did exist. They would never capitulate. On the contrary, they were prepared, for the sake of world peace, to reaffirm their independence, established on the everlasting foundation of armed neutrality.

Actually, all I remember are shreds of words that I am now piecing together; I came like I had never come before, it seemed to go on forever, and as I let go of Nora, "When the Morning Skies Turn Red" was sounding again from the loudspeaker. We stood up. I was bathed in sweat. We went to the laboratory, both of us naked. She took a sample of my blood and examined it. "You'll stay alive," she said. "And you?" I asked. "The Administration examined me," she said. "I was lucky. Like you." Again I attacked her, dragging her down to the floor next to the lab table, but again I went into a rage, because as I tried to take her, she said in a cold, matter-of-fact voice: "A functioning government without a people is really ideal for the government," and then she laughed and didn't stop laughing, and I let go of her. "How many people work in the Administration?" I asked after I had calmed down. "Twenty or thirty, no more than that," she replied. Then she got up and stood before me. "Where does Edinger live?" I asked, still sitting on the floor, naked, exhausted. She regarded me thoughtfully. "Why do you want to know?" "No reason," I replied. "In Bethlehem.* In a penthouse," she finally said. "Do you know his first name?" She hesitated. "Jeremias," she said then. I went to the computer. Only a few Edingers were listed, among them Jeremias Edinger. I quickly scanned the facts: philosophy major, no degree. Environmentalist, draft resister, death sentence, commuted to a life sentence by parliament. I went back to the radio station, closed the door, the code lay in the secret compartment. I returned to Nora, got dressed. She had put on her dressing gown. I went to the arsenal, selected a pistol with a silencer, told her to keep the key and lock the place up, and that I was going to do something that might be dangerous. Nora said nothing. I left the government building through a door on the east wing.

There was only one skyscraper still standing in Bethlehem, though actually it looked more like a ghostly scaffolding. I entered the building, everything was

*District in the city of Bern, the capital of Switzerland.

burned out on the ground floor, the elevator shafts were empty, the only lighting came from the extraordinarily bright night sky. I was already starting to think I was wrong and the building was uninhabited when I discovered a ladder. I climbed it up to a flat roof directly adjoining the dark surface of a penthouse. There was light shining through the cracks of the door. I knocked. I heard steps in the penthouse, then the door opened and a silhouette appeared in the bright bluish rectangle. "Is Jeremias Edinger here?" I asked. "My dad is still in the office," a girl's voice replied. "I'll wait for him downstairs," I said. "Why don't you wait with me," the girl said. "Come in. My mom isn't home yet either." The girl went into the penthouse, and I followed her with my hands in my coat pockets. Opposite the door was a huge glass wall, and I understood why the interior of the penthouse appeared to be lit. Behind the glass wall stood the bright sky, a translucent bluish silver, not because the moon was shining but because the mountains appeared to be phosphorescent. The Blümlisalp was so radiant that it cast shadows. I looked at the girl. She resembled a ghost in that light. She was thin, her eyes were very large and her hair was the same color as the Blümlisalp. There were two beds by one of the walls. In the middle of the room stood a table with three chairs. Two books were lying on the table, *Heidi* and Schwegler's *Brief History of Philosophy: An Outline.** By the opposite wall stood a stove, and there was a rocking chair by the glass wall. The girl lit a candelabrum with three candles. The warm light transformed the room. A child's gaily colored pictures hung on the walls. The girl was wearing a red gym suit, her eyes were large and cheerful, her hair was white blond, she must have been around ten years old. "You're scared," she said, "because the Blümlisalp is shining so brightly." "Well, yes," I said, "I am a little scared." "The shining has gotten stronger over the past few weeks. Dad is worried," the girl said. "Dad thinks I should leave with Mom." I looked at the drawings. "*Heidi*," the girl said. "I made pictures for the whole story. That's Alp-Öhi over there, and that's Peter the goat-boy. Won't you sit down?" the girl asked. "On the rocking chair, it's for guests." I went to the glass wall, looked out at the Blümlisalp and sat down on the rocker. The girl read *Heidi* at the table. It must have been around three in the morning when I heard steps. A tall, fat man appeared in the door. He looked at me briefly and turned to the girl. "What are you doing up at this time, Gloria?" he said. "Close the book and go to bed." The girl closed the book. "I can't sleep before you come home, Dad," she said. "And Mom isn't home yet." "Your Mom will be home any minute," the tall, heavy man said, and came toward me. "My office is on Eigerplatz," he said. "I have something personal to talk to you about, Edinger,"

*Albert Schwegler (1819–1857), German philosopher and theologian.

I said. "Don't you want to introduce yourself?" he asked. I rocked in my chair. "My name is irrelevant," I replied. "Fine," he said, "let's have some cognac." He went to the stove, bent down, pulled out a bottle and two brandy glasses. He came back into the room, stroked the girl's hair (she was already in bed), blew out the candles, opened the door, motioned for me to follow, and we both stepped out onto the roof, which lay before us like a flat plain strewn with scattered ruins, shrubs, and small trees. We sat down on the remains of a chimney, looking down on the ruins of Bethlehem. Behind one of the collapsed skyscrapers in the distance, the city with the narrow, upward-striving silhouette of the Münster was barely visible. "You were a soldier?" "I'm still a soldier," I replied. He gave me a glass, filled it, and then filled his own. "From the French Embassy," he said. "The glasses too. Crystal." I asked him if the Embassy was still there. "Just the cellar," he replied. "The Administration has its own secrets," he added. We drank. He asked me what I had been before. "A student, with old Katzbach," I replied. "I was in the middle of a dissertation." "I see," he said. "About Plato." And then he asked: "What part of Plato?" "*The Republic*," I replied, "The seventh book." He said he had studied with Katzbach too. "I know," I said. "You know all about me," he remarked, but without surprise, and drank. "What happened to Katzbach?" I asked. His apartment had caught fire when the bomb fell, Edinger reported, swirling the cognac in his glass, "too many manuscripts." "Philosopher's luck," I said, "there's nothing left of the German department either." Only Schwegler's book, he said, that was the only thing he'd been able to find there. "I saw it on your table," I replied. We fell silent, staring out at the Blümlisalp. "Have yourself examined tomorrow," Edinger said, "on Eigerplatz." "I'll live," I replied, "I've already been examined." He didn't ask who had examined me, poured me some more cognac and himself, too. "Where is the army, Edinger?" I asked. "We mobilized eight hundred thousand men." "The army," he said, "the army." He drank. "A bomb fell on Innsbruck." He drank again. "It took a while to explode. You're coming from the army. Then you were lucky." We were silent, stared at the city, drank. "We will probably have to give up this country," Edinger said. "Probably Europe altogether." What had happened in central and southern Africa, he said, was beyond description. Not to even mention the other continents. So far, there was no sign of life from the United States. There weren't more than a hundred million people left on the planet. While before, it was ten billion. I looked at the Blümlisalp. It was brighter than the full moon. "We have founded a World Administration," he said. I swirled the cognac in my glass. "We?" I asked. He did not answer right away. "You refused to serve in the army, Edinger," I said, raising my glass in the direction of the Blümlisalp. A spectral glow lit up the mountain. "You are alive because the prison walls protected you. A joke. If the parliament had had any guts, you would have been shot long ago." "I guess you would have had the guts," he said. I nodded. "You'd better believe it, Edinger." I took a sip, relished it. A dull explosion resounded from the city. The silhouette of the Münster tilted. There followed a far-away thundering, and a bluish cloud of dust rose, descended. The Münster was gone. "That was the Münster terrace collapsing. It tore the Münster down with it," he said indifferently. "We've been expecting this all along. By the way, you're right, Colonel," he continued. "We draft resisters founded the Administration here, elsewhere it's the dissidents or the victims of the antiradical laws." Edinger had given himself away. He knew who I was. But for the time being, that didn't matter. It was more important for me to find out more about the Administration. "So there are other branches of your World Administration in other places," I said, "and that's why you're so well informed, Edinger." "By wireless," he said. "There's no electricity," I interjected. "Some of us are handy," he replied. His face was ghostlike in the unnatural light, and something inexplicable was emanating from him, something strangely rigid. "At one point I thought I saw an airplane," I reported. He drank. "From the Central Administration in Nepal," he said. "They use it to test the radioactivity." I thought about this. There was something wrong with this story. "You know who I am, Edinger," I remarked. "I knew you would come, Colonel," he replied. "Bürki prepared me." We sat silently. "Did he give you the key, too?" I asked. "He did," he said. "And Nora?" I asked. Nora didn't know anything about it, he said. Finding the bunker under the east wing wasn't hard. He had listened to some of the government's speeches, and then he had given the key back to Bürki. Bürki had died, and the key, he said, had come into my possession via Zaugg, Stauffer, Rüeger, and Hagedorn. "You're well informed," I said. He drained his glass of cognac. "The Administration is well informed," he replied. I pointed at the glowing Blümlisalp. "That's where the Administration is, Edinger," I said, "a functioning government, a functioning parliament, a functioning bureaucracy. Once we liberate them, we'll have a better Administration than your World Administration of draft dodgers and dissidents. I bet it's a marvel of improvisation. Pour me another drink, Edinger." He poured out some more cognac. "There's one thing you're probably starting to realize, Edinger," I continued, "I'm stronger than you are." "You mean because you have a weapon?" he asked and drank. "I handed over my gun to the madam of the whorehouse your Administration set up in the government building," I said. He laughed. "Colonel, in the bunker under the east wing you had access to a weapons depot. And to the code." I was taken aback: "What do you know about the code?" He did not answer right away. He stared at the

Blümlisaslp, and again that strangely rigid quality appeared in his big, heavy face. Bürki had shown him the code in the secret drawer under the east wing, he said, and then they had all put their heads together and deciphered several secret messages the government had issued from the Blümlisalp. Incidentally, he said, that was only possible because the underground cable was undamaged, the radio transmitter in the Blümlisalp had been disabled by radioactivity, so the government could only be reached from the east wing of the government building. The government was desperate, he said. They had tried in vain to get in touch with me, and had now given up trying. They had hoped I would liberate them, and now they were addressing their plea to those who they were convinced had won the war, to the enemies, unaware of the fact that there were no victors, that everyone was vanquished; that the soldiers of all armies had refused to go on fighting and had shot their officers, that the World Administration had assumed power and that those soldiers who had survived the catastrophe were now trying to make the Sahara arable: perhaps this would be a way for the human race to survive after all. He fell silent. I had listened to his report and was now considering my options. "What do you suggest I do?" I asked. He emptied his glass. "The people in the Sahara are working to survive," he said. It wasn't clear, he continued, whether the radioactive fallout would reach them, it wasn't out of the question. The people were trying to irrigate the desert with unbelievably primitive instruments. They were working like cavemen. They hated technology. They hated everything that reminded them of the old world. They were in a state of shock. It was this state of shock, he said, that we had to overcome. "You studied philosophy just like me," he said. "I have Schwegler's book. Remember? We used to laugh at his *Outline of Philosophy*. But maybe you could teach the people in the Sahara that thinking isn't just dangerous." He fell silent. This suggestion was grotesque. "Learning to think with Schwegler," I laughed. "It's all we have," he said. "This is the only possibility you have to offer me?" I asked. He hesitated. "There is another one," he finally replied, "but I don't offer it gladly." "And what would that be?" I asked. "Power," he said. I observed Edinger thoughtfully; he was hiding something from me. "You want to include me in the Administration, Edinger?" I asked. "No," he replied, "you can't be included in the Administration, Colonel." He turned his heavy face toward me. "The Administration is a court of arbitration, that's all it is. Every individual is free to decide whether he wants powerlessness or power, whether he wants to be a citizen or a mercenary. But you can choose. Your choice must be accepted by the Administration." I gave that some thought. "What does a mercenary's power consist of?" I asked suspiciously. "It consists of what all power consists of," he replied, "power over people."

"Which people?" I inquired further. "People who fall into the hands of mercenaries," Edinger replied obscurely. "Stop beating around the bush,
Edinger," I said. "You lack perspective, Colonel," he replied. "World War
Three isn't over yet." "Really?" I said. "Where is it still going on?" Again he
hesitated, staring into his glass. "In Tibet," he finally replied. "People are continuing to fight there." "Who?" I asked. "The mercenaries." I was finding all
of this quite unbelievable. "Who attacks the mercenaries?" I asked. "The enemy," Edinger replied. "Who is this enemy?" I wanted to know. "That's the
mercenaries' business," he replied evasively. "The Administration doesn't
get involved in their business." Our conversation was turning around in
circles. Either the enemy had to be stronger than Edinger wanted to admit, or
the war in Tibet was a trap. I couldn't afford to take a risk. "Edinger," I said, "I
was the liaison officer of our army under the Commander. When the Allies
capitulated and the staff celebrated this capitulation, the Commander sin-
glehandedly shot his staff." "So?" Edinger asked. I looked at him. "Edinger," I
said, "by the side of the road to Zernez there were more than three hundred
officers. Shot by our soldiers." Edinger drained his glass. "Our soldiers don't
want to fight anymore," he said. I pulled out the pistol with the silencer. "Pour
me another drink, Edinger," I said. "I don't care about the soldiers in Tibet,
and I don't give a damn about your Administration either. All I care about is
the government, the Blümlisalp. The country is full of dying people. I'll use
these people, who are dying anyway, to save the government." Edinger filled
his glass and swirled it. "You will go to Tibet nonetheless, Colonel," he said
calmly, putting the bottle down next to himself on the flat roof, and tasted the
cognac. "Stand up," I commanded, "go to the edge of the roof. You are a draft
dodger and a traitor." Edinger obeyed, and turned back to me once more by
the edge of the roof, a silhouette against the radiant backdrop of the Blümlisalp. "The Blümlisalp," he said. Then he laughed and asked me: "Do you
know what this makes me think of, Colonel, when I see the Blümlisalp shining like that?" I shook my head. "It makes me think of what I said at my trial,
when I was sentenced to death. I suggested that, with the money we would
save by getting rid of the army, we could do something crazy: build the
biggest observatory in the world on the Blümlisalp." He laughed. He waved to
me. Then he emptied his glass, threw it down into the ruins below him, and
turned his back to me. "In the name of our government," I said, and fired three
shots into the silhouette. It dropped away. The bright night sky before me was
empty. I heard Edinger's body hit the ground far below. Then I started to feel
that something was missing. I picked up the bottle and threw it after him.

I felt someone standing behind me. I whirled around, with the pistol in my hand. It was Nora. She was wearing overalls, the kind workers wear. Her hair was draped over her shoulders. In the eerie light, it looked as white as the girl's hair in the penthouse. "Nora," I said, "I killed the traitor Edinger. It wasn't necessary for you to follow me." She didn't say anything. I walked just a few steps to the edge of the roof, and turned around. "Nora," I said, bewildered, "I'm missing something, and I don't know what it is." "I've been here for a long time," she replied. "I listened to you. Gloria is my child, and Edinger was my husband." I stared at her. "There was nothing about that in the computer," I said. "If it had been in the computer, I wouldn't be working for the government," she replied, walked past me to the edge of the roof and looked down. "I'm glad you killed him. When the bomb fell, he was working with other prisoners in the bog. There was no way to save him. He suffered terrible pain. He had to go through hell." She turned around and came up to me. "I know what you are thinking now, because you can only think in one category." She stopped in front of me, a dark shape framed by the continually brightening sky. "But I am not a traitor. Edinger was my husband and nothing else. A man. But I thought he was a fool. I believed all that nonsense about national defense. I was pregnant when he was sentenced to death as a draft resister and then to life in prison. That was eight years before the war broke out. I had made it possible for him to study. He called me his Xanthippe, jokingly. That woman, he said, had done more for philosophy than all other women. What compelled him to resist military service was intellectual honesty: what one thinks, one must carry out, he said; there is no need for conscience, but thought is a necessity; conscience and thought are the same thing. He loved our country, but he accused it of dodging thought. He didn't hate anyone. But I felt abandoned by him. I was afraid. My instinct told me that we need a national defense. He told me that the government, the parliament, and the government bureaucracy would be the only survivors. He foresaw all the things that eventually happened. I didn't believe him. When he was put in jail, I began to take revenge: I went to bed with every one of you." It had gotten so bright that I could see her face now. It was stony and perfectly calm. "And because I took revenge against my husband, whom I loved, and because I went to bed with every one of you of the higher military administration, I became a patriot, and I remained a patriot even when everything Edinger had foreseen came to pass." She smiled, and suddenly a new quality came into her face, a tenderness I wouldn't have thought her capable of. "I am such a patriot that I took part in the brothel he set up in the government building. That, too, he did for purely logical reasons: because the dying need a brothel. He was the one who convinced the Salvation

Army, too." She laughed. "And so I became a prostitute in order to wait for you and for your assignment. I thought Edinger didn't know anything about this, but now I know that he did." "You were a matter of indifference to him," I said. She looked at me. "Every night around this time I would come here. He was in such pain he could no longer sleep, but never have I spent a more beautiful time with another human being than during these hours before dawn. We talked, and when he reached for the book he had found in the ruins of the university, I knew he wanted to go on thinking, and I went to sleep. He told me once that he had reconstructed philosophy, from one silly manual. Sometimes a deaf-mute came to visit him at night. Together they reconstructed mathematics, physics, and astronomy. Everything could be reconstructed, he said, because no idea can be lost." I stepped up to the edge of the roof and looked down. Far below, I saw Edinger with his arms and legs spread out. I couldn't make out whether he was on his back or not. "Whether Edinger was a genius or not," I said, returning to Nora, "is something we don't have to worry about any longer." "You want to organize the dying," she said. I told her I had to carry out my assignment, and that was why I wanted to get in touch with the government under the Blümlisalp as soon as possible, before the Administration could stop me. "You can no longer do that," she said calmly. "After you left the bunker under the east wing, I switched on the automatic detonator and followed you. I saw you going to the penthouse. I waited outside. Edinger didn't see me either. I stood behind you when the explosion went off. The rest of the dome remained standing. But the Münster came down. There is no way to reach the government any more." I stared at her, horrified. I no longer understood anything. Nora had lost her mind. She looked at the Blümlisalp. "When we were in the room and I heard the voice of the commentator and then the speech of our Chief, I suddenly understood that Edinger was right," she said. "I took you!" I screamed. She approached me and stopped in front of me. "Colonel," she calmly said, "did you not understand what the Chief said?" "I took you!" I screamed at her. "Could be," she said. "I don't care what you did with me. But I listened to that speech and suddenly understood what they had done to us: a government, a parliament, a bureaucracy that consider themselves the people, for whom the people are just a pretext for getting themselves out of danger, it's just too ridiculous for words; Colonel, let them sit for all eternity under their Blümlisalp! And now you come along with your idiotic idea of getting the dying to scrape this government without a people out of the grave they dug for themselves. Do you still not understand that every patriotism is ridiculous? What is this government still there for? And do you think this is the only government sitting in its Blümlisalp? Edinger claimed that the governments of the whole world are trapped in their bunkers, governments like ours, governments without a people and without enemies." Suddenly I understood what I had been missing ever since I had killed Edinger. "The enemy," I said slowly. "I no longer have an enemy." I was suddenly unspeakably tired and without hope. It had become bright as day, the Blümlisalp grew hazy. It was morning. The girl slipped past me and hugged her mother, who was standing before me, proud and beautiful. "Go to Tibet," Nora said, "to the Winter War . . ."

[*Here the inscription breaks off. Parts of its continuation were found in a far-off tunnel.*] . . . been confused for some time (months, years?). Not because I live in complete darkness; I know my way around and can always find the way back to my ammunition and my provisions. At any moment, of course, the enemy can enter the system of tunnels that was under my control when the lights were still working—and maybe he's here already—but he'll find it more difficult to find me. Writing, too, is becoming difficult: sometimes I have to touch the tunnel wall with the tiny part of my right upper arm that is not yet a mechanical replacement, or sometimes with my cheeks, to feel whether I have already covered it with writing. I estimate by the revolutions of the wheels on my wheelchair that the lines I am writing are two kilometers long, and I now only write two lines in a row. But what troubles me is neither the possibility of an enemy attack nor my personal discomforts. I have accepted my situation. It fills me with pride, for I have taken over Edinger's position: in this labyrinth beneath Chomolungma I am the only defender of the Administration. I am atoning for Edinger's death; even though what I gave him was a coup de grace. His suggestion to teach philosophy to the people irrigating the Sahara is understandable. He was trying to reconstruct philosophy. But Nora was right: given my function and my fate in the Winter War, I am more useful to the Administration here. It may be cruel, but it makes sense. I remember that night beneath the peak of Gosainthan in the Commander's headquarters when we heard "When the morning skies turn red." On short-wave radio. The transmitter on the Blümlisalp must have accidentally pierced the fallout for a moment. We also heard a speech by the president: he said he was prepared to negotiate with the enemy on honorable terms. The thought that I had served this government was embarrassing. Occasionally we heard other national anthems and other government leaders expressing their readiness for peace. There was one man who went on endlessly and desperately in Russian, but we didn't know any Russian. He finished by announcing his country's capitulation in all the various languages. The Administration that I am now serving will never consider such options. It will never surrender to the enemy. But what confuses me is an event that I don't understand. Not that the Winter War could have taken a turn that would prove fatal to the Administration: that is out of the question. I believe in our final victory. I have no doubt about that. But recently, after advancing with my inscriptions to a point that must have been near the brothel, which was closed down a long time ago, I noticed a far-off light. It could have been the enemy, of whom I had seen no sign for years. Maybe they were preparing a major offensive. I rolled forward cautiously and found the great hall of the brothel lit up bright as daylight and full of people: men, women, entire families. Many were taking photographs, and others, uniformed men, were explaining the layout. I was so surprised that I rolled right into the crowd. Blinded by the light, I almost fired at them, but I recognized just in time that I was not among enemy soldiers but among travelers. I fired off a warning burst from my submachine gun: the travelers were in danger, they could be attacked by the enemy. It was careless to permit and organize this visit to the old brothel. The travelers ran off through a large tunnel with screams of terror. I rolled after them, it could have been enemies disguised as travelers. The tunnel was lit, like the brothel, and the ground was paved. Suddenly I reached an open space. Mercenary soldiers with oxygen masks and submachine guns were staring at me from a rock cavern. I fired. I heard the sound of breaking glass: the soldiers were wax figures, exhibited behind a glass pane and artfully illuminated. I was in a large exhibition hall. Behind further sheets of glass, I saw scene after scene from the Winter War represented by wax figures. I recoiled when I recognized the Commander and myself behind one of those panes; there was a reproduction, exact to the most minute particulars, of our command post inside the peak of Gosainthan. I was in a museum. In a rage, I sprayed the displays with bullets. I saw the shadowy forms of uniformed people running, they were museum personnel. I rolled after them and suddenly found myself facing the exit. Outside, a park full of rhododendrons, a blue, cloudless sky, a man in a white smock, bald, with glasses, waving a white cloth, as if he were a doctor. I shot him down and rolled back through the museum into the tunnel and into the abandoned brothel. With the mechanical claw where my right hand used to be I picked up a pamphlet from the floor. It was a "Guide through the mercenaries' brothel in Gasherbrum III," the "shining wall." I picked up more pamphlets, all of them with the same title. It took me several days to reach the old cave.

An impenetrable darkness surrounds me as I scratch this inscription into a new tunnel. I am not disconcerted by the enemy's advance. I am irritated, because I had always assumed that the brothel was under Kanchenjunga, in the "five treasure chambers of the great snow," in the eastern Himalayas; but Gasherbrum, the mountain of which the pamphlets claim that the brothel is underneath it, is in the Karakoram range, six hundred miles off to the northwest. It's possible, of course, that these pamphlets were deliberately forged by the enemy. Whatever the case, it is no longer safe for me to stay here. I remember a cave where, as a Lieutenant, I mustered my first raiding party, a cruel selection: no more than a third of the soldiers survive. I have decided to visit this training camp, perhaps I will find my unit again, even though there is the danger that the camp has been occupied by the enemy, a possibility I now have to reckon with. The fact that travelers are visiting the brothel the way people used to visit excavations does suggest that the battles are raging far to the west now, but the enemy may have conquered large parts of the areas governed by the Administration, though of course I don't believe this. Nevertheless: I shot the man in the white smock, even though he was probably a member of the Administration. Maybe he was an enemy after all. I am concluding the inscription in this tunnel. [*End of the inscription.*] Cautiously I rolled into the tunnel system that leads to the training camp, equipped with provisions that would sustain me for several days. I still remembered exactly how to get there—without a perfect memory survival in this war is impossible. At a crossing of two tunnels, which announced itself by the almost imperceptible draft that arises at every crossing, it seemed to me as if I heard a scratching sound in a neighboring tunnel. I slowly rolled into the tunnel, inch by inch, stopped, the scratching sound had stopped. Instead, it seemed as if something was rolling toward me. Then silence. I rolled forward cautiously, again inch by inch, stopped, listened: again that rolling sound was coming toward me, and again there was silence. I rolled further, stopped, listened. This process of rolling closer to each other lasted for hours. Suddenly someone was breathing right in front of me, I remained motionless, holding my breath. The breathing started again. Since there could be several other enemies nearby, it was better not to use the submachine gun. I swung out my right claw and missed, rolled forward, swung again, it sounded like steel clashing against steel. I struck again, fell out of my wheelchair, rolled around on the ground with something else, pounding at it again and again, striking steel at times and soft parts at others. Then the other thing stopped moving. I searched for my wheelchair. It was a jumble of steel parts. I crawled on my stumps, searched, fell into a shaft, struck against something with my face, rolled about and fell into another shaft. I must have lain unconscious for a long time. When I came to, I was lying in something sticky that was covering my face. I wanted to shoot—I could have fallen into the midst of the enemies—but my left arm prosthesis was missing. I was weaponless.

I still am. It seems I am in a cave. I can feel that my face is a bloody pulp. The ground is rubble. With a great effort I drag myself alongside the wall of the cave, which must be immense. Sometimes the draft is icy, sometimes there is an unbearable heat: probably I am very close to the huge workshops where the weapons are manufactured; whether these are our weapons or those of the enemy, I don't know. My position is hopeless. Crawling on the ground, with only myself to rely on, following the wall of this enormous cave, which often winds about in the strangest way, I can now ask myself the question I never permitted myself while the fight was on: who is the enemy? The question no longer has the power to paralyze me, nor does the answer. I have nothing more to lose. That is my strength. I have become invincible. I have solved the riddle of the Winter War. Even though I no longer have a wheelchair, even though my submachine gun prosthesis lies somewhere behind me in one of the tunnels, I am using the steel stylus to scrape my insight in minuscule letters into the rock, not so that it will be read, but to give clearer shape to my thoughts. For by digging them into the rock, I am digging them into my brain: the path that leads to knowledge is difficult to walk, even more difficult than the paths I have traveled since tumbling down a filthy staircase in a small Nepalese town. Without taking the risk of fictions, the path to knowledge cannot be trodden. Thus, in the absolute darkness that reigns around me, I imagine a light; not the absolute light, but a light that corresponds to my situation: I imagine people in a cave, people who have been bound in chains by their necks and thighs from an early age, so that all they can do is sit still, looking straight ahead at the wall of the cave. They are holding submachine guns. Above them, a fire is shining. Between this fire and the chained people there is a transverse path. Alongside this path I imagine a little wall. On top of this wall, powerful prison guards would bring out people who would also be chained and would also be holding submachine guns. But then, as I go on digging my inscription, sliding along on the rubble covering the floor of the cave, I ask myself whether I ever see anything more of myself or the others than the shadows cast by the fire on the wall of the cave before me, and whether those shadowy figures aren't the only truth I can recognize; yes, and if a voice were to call out to me from somewhere, telling me that these shadows, which after all exhibit shadows of submachine guns, are my enemies, whether I would not shoot at the wall of the cave before me and thus—since the bullets would ricochet off the wall—kill those who are, like myself, chained by their necks and thighs; and whether they, because they believe and act as I do, would also kill me. But if my chains were removed and I were suddenly made to stand and turn my head and walk about and look into the light, and if that glaring light were painful and I were unable to look at these people whose shadows I used to see, people in the same situation as myself: would I not be of the opinion that the shadowy forms I had seen earlier were more real than those I was now being shown? And if I were forced to look into the light itself, the pain would make me run away and turn back to those shadow men I was able to look at; and I would persist in thinking that these were really more distinct than those I had been shown, for these were my enemies; and would I not start shooting again, to kill them again and have myself killed by them again and again? I need not give myself any further answers. I remember puzzling over this same simile long ago; maybe I read it somewhere, or else I imagined it, I no longer know. Probably I invented it while I was scratching in the rock. The fire that casts the shadows must have come into being an immensely long time ago. It's with good reason that fire strikes fear in every beast; fire is an enemy, and man's enemy is his shadow. That is why I shot Edinger and the man hanging in the cave, that is why I killed the Commander: they no longer believed that the shadows are enemies; they believed the shadows were chained men like myself. And now that I think this, I suddenly understand the Administration: having emerged victorious from the three world wars, it administers a human race which, because it is being administered, has lost its meaning: the beast that is man has no meaning, its existence on earth no longer has a goal. What is the purpose of man? is a question without an answer. The will to sustain man and earth is lacking. Man suffers in other respects as well, he is in the main a sickly beast; but his problem is not suffering itself, it is that there is no answer to the cry, "Why this suffering?" Man, the bravest of beasts and the one most inured to suffering, does not reject suffering as such; he wants it, he will even seek it out, provided he can be shown a meaning for it, a meaning for suffering. Life's meaninglessness, not suffering, is the curse that the Administration was unable to dispel, short of restoring to man the very meaning from which, grotesquely enough, it liberated him: the enemy. Man is only possible as a beast of prey. Even though no heavier fate can be imagined than that of the beast of prey, hounded by the most ravenous distress through the web of tunnels beneath Chomno-Lungma, Chooyu, Makalu, and Manaslu, or beneath Gosainthan, rarely satisfied, and even then only in such a way that the satisfaction becomes a torment, in lacerating struggles with other beasts of prey or in the disgusting greed and glut of the subterranean brothels. To cling to life so blindly and madly, for no higher prize; far from realizing that one is being punished, let alone why, but craving that punishment as if it were happiness itself—this is what it means to be a beast of prey; and when Nature herself is driven to prey and to plunder, she signals thereby that this is necessary for her release from the curse of life and that ultimately, in that savage compulsion, existence holds up a mirror to itself, in the depths of which life no longer appears senseless but is revealed in its metaphysical significance. But consider the following: where does the beast of prey end—this cruel, bloody, predatory ape called man—and where does the Superman begin? In him who can survey the hell of the cave into which he is banished; who does not succumb to the illusion that the shadows are those of his enemies and not his own shadow; who tears away even this most subtle veil behind which the truth lies hidden: the goal of man is to be his own enemy—man and his shadow are one. He who understands this truth inherits the world, he restores to the Administration the meaning it lost. The lord of the world is myself. In the overpowering glare of the light I see myself rolling through a tunnel in my wheelchair and arriving at a cave; and from an opposite tunnel I am rolling toward myself, both of us now have two submachine guns in place of arms, there is nothing more to be scratched into the wall, we point our four submachine guns at ourselves and simultaneously shoot.

[*The mercenary's body was found by mountain climbers on a rocky slope at the foot of Gasherbrum III, 7,952 meters, in the Karakoram. The mercenary had dragged himself alongside the cliff for about 150 meters, scratching his inscription with his right prosthesis into the cliff and onto larger stones that he apparently also took for the rock wall of Gasherbrun III (which is very steep hereabouts) or of some other mountain. His face was a bloody mass of flesh. He must have been blind. In addition, the body had been attacked by a scavenger (a vulture, a jackal?), but was then left in peace. The inscription was hard to decipher as, very soon after it was begun in the tunnels of Gasherbrum III, it was almost exclusively written from right to left instead of from left to right, and likewise on the opposite wall, probably as a result of the man's being ensconced in a wheelchair: it would have been easier for him to write this way in the dark. Outside, on the rocky slope, at the foot of Gasherbrum III, he must have continued his chiseling: a single row, 150 meters in length, of very small and often nearly indecipherable letters without any spaces between the words and without punctuation. The concluding passages confirm his earlier studies in philosophy. They appear to be reminiscences: a collage of Plato* (Republic, *simile of the cave) and Nietzsche* (On the Genealogy of Morals, Schopenhauer as Educator). *Having nearly lost the capacity to think for himself, all he had left were quotations. Unwittingly he constructed, not philosophy, but his own philosophy. At least we* *must make this assumption in view of our accidental discovery in Jamestown (Australia) of a library, apparently belonging to a philosopher, our most important supplement to the Schwegler book. (In addition to Plato's Republic and Nietzsche's Collected Works, the library also contained The Myth of the Twentieth Century by Rosenberg.* Since neither Nietzsche nor Rosenberg are mentioned by Schwegler, contemporary scholarship considers them to be philosophical fictions.) But this inscription is contradictory. Due to the difficult situation in which the human race still finds itself after World War Three, the Administration was not able to finance more than one scientific expedition to the Gasherbrum massif. Shortly after completing their work, the massif collapsed; the mercenaries must have thoroughly hollowed it out. Why they believed themselves to be in the Himalayas is impossible to determine. The inscription itself is no longer extant, all that we have is a transcript. Several scholars believe that the inscription was written by two "I"s. The number 6023 10²³, which the deaf-mute wrote on the blackboard, can also be read as being identical with Loschmidt's constant, 6.023 × 10²³. Incidentally, we owe the rediscovery of this constant to the inscription. The other "I," then, would be the deaf-mute. Knührböhl, Hoppler, and Arthur Poll believe that this deaf-mute was Jonathan, and that he, too, scratched inscriptions into the rock. They find it noteworthy that he is not mentioned later on. Nora, they point out, tells the "Colonel" that Edinger and the deaf-mute have reconstructed mathematics, physics, and astronomy; the "Colonel" is preoccupied with the question of the enemy; but a part of the inscription shows a preoccupation with the fate of humanity, associating this question with the evolution of "suns"; it is not conceivable, in these scholars' opinion, that this part of the inscription was written by the "Colonel." Others, like Stirnknall, de la Poudre, and Teilhard von Zähl, find it significant that there is no "Edinger" in the Administration's registry. In their opinion the inscription is a kind of dream invented by the Colonel to alleviate his hopeless situation, splitting himself up, as it were, into two mercenaries, a man of action and a thinker. It is worth noting, in this connection, that we have no concrete information about the vanished continent of Europe. Only its music has been preserved. It was the supreme achievement of this continent. The tune called "When the Morning Skies Turn Red" is also extant. However, we do not give credence to an amateur radio operator's claim that he recently heard this tune on the short wave band: the man is a notorious alcoholic.]*

---

*Alfred Rosenberg (1893–1946), Nazi ideologue and racist theoretician. Found guilty at the Nuremberg trials and executed.

The Bridge

The truth is a statement that should correspond with the facts, it is a true statement concerning reality and is therefore identical with reality—a somewhat simple but robust definition. Interpretative reason either deduces a truth from another truth that is in turn deduced from a further truth and so on, all the way back to a truth that is not a deduction; that is, reason interprets deductively, or else it employs fictions, hypotheses, and theories in an inductive fashion. Deductive reason bets on certainty, inductive reason takes risks. Deductively interpretative reason is the reason of the gods; they know the truth, they deduce the particular from the universal. But human life moves in the realm of induction and not of deduction, in the unpredictable and not the predictable, and it is precisely the unpredictable (which we call chance because it befalls us much as a meteor falls toward us from space) that, in retrospect, after it has demolished us, assumes a predictable character. To stay with the meteor: truth as fact restates the law of identity: a meteor is a meteor; the interpretation of a meteor as a lump of iron hurled at the earth by Zeus from the top of Mount Olympus is a deduction. Without the belief that there is a Zeus on top of Mount Olympus, the interpretation does not take place; also, this assumption permits us to deduce an unlimited number of further interpretations concerning the meteor, for example that Zeus tossed down this piece of iron on a whim, because he was bored in his infinite world, and so on; if the deductive interpretation wants to take Zeus himself into account, it is forced to take all of mythology at face value, that is, to take myth as the basis for its deductions, from Gaia's first emergence from chaos and the birth of her son Uranos to the primal pair's incest and the castration of Uranos by his son Chronos, and so forth. We can spare ourselves the rest of those horror stories. But the interpretation of the meteor as an astronomical phenomenon is at first a deductive interpretation, because it presupposes a chain of inductive interpretations, of previously erected theories that proved to be erroneous and engendered new ones; but then it gives rise to a series of new inductive interpretations, of hypotheses that become more and more abstract but never arrive at absolute truth, just as the fractions between one and zero never arrive at zero—though I know there are many physicists who hope some day to arrive at this zero: their physical world-formula would then be a metaphysical one as well.

More concretely: if the twenty-two-year-old student F. D. had been killed by a meteor on October 15, 1943, three hours, forty minutes, and seventeen seconds after midnight, Swiss time, as he was staggering home drunk across Kirchenfeld Bridge in the direction of the Museum of History in Bern and stopped to pee through the iron railing into the river Aare when the meteor struck him—coincidentally observed from the Gurten, a hill on the southern side of the city, by an equally inebriated student of astronomy who had wanted to photograph the Orion nebula, which stood in the south—this statement would by and large coincide with the truth and would be arguable only insofar as the precision of any recorded moment can be disputed and the notion that F. D. was on the way "home" is purely a matter of conjecture. But the interpretation of this statement would not be a simple matter. The victim of the accident, F. D., would have to be closely examined and the connection between the accident and the astronomy student's accidental snapshot would have to be established beyond any doubt; an unbroken chain of circumstantial evidence would be needed, all in all a rather taxing exercise of reason. However, these data would permit the calculation of the meteor's path, despite the extreme brevity of its flash, a mere second. Also, the provenance of the cosmic missile could be ascertained: it would have been a particle of the proto-sun that eventually developed into our sun. The interpretation of the improbable accident would turn out to be deductive, since the possibility of calculating the meteor's path presupposes a knowledge of the laws of gravity. The ridiculous rock fragment that felled this ridiculous F. D. had been wandering around the solar system for six billion years—since its beginning, that is—before being diverted by some Matterhorn-sized mini-planetoid,* getting sucked into the earth's gravitational field, and plunging down so unfortunately, though quite lawfully, that the cosmic accident looked like a planned murder. With some qualifications, however: even though the accident can be described in a simple sentence and gives rise to

Matterhorn: Probably the most famous Swiss mountain.

an equally simple, if strange, interpretation, the more inferences we make concerning the factors that made the accident on the Kirchenfeld Bridge in Bern possible, the more we enmesh ourselves in increasingly complex interpretations; while the laws of gravity are still within our ken, gravity itself already raises some questions, as does the origin and development of the meteor. The answers to these questions—which is to say, the interpretations—become merely probable instead of true, until in the end they issue in mere possibility, mere hypothesis. Where, in a mere fact, truth and interpretation are still identical, the interpretive reconstruction of the fact drives them further and further apart. The possible need not be any more true than the logical.

Truth is such a difficult problem that most people don't see any problem in it at all—especially my godfather with regard to the truth about F. D., unlike science, which would have had a far more difficult time with the drunken student than with the meteor. But if, after the cause of death had been determined, someone had taken my godfather to the Medical Examiner's Office and shown him F. D.'s body, he would have given short shrift to the truth. As a former missionary on the African Gold Coast and a popular prison and jailhouse preacher as well as a pastor for the deaf and dumb, he would have found in the student F. D. not only an argument for the existence of God: "There was a man who, leaving the alehouse, drunk, declared that there is no God," I heard him preach to the inmates of the prison of Basel, who were sitting across from us, each man separated from the others by a kind of cell (it was 1947; embarrassed, I had sat down on the speaker's podium next to the prison director), whereupon, looking like a blend of Bismarck and Clémenceau,* their combined body-mass compressed into a single quadrangular block, he bellowed: "Boom, a flash of lightning and the man was dead. Therefore there is a God." (And as we walked home, to a house that was ripe for demolition, situated in the suburb of Sankt-Alban, he made the following deduction: "Had you gotten your doctorate, your first play wouldn't have bombed in Zürich, it wouldn't even have occurred to you to write one.") No, my godfather would also have stated the reason why the meteor, instead of continuing to wander around the solar system, had collided with F. D. and not with a single one of the earth's other inhabitants, which at the time numbered two and a half billion: "That is God's

---

*Otto von Bismarck (1815–1898), German chancellor known as the founder of the German empire; Georges Clemenceau (1841–1929), French statesman and prime minister of France from 1917 to 1920.

punishment for the poor fellow's refusal to become a minister, as his father and especially his mother had hoped, and for having relations with a Catholic painter. He didn't know any French and she didn't know any German, so you can imagine the un-Christian tenor of their conversation. God had to put a stop to that," my godfather would have said, whereupon he would have left the medical examiner's office and wandered off in the direction of Thorberg Prison, talking to himself in some African language, of which he knew many.* Which would of course leave the case of F. D. unsolved. Even if the various effective causes that steered the meteor in the direction of the student's skull had been thoroughly reconstructed, if there were laws in operation that were known and that could be applied, the investigators would still be in the dark as to the motives that inclined F. D. to stagger across Kirchenfeld Bridge at nearly four o'clock in the morning. One of his friends would have remembered F. D.'s leaving a basement pub in the Old Town with the angry words "I object to being taken seriously," while another carouser would have described F. D. as a chaotic wastrel, a cynic to whom nothing was sacred, who had apparently read too much Nietzsche and was therefore thinking of studying philosophy, typical; another fellow would have claimed that the only reason F. D. hadn't become a Nazi was because the Nazis, according to F. D., were not extreme enough, my God, even the devil was too pious for him; a teacher of art history would have said that F. D. had visited him shortly before midnight, that they had drunk a bottle of wine, and that he had read out loud to F. D. some passages about hell in Dante's *Divine Comedy;* the manager of a supermarket, on the other hand, would say that he had heard F. D. come home at one-thirty in the morning, since he, the manager, lived underneath the student's garret apartment—which, incidentally, was covered with grotesque murals—yes, he could swear that F. D. had entered his room, evidently he must have left his room later to go back to the city. Also, a failed writer in Zürich would have written that he had always predicted that F. D. was heading for a catastrophe, while a famous professor of psychiatry would have declared that F. D. had consciously stepped under the meteor, and that he, the professor, had predicted to F. D. that he would eventually commit suicide.

All these statements would not have added up to a logical pattern; instead, they would have encouraged the supposition that F. D.'s movements were simply a random drift from one whim to another, and that therefore the motives that led him to the Kirchenfeld Bridge were impossible to interpret.

Thorberg Prison: Swiss prison on the outskirts of Bern.

While the meteor's path was causally determined (so the argument would run), F. D.'s path was subject to chance, which is to say that its causality can no longer be reconstructed and can therefore no longer be interpreted, either. Chance events, therefore, are also possible: maybe F. D. actually intended to go directly to his house in the Old Town, but as he crossed the Casinoplatz he encountered a hedgehog scurrying across the wide stretch of asphalt in the direction of the bridge, a grotesque little piece of life, unreal among these surroundings. It occurred to F. D. now to follow the hedgehog, and when the animal had scrambled down the embankment, F. D. wandered, lost in thought, onto the bridge and under the meteor. In short: F. D. is an infinitely more complex phenomenon than a meteor. Certainly F. D. can be regarded in the same way as the cosmic object. As a human specimen: just as the meteor originated in a supernova that once polluted the hydrogen mist, F. D. is a descendant of impish little lemurs who cavorted in the trees millions of years ago; but while the little meteor remained what it was when the tremendous energy of the supernova baked it into existence, F. D. evolved, like every human being, into a creature that was both rational and irrational. The little lemur F. D. metamorphosed his way through the aeons until he became homo sapiens, changing from a complex organism into ever more complex organisms, dragging his inherited animal traits along with him as he progressed, equipped with a cerebral cosmos, a formation of such complexity that F. D.'s behavior was subject to the influence not just of a few meager logical considerations, but of predominantly unconscious motives, erratic moods, preprogrammed patterns of some aboriginal ancestor's unpredictable behavior, and also by sudden whims, for example the thought of peeing into the river from the middle of the Kirchenfeld Bridge, just as he used to enjoy standing on the Kirchweg Bridge and peeing onto the train that ran from Bergdorf to Thun, which was already electrified then, and responding to a peasant woman's question as to why he was doing that: "I want to see if I'll croak." Back then, the high-voltage current had not hit him, but now the meteor had. To be sure, the unfortunate student could have been interpreted as a rational being, statistically accountable and anatomically dissectable (F. D.'s recent bout with hepatitis and a consequent raising of his sugar level would have come to the forensic physician's attention, along with signs of incipient corpulence), sociological (son of a pastor) and psychological (protracted puberty) observations would also have been possible, and as an irrational creature, that is, as the individual F. D., he could have been given a retrospective psychoanalytic interpretation as well, why not. But all these interpretations would have been mere approximations, speculative guesses that would not have permitted even the most cautious hint of a law that might have compelled F. D. to step under a meteor.

The truth escapes us categorically in the case of F. D. Nevertheless, truth makes absolute claims, while reason contents itself with a relative correctness. F. D., demolished on that bridge (which fortunately suffered no damage), is therefore only an insignificant part of the truth, which wants to be more: it aspires to totality, and as such, truth wants to reign supreme not only in the past and the present, but also in the future. But with this demand for eternity, truth moves beyond the realm of humanity into the realm of the gods. As soon as man separates truth from himself, the better to find his meaning in it, truth no longer resides in man, but outside him. In order to learn the truth about himself, man would have to be able to double himself, more successfully than I have doubled myself in F. D.; he would not only have to confront himself as a *doppelganger* but also as himself turned inside out, as the truth outside himself. Thus the challenge on the frieze of the temple of Apollo, "Know Thyself," presupposes that one seeking self-knowledge already knows himself, for knowledge of any particular presupposes a universal from which that particular can be deduced.* This is possible in the realm of pure logic. For example, there is a story about a rabbi who, plagued by a chronic intestinal illness and finding himself in a place where it was forbidden to think of God, reconstructed Euclid's geometry in his mind, never realizing that it already existed: unbeknown to himself, geometry was already within him, it presented itself as a consequence of the intrinsic modalities of logic, of the a priori within thought itself; one of the most beautiful and apposite stories about mathematics. Existentially, things are different. F. D. as a general idea, let's say as "man in himself," belongs to the realm of logic, of statistics, for instance, which permit an assessment of F. D.'s life expectancy in view of his state of health, but cannot bar him from having to fear an earlier death or seeing grounds for hope of a longer life. But if we want to deduce F. D. as the uniquely particular F. D. from a universal F. D., we are faced with the impossibility of deducing the existential from the logical. We would then have to stipulate that there is not only a unique and particular F. D. but also F. D. as a universal—an evident absurdity, unless God has a universal idea of every single mortal on the face of the earth, an idea that would yield as one of its

---

Temple of Apollo: The Delphic Temple in Greece.

possibilities the particular, individual human being, which raises the question of whether this God still finds it worth his while to think about every single one of the possible human beings. It isn't worth his while. He is occupied with ideas.

And so, not being able to deliver the truth about F. D., I have no choice but to render possibilities about him; to add to the stipulated F. D. 1 (who was struck by a meteor as it hissed its way earthward from outer space to the Kirchenfeld Bridge three hours, forty minutes, and seventeen seconds after midnight, Swiss time) another F. D., an F. D. 2, who also arrives at the bridge, like his double, but hesitates to step onto it. Not because he has contemplated the possibility of being struck by a meteor on the bridge. Admittedly, F. D. 2 would have always been fascinated by astronomy (much like F. D. 1 and myself, by the way), but the possibility of being demolished by a meteor is not only too improbable, it is also too general: a meteor could have struck any F. D. we care to stipulate in any place we care to imagine, in front of the bridge or in the basement pub or in bed; I, too, could be hit by a meteor as I write these words; it's uncanny how many meteors plunge to the earth every year, at least five million tons, all told, if we include cosmic dust. It is not the thought of a meteor but the bridge that causes F. D. 2 to hesitate to set foot on it like F. D. 1. Now I don't want to say anything against the Kirchenfeld Bridge, this honorable iron construction from the previous century. Unlike the concrete bridges leading from the city to the other side of the Aare, there is something buoyant about it, and in the rush hours a vibrancy as well, especially when you look down from it into the green river, something seductive. You can understand why people jump off it every once in a while. That is why, on my way to the city or back, I always preferred to cross this bridge; I loved it and preferred it to the boring Nydegge Bridge, which is too plain and too solidly constructed to give rise to the adventurous feeling the Kirchenfeld Bridge gave me: the sense that it could collapse at any moment and especially at the moment when I was crossing it. It's not for nothing that it leads to the diplomats' quarter. F. D. 2 would have loved this bridge also; indeed, just like me, he would have hesitated each time before setting foot on the bridge; in fact it is conceivable that it was this brief moment of hesitation that would have saved F. D. 2: the meteor would have missed him by a few centimeters. The cause of his hesitation would not have resided in anything objective, but rather in a subjective factor, in the feeling this bridge had always aroused in him, and for the sake of which he loved to cross it. He would have hesitated in order to amplify this feeling even further, tempted by the gradually dying night. Dawn is already beginning to break (how else could F. D. 2 have spotted the hedgehog?), a leaden whiteness glows behind the dark, the Gurten stands out as a stark silhouette:* the hill on which the drunken student of astronomy is fever-ishly fidgeting with his apparatus; the bridge becomes unreal, stretches endlessly over an abyss, becomes so menacing that the entertaining ques-tion "Is this bridge really sound?" is as inescapable as the ghostly eruption of the morning; a question that tempts F. D. 2—after another brief moment of hesitation, of pause and wonder—to step onto the bridge precisely be-cause of that question: for by casting doubt on the safety of the iron con-struction, F. D. 2's walk is turning into an adventure, especially since—F. D. 2 was about to pee into the depths, out of sheer high spirits—something suddenly—a lightning flash or a missile—steeps everything in a glaring light, the house of parliament, the river, Helvetia Square, the Museum of History. F. D. 2, blinded by a plunging mass of light, feels something falling on the iron railing, smashing it and dropping into the river far below with a hiss, while the Kirchenfeld Bridge shakes and then vibrates slightly. "The Germans," F. D. 2 thinks, "or an American airplane," and runs—even though this makes little sense—not back, but across the bridge with an open fly to Helvetia Square, despite his incipient corpulence and his my-opia, which is still on record with the military authorities (officially he shouldn't have been able to see the hedgehog on Casino Square before step-ping on the bridge), wondering, as he runs, why there is no booming sound or report from a gun, just a powerful hissing or roaring. But when, after passing the school belfry, bathed in sweat and breathing heavily, he espies, on the head of the full-bosomed, broadly seated Helvetia, the lid of a milk-can, shimmering in the light of dawn, with which, climbing the monument a month ago, also at night and not yet recovered from his hepatitis, he crowned the mother of our nation, an adornment to which no one appears to have objected yet (and that lid was to remain there for another full month, indicative of the low regard in which the mothers of nations are held even in patriotic times), he calms down. Around him a stillness that, due to this proximity of Helvetia crowned with her milk-can lid, feels warm and moth-erly. Not a sound, let alone an alarm—something happened, a short circuit perhaps, most probably nothing warlike. It never occurs to F. D. 2 that it could have been a meteor, this possibility is just too unbelievable; thirty years later it didn't occur to me either that someone could have shot at me from a distance, even though that event was a good deal more probable than

---

*Gurten: Long hill to the south of Bern.

a meteor hurtling down from the sky could be under any conditions: I had swum out to sea on the outskirts of Eilat,* Arafat had addressed the UN in New York that morning,† soldiers with submachine guns stood on the roof of the hotel, I was swimming in the direction of an oil tanker, the water was clear as glass, Jordanian Aqaba was palpably near,‡ when suddenly, a few feet away from me, a water spout shot up from the sea, I thought it was a fish, and swam back to the hotel, and only much later did it occur to me that someone in Aqaba could have aimed at me and pulled the trigger; but, thinks F. D. 2, trotting home from Helvetia Square through the English Garden, he probably shouldn't have walked across the bridge after all.

The logician F. D., on the other hand—I might as well call him F. D. 3 to distinguish him from the other two—doesn't need the break of dawn or the counsel of experience to come upon the idea that the Kirchenfeld Bridge could collapse if he crossed it. When F. D. 3 enters his garret on the night of October 14 to 15, 1943, at one thirty a.m. (the manager of the supermarket was mistaken), he makes the decision to study philosophy. He has always been interested in philosophy, but since he wanted to become a painter and had spent the winter, like F. D. 1 and F. D. 2 (and me, too, by the way) in Zürich attempting to write, he was at a loss as to what he should do: the university was a waiting room to him, as it was to F. D. 1 and F. D. 2 (and to myself at the time). But while F. D. 1 lives his life with chaotic abandon, and F. D. 2 still hopes to become a painter or writer (already then he hates the word "poet"), F. D. 3 is now, at one thirty a.m., determined to drop writing and painting, stop chasing his dreams, and instead learn to think as one learns a craft. Thrilled by his idea, he closes the door again, walks down the stairs, past the door of the supermarket manager (who has fallen asleep again), leaves the house, and goes down Haspel street and across Nydegge Bridge to the Old Town. He decides to live only by logic from now on. But no sooner has he left Nydegge Bridge behind him than he begins to suspect that it wasn't entirely logical to cross the bridge without any forethought. Pondering this question, he walks through the darkened Old Town to the university, where he studied literature (in a manner of speaking) a year ago, and goes back again, mechanically, still mulling over his problem, when suddenly—he hasn't noticed the hedgehog—he finds himself confronted with the Kirchenfeld

---

Eilat: Northernmost city in Israel.

†Yasser Arafat (1929–2004), leader of the Palestine Liberation Organization and joint winner of the Nobel Peace Prize of 1994.

‡*Aqaba:* Town in the northwest of the West Bank.

Bridge and hence with his problem, for every bridge is a bridge, and the possibility of its collapsing cannot be logically discounted: logically, it could collapse at any moment. Therefore every act of walking across a bridge requires a certain measure of belief that the bridge won't collapse while being trodden. This measure of belief depends on the condition of the bridge, although there are other factors that could cause the bridge to collapse: an earthquake, a charge of dynamite, or a far larger meteor than the one that three minutes later would kill F. D. 1 and barely miss F. D. 2. If the Kirchenfeld Bridge is in good repair, if buses (trams at that time), trucks, cars, and people on motorcycles and bicycles drive across it every day, and if in addition hundreds of people walk on the footpaths alongside the balustrades on each side of the bridge, then it takes no more than a tiny measure of belief to walk across the bridge at night, but still, it's a measure. It's this measure of belief that the logician F. D. 3 can't get over, since he intends to live by logic. He takes seriously the premise that the bridge can collapse, and concludes: "If it is always possible for the bridge to collapse, then at some point the bridge will collapse, for 'always' is an infinite number of 'nows.'" He stares into space. "But if I were to walk across the bridge," he mutters, "the time it would take me would also divide into an infinity of nows. Now is timeless. Every measure of time, even a fraction of a second or a fraction of that fraction, and again a fraction of the previous fraction, divides into an infinite number of nows." He is feeling dizzy, he is arriving at ever smaller fractions. The morning has long since arrived, he has not noticed the fall of the meteor, an infinity of nows is whirling through his head like a tornado. "Therefore the bridge, which will collapse at some point, a point that is a now, will collapse while I walk across the bridge," he finally concludes as the first tram drives past him across the Kirchenfeld Bridge. Thus F. D. 3 has not only argued like the Greek philosopher Zeno, 490–430 BC, but is also behaving like Zeno's flying arrow:* "For if everything is always at rest as long as it occupies a space that is as large as itself, and if what is in motion is always in the Now, then the moving arrow is at rest." It is now 1990 AD, and F. D. 3 is still standing in front of Kirchenfeld Bridge. All the countless millions of people that have walked and driven across that bridge since he stopped there have not been able to move him from the spot: the logical alone is real, the illogical is mere appearance. He is still pursuing this thought: the Kirchenfeld Bridge, too, is nothing but an appearance, the city, he himself, the earth, the whole, the big bang. There is nothing but a single point, a

*Zeno, a Greek philosopher from Elea (Velia), was famous for his paradoxes of multiplicity and motion.

unique singularity, and there is no reason why it should expand into a cosmos, let alone make it possible for life to exist.

Let us imagine an F. D. 4 who is as determined as F. D. 3 to study philosophy and to live logically. Astonished, he gazes after the tram that is driving past him across the Kirchenfeld Bridge, filled with employees of the various embassies, with Germans, Englishmen, Americans, Italians, with Germans in the British secret service and Englishmen in the German secret service, and so forth, all combinations are possible; with people who, in 1943, were they not in neutral Switzerland, would have to beat each other up at the very least, since they are in a state of war with each other. F. D. 4, seeing that the bridge is not collapsing, even though it takes the tram some time to cross it, time that is made up of an infinite number of nows, and that moreover the combined weight of the tram and those peaceful mortal enemies inside it is considerably greater than the weight he would add to the bridge if he were to cross it alone, concludes that there must have been an error in his calculations, since otherwise the Kirchenfeld Bridge with the tram and the embassy personnel would have long since fallen into the river and onto the soccer field. Like F. D. 3, F. D. 4 remains standing in front of the bridge, but unlike him, he is not perpetually bound by the same chain of logically interlinking ideas; instead, F. D. 4 is desperately trying to refute the axiom according to which the bridge could collapse, and to find a logical way out that would permit him to cross the bridge with absolute certainty and without even the faintest trace of belief that it will continue to stand, thus equating logic and reality. He has not succeeded to this day. The little grain of belief he would like to think away cannot be thought away. Like F. D. 3, he is still standing in front of the Kirchenfeld Bridge.

F. D. 5, on the other hand, at the sight of the tram, and captivated, like F. D. 4, by the fact that it has reached Helvetia Square, decides to drop logic and with it his study of philosophy, and without hesitation walks home across the Kirchenfeld Bridge, not without occasionally stamping the pavement or giving the balustrade, which is damaged in one spot, a swift kick, out of anger at having gotten himself entangled in a web of meaningless thoughts. His belief that the bridge will not collapse as he crosses it has grown to such a degree that he believes his believing this isn't a belief, but a certainty.

F. D. 6, his confidence in the value of purely logical reflection somewhat shaken by the tram, also crosses the bridge like F. D. 5, but he does so thoughtfully, examining the damaged balustrade, turns around again on

Helvetia Square, goes back to Casino Square, then back to Helvetia Square, and only then goes home, reflecting on the experience he just had and wondering what it might mean. He knew that the bridge would collapse sometime, but he also firmly believed that it wouldn't collapse as he crossed it. He's not quite sure whether he still wants to study philosophy; he suddenly would like to become a physicist, and he's annoyed at himself for busying himself with Greek and Latin instead of mathematics.

F. D. 7, determined to let himself be guided by logic, arrives at the Kirchenfeld Bridge at 3:40 a.m. and walks into a barrier, almost falling over it. It occurs to him that the barrier wasn't there yet when he left the basement pub a few hours ago. He walks to and fro in confusion, and then, in the glaring light produced by the meteor as it comes hissing down (F. D. 7 is so confused by the barrier that he doesn't ask himself where this abundance of light comes from), he reads on a wooden placard that the bridge is in danger of collapse and that anyone crossing the barrier is not only breaking the law but taking his life into his hands. Forgetting his resolution to act only according to logical principles, he climbs across the barrier, overcome by a boundless lust for adventure, runs across the bridge and back again, and so forth several times, until fear of the bridge's collapsing makes him suddenly stop. He goes home, bathed in sweat and breathing heavily, and doesn't calm down until he reaches the junction of Kollerweg and Muristalde. The belief that the bridge would not collapse as he walked on it had become a risk that enticed him to walk on it, even though logic told him that the bridge could collapse.

As he climbs over the barrier and steps onto the Kirchenfeld Bridge, F. D. 8 feels it beginning to sink; horrified, he no longer believes he can get to the other side. He swings himself back to safety across the barrier, and the bridge, illuminated by the roaring descent of the meteor, thunders down into the depths. F. D. 8's belief has abandoned him.

As he climbs over the barrier and steps onto the Kirchenfeld Bridge, F. D. 9 feels it beginning to sink, just like F. D. 8, but he runs, in defiance of all logic, downward along the sinking bridge, running so fast he does not notice the fall of the meteor, in the mad belief that he will make it to the other side, then up the rising incline as the bridge begins to fold in the middle, until, arriving at Helvetia Square, he climbs onto the lap of his nation's tin-crowned mother and sees the bridge collapsing with a crash. F. D. 9's belief has been borne out. Never in his life has he been as happy as when he was running across the bridge.

F. D. 10, who has climbed across the barrier in the belief that nothing can happen to him, notices, as the bridge collapses beneath him, a patch of lawn shooting toward him in the glaring light of the meteor, and thinks: "This is typical of me." His belief was nothing but thoughtlessness.

F. D. 11, having climbed across the barrier without reading the warning while simultaneously resolving to become a writer after all, casually ambles along on the bridge, so fascinated by his decision that he, too, does not notice the meteor, whereupon, apparently floating through the air, he crosses the gaping abyss as the bridge collapses beneath him, and arrives on Helvetia Square. He doesn't notice that the bridge has disappeared until he decides to return to Casino Square, determined not to go home after all and to enjoy his decision. He is confused. He doesn't know how he managed to cross a bridge that is lying far below him in the river bed and on the Dalmazi Quai, perhaps by a miracle, but he could also imagine that the bridge didn't collapse until after he had crossed it, and that, steeped in his dreams, he failed to hear the noise. Relieved, he climbs onto Helvetia, removes the milk-can lid from her head, and tosses it down onto the ruins of the bridge, joyfully exclaiming that he has found something to write about.

F. D. 12, determined to study philosophy, stands in front of the barrier and reads the warning. He thinks that every bridge can collapse, with or without warning, and that if he sets foot on the bridge now, it will be because he believes it won't collapse when he sets foot on it, and if he does not set foot on it now, it will be because he believes it will collapse when he sets foot on it. But because belief is belief regardless of what the belief is about, he sets foot on the bridge, and as he sets foot on it, both he and the bridge drop into the abyss. Belief is not belief.

F. D. 13, finally, goes home after reading the warning sign, and begins to draw the Kirchenfeld Bridge in the process of collapsing, sometimes at night with himself on top of it, sometimes by day with its load of trams and people all dropping into the abyss, page after page, and is still drawing the collapsing Kirchenfeld Bridge today.

Looking at the various F. D.'s, we notice that there are rational and irrational beliefs. That a bridge that has just been crossed by a tram will not collapse when I cross it is a rational belief, even though the possibility exists that the bridge will collapse. But this possibility is so improbable that my crossing the bridge doesn't even represent a risk. If I run across a bridge while it collapses, my belief that I can reach the other side is an irrational belief. The possibility of the bridge's collapse is not only probable, it has become a fact. My running across it entails a suicidal risk. The dialectic of belief, therefore, is played out between rational and irrational belief and not between reason and belief, for there is always an element of belief in reason. Without belief there could be no conjecture, which is always a crossing of the bridge between assured ground and uncertainty; if not for the belief that this bridge does not lead to a void but to virgin soil, if not for the belief that things might be as I imagine them, if not for this bridge of belief from a finding to a hypothesis that permits an old interpretation or demands a new one, there could be no science. Precisely for this reason, F. D. 3 and F. D. 4 are not mere fictions. F. D. 3, who does not dare to cross the bridge for fear that it might collapse, is a character we reencounter in politics. Thus no one dares to disarm because the other side isn't disarming either. Both sides trade off reasons for not disarming (for not crossing the bridge). The logic of rearmament becomes absurd. The already existing armament programs are supplemented with rearmament programs, the explanation being that in a few years, when these new programs have been carried out, one will have caught up with the other side's lead in the arms race and thus be secure, only to note with indignation, once the new rearmament program has been carried out, that the enemy has built up his defense capability even further in the meantime, thereby necessitating a further rearmament program, and so on ad infinitum. The logic of rearmament compels ever new arguments for further rearmament. Its inner contradiction resides in the suppression of the question of why the enemy didn't attack a long time ago, while one's military buildup was still under way. Concealed in the argument, therefore, is a belief, which cannot be justified logically, because it is inherently impossible to justify any belief on logical grounds, no matter how rational it is— let alone a belief as irrational as the one required for rearmament: namely that the enemy won't really attack but that, since in terms of purely formal logic there is always a possibility of his attacking, he will exploit this possibility to justify his own military buildup. What is outrageous about this arms race logic is its dishonesty. But other arguments also conceal logical contradictions and therefore beliefs, for example the argument of deterrence by fear. This argument presupposes a rational enemy who is not desperate, and it falls apart when the enemy has either become irrational out of desperation or when he thinks that we have become careless out of desperation. The theory that the enemy can be destroyed by the arms race itself is founded in a belief that overlooks the possibility that this very threat could force the enemy to attack before the arms race destroys him, since that manner of destruction can only befall him if he does not attack. The arms race is irrational, and only with great difficulty is the specter recognized as such; each side declares that the arms race has been necessary and that, within limits, it still is. And so it will continue. In this or in another form, because we can't get around the irrational. Absolute certainty exists only in pure logic, as in Pythagoras' theorem. On the empirical level, absolute certainty exists only in absolute fact (but not in its interpretation). The absolute fact lies in the past. My ramming a car into a tree while attempting to start it on January 19, 1982, at eight p.m. did not become a fact until after I had slammed into the tree: a present occurrence is only recognizable and interpretable as a past event, even if it is an ongoing condition, for everything that lasts changes, and a change can only be registered after it has occurred. A future event, on the other hand, is merely probable, and probability includes improbability: what is probable is still within the range of what we can approximately predict, it will probably take place, but it doesn't have to take place; the improbable, on the other hand, which may also take place but is not required to do so, lies completely outside the bounds of predictability. But since a future event, as soon as it takes place, represents a possibility in the chain of probabilities and improbabilities that has become a reality, and because what applies to a future fact applies to any fact, including a past fact, we may venture the proposition that reality is an improbability that has taken place. But this proposition comprises all of reality, whatever it may be, regardless of whether or not I slammed into a tree, regardless of whether or not I exist, indeed regardless of whether or not life exists. The proposition, therefore, is cosmological, and it states that the world's being as it is is improbable, which does not dispute that it is as it is. Now if F. D. 4 (who expects the improbable and believes that the Kirchenfeld Bridge could, against all probability, collapse if he crossed it) has a second bridge built next to it and, since that bridge, too, could collapse, a third one, and so on, one Kirchenfeld Bridge next to the other, he will never get to the other side. He will always find a new reason for building a new Kirchenfeld Bridge, however monstrous: haunted by the certainty that the bridge could indeed, however improbably, collapse if he crossed it, he takes refuge in the belief that there is a bridge that would stand firm under all circumstances, even such as are not improbable at all, if he crossed it.

F. D. 4 continues building one Kirchenfeld Bridge after another, but it makes little sense to still call it that, as the bridge no longer leads to the churchyard that gave it its name, but to a field near Grenchen, on the right bank of the Aare, and still he keeps building, between Aarau and Olten at this point,* because, contrary to what he believes, absolute certainty as required by logic is not realizable on the empirical plane, which leads to the frightening question whether what one believes in can be realized at all; frightening because F. D. 4's undertaking is only apparently that of a fool. F. D. 4 is not an isolated case. No matter whether we are talking about nuclear deterrence, about atomic power plants, about the storage of nuclear waste, about the ravaging of our planet, and so on, those who believe in these practices always insist on our believing that what they are doing is absolutely safe. In broaching the issue of belief, we have entered upon a human force field that can teach us the meaning of fear. It is not what people believe about God but what they believe about themselves that determines the fate of mortals.

*Aarau and Olten: Towns to the northeast of Bern.

Switzerland—A Prison

A Speech for Václav Havel [1990]

Dear Mr. President,
Dear Václav Havel,*

I, too, participated in the protest meeting at the State Theater of Basel after the forces of the Warsaw Pact had invaded Czechoslovakia in 1968,† and I ended my speech with the following words: "In Czechoslovakia, human freedom has lost a battle in the fight for a more equitable world, but not the war itself: the war against the dogmatists of violence continues, whether they wear the mask of communism, of ultracommunism, or that of democracy. The people of Czechoslovakia have shown us how to conduct this struggle, if necessary, in a technologically developed country, where there is no possibility of escaping into the jungle. Opting for survival, they did not send out their troops, did not act out a Nibelungen romance of self-destructive heroism;‡ and yet, with their nonviolent resistance, they have dealt a blow against a power system, perhaps a deadlier blow than we can imagine." More than twenty years have passed since then. In Vietnam, the United States not only lost the war, but also its honor. The power of the dogmatists in Eastern Europe has collapsed, the military blocs of both sides have become useless with all their ferocious weaponry; both sides have lost the target presented by an external enemy; the two superpowers find themselves increasingly confronted with themselves instead of each other; and in you, dear Havel, nonviolent resistance has found its representative, and Czechoslovakia its

---

*Czech playwright and dissident Václav Havel (b. 1936) became president of Czechoslovakia in 1989 and subsequently of the Czech Republic in 1993, a post he held until 2003.

†*The Warsaw Pact:* In 1968 an attempt by the then Czech government to wrest more freedom from the Warsaw Pact was put down by force with the entry of troops and tanks into Prague. The action was known as "the Prague Spring."

‡*Nibelungen romance:* A reference to the medieval German epic *The Lay of the Nibelungs,* in which the Burgundian armies are slaughtered by the Huns.

head of state. Here you have received the Gottlieb Duttweiler Prize,* the prize of a man who was as popular in Switzerland as he was controversial, who turned his large capitalist enterprise into a cooperative and founded one of the few parties in Switzerland that can still be regarded as being part of an opposition, although we must be careful, because in this country we even have an Automobile Party that regards the automobile as a sacred symbol of freedom, and considers itself an opposition party. You, dear Havel, received the prize, as it says in the explanatory statement, because your name stands for civic courage, honesty, and tolerance of other viewpoints, the indispensable basis for the free development of the individual in a democratic state. A beautiful prize, a Swiss prize, but somehow impossible to reciprocate. I cannot imagine your giving a Swiss draft resister a Václav Havel Prize for civic courage, honesty, and—I'm not sure now—in what sense were you tolerant of the regime you were protesting against? Surely only in that you rejected the opportunity to leave your country and submitted to your punishment and went to jail. By doing so, you brought about the downfall of a regime, while our draft resisters . . . —let's face it, we Swiss are a belligerent nation that has not been attacked for almost two hundred years, but would defend itself if attacked, and to prove that it would defend itself, it locks up those who have the civic courage and the honesty to declare that they would not under any circumstances defend themselves if attacked. In the view of our military court, the only extenuating factor would be a religious inclination, but in a case of political conviction—like yours, dear Havel—here, in Switzerland, the whole severity of the law is brought to bear on the conscientious objector, as it was brought to bear on you in Czechoslovakia. Our conscientious objectors, therefore, are the dissidents of Switzerland. So far, they have not accomplished anything. Now, as a Swiss, I don't want to boast of our military prowess; true, the Hussite Wars under the blind General Ziska caused Europe to shake in its boots,† but already a hundred years before Hus was imprisoned in Gottlieben and was burned alive in Constance, a Swiss army under Rudolf von Habsburg, a native of Aargau, defeated King Ottokar II of Bohemia in the battle of Dürnkrut on August 28, 1278, the same Bohemia that fell definitively to the Habsburgs in 1526, remaining subject for four hundred

*Swiss entrepreneur and politician Gottlieb Duttweiler (1888–1962) established a prize administered by the institute named for him, which is awarded at irregular intervals to the person who in the opinion of the jury has made significant changes in political life.

†The Hussite Wars took place between 1416 and 1434 in Czechoslovakia between the supporters of Johann Hus (executed in 1415) and the king of Bohemia. Hus was an anticlerical reformer regarded as a revolutionary by the king. The wars had a lasting effect and were significant for many innovations in military tactics.

years to that most successful of all emigré Swiss families, whom we nevertheless victoriously prevented from returning to their homeland—just think of Morgarten and Sempach.* Just as the collapse of the old Confederacy in 1798 initiated the founding of the new Confederacy, modern Czechoslovakia emerged from World War I in 1918. Both states are products of defeat: our own defeat in the case of Switzerland, the Austro-Hungarian Empire's defeat in the case of Czechoslovakia. Then came Hitler. In the Bern Münster, a special service was given in 1938 to thank the Lord that the Great Powers had abandoned Czechoslovakia. That country did not defend itself, the Sudetenland was occupied, and a little later the Czech Republic was turned into a protectorate and Slovakia into a vassal state. The question presents itself: Would Switzerland have defended itself in the same situation? This question is impossible to answer. Switzerland was never in this position. For the Czechs, the situation was catastrophic: the name Lidice says it all†—they had to work for Hitler, and the Jews were gassed. We were not attacked, but we also had to work for Hitler, and the Jews whom we turned away at the border were also gassed. After the war, Czechoslovakia fell victim to Stalin and to his successors' policies; after the DDR and Hungary, this country, too, was violently prevented from reforming socialism, from giving it a human face. You, Václav Havel, wrote about this in your essay *Event and Totality:* "In the fifties there were huge concentration camps in our country, and inside them were tens of thousands of innocent human beings. Simultaneously, on the building sites of the younger generation, enthusiastic devotees of the New Faith massed together to sing songs about reconstruction. There was torture, there were executions, dramatic escapes across the border, conspiracies—and at the same time, hymns were written in praise of the supreme dictator. The President of the Republic signed the death warrants of his closest friends, but strangely, it was possible to run into him in the street now and then. The songs of idealists and fanatics, the ravings of political criminals and the suffering of heroes have been part of history from time immemorial. The fifties were an evil time, but such times have been frequent in human history. It was still possible to classify the fifties with those other periods, or at least to consider them comparable; they were still somehow reminiscent of history. I would not venture to claim that nothing happened during that time or that it was ignorant of events as such. The fundamental programmatic document of

---

*See chapter 1, note 23.

†Lidice is a village in Czechoslovakia that was destroyed by the Germans in 1942 as revenge for the assassination of Richard Heydrich, the Reichsprotector of Bohemia, by Czech resistance agents.

the political regime that was installed in Czechoslovakia after the Soviet invasion of 1968 was called *Lessons from the Years of Crisis*. There was something symbolic in that: this regime truly did teach itself a lesson. It realized what could happen if it opened the door just an inch to a plurality of opinions and interests: its own totalitarian nature was at risk. That lesson learned, the state set aside everything except its own preservation: all the mechanisms of direct and indirect social manipulation assumed a life of their own and developed forms that had never been seen before; nothing could be left to chance. The last nineteen years in Czechoslovakia could almost serve as a model of a fully mature or late totalitarian system: revolutionary ethos and terror were replaced by numb immobility, anxious alibis, bureaucratic anonymity, and mindless stereotypes whose only meaning consists in becoming more and more perfectly what they are. Today, the enthusiastic songs and the cries of the tortured are no longer heard; injustice now wears silk gloves and has moved from the infamous torture chambers to the plush offices of bureaucracy. One no longer sees the President of the Republic in the street, except perhaps behind the bulletproof windows of his car as he rushes off to the airport, surrounded by a police convoy, to welcome Colonel Qhadafi.* Thus the late totalitarian system is supported by such subtle, complex, and powerful instruments of manipulation that it no longer needs murderers and their victims. It has even less use for zealous utopians who sow unrest with their dreams of a better future. The concept this era has invented for itself — 'really existing socialism'—indicates who is excluded from it: the dreamers." And when you, Václav Havel, this time as president of your country, in your New Year's address of 1990, described the content of your dreams in some detail, as follows: "Perhaps you will ask me what sort of republic I dream of. My reply is: I dream of an independent, free, democratic, economically prosperous and at the same time socially just republic, in short a humane republic that serves human beings and therefore has reason to hope that human beings will serve it in turn. A republic of universally educated men and women, because without them, none of our problems can be solved, be they human, economic, ecological, social, or political problems," there are many Swiss who dream that they themselves live in such a republic, live, as it were, in the dream you, Václav Havel, are dreaming. But the reality within which these Swiss dream their dream is different. As a playwright, dear Václav Havel, you depicted the reality in which you lived before the collapse of political dogmatism, in plays that are regarded by many critics as theater of the absurd. For me these plays

*Muammar Abu Minyar al-Qaddafi (b. 1942), ruler of Libya since a successful coup in 1969.

are not absurd, not meaningless; for me, they are tragic grotesques. For the grotesque is an expression of the paradoxical, indeed nonsensical, state of affairs that comes about when an essentially rational idea like communism—can one imagine a more equitable social order?—is transplanted into reality. Early Christianity was communistic also, and look at what happened to Christianity! Man makes everything into a paradox; meaning turns into absurdity, justice into injustice, freedom into bondage, because man himself is a paradox, an irrational rationality. Thus Switzerland can be juxtaposed with your tragic grotesques as another kind of grotesque: a prison, albeit very different from the kinds of prisons into which you were thrown, dear Havel; a prison in which the Swiss have taken refuge. Because there was mayhem outside the prison and because only in prison can they be safe from attack, the Swiss feel free, freer than other people, free as prisoners in the prison of their neutrality. There is only one problem for this prison, namely that of proving that it is not a prison but a bulwark of freedom, since seen from outside, a prison is a prison and its inmates are prisoners, and prisoners are not free. To the outside world, only the guards are free, for if they were not free, they would be prisoners. In order to solve this contradiction, the prisoners have introduced universal guard duty: by being his own guard, every prisoner proves his freedom. The Swiss, therefore, have the dialectical advantage of being at one and the same time free, a prisoner, and a guard. The prison needs no walls because its prisoners are guards and guard themselves, and since the guards are free, they make business deals among themselves and with the whole world—and how!—and because, on the other hand, they are prisoners, they cannot join the UN and are worried about the European Common Market.* If you live dialectically, you run into psychological difficulties. Since the guards are prisoners, too, it is possible for them to suspect that they are prisoners and not guards, let alone free; therefore the prison administration created dossiers of everyone they suspected of feeling imprisoned and not free; and because they suspected many people of feeling this way, they piled up a mountain of dossiers that on closer inspection turned out to be an entire mountain range, mountains beyond mountains of dossiers. But since the dossier mountain range was only to be used if the prison was attacked, and since it never was attacked, the guards, when they found out about their dossiers, suddenly felt like prisoners and not free; that is, they felt the way the prison administration didn't want them to feel. But in order to feel free again, and to see themselves as guards and not prisoners, the prisoners asked the prison administration to tell them who had made the dossiers. But since the

*Switzerland became a member of the United Nations in 2002.

dossier mountain range is so enormous, the prison administration eventually decided that it had made itself. Where everyone is responsible, no one is responsible. What produced the dossier mountain range was the fear of no longer being safe in prison. This fear is not groundless. Who would not want to be in a prison where the inmates are free? Thus the prison became a global attraction. There are many who attempt to become prisoners—which they may, provided they have the necessary means, for freedom is a precious thing, and conceivably people without means could seek that security in prison to which only free prisoners are entitled—and many are turned down. The prison administration is not in an enviable position. On the one hand, there are not enough free prisoners to keep the prison clean, to polish the luxury cells, the hallways, the prison bars themselves, so people have to be let in from outside who will renovate, restore, reconstruct, and maintain the prison just in order to make a living, while prisoners who also earn a living but are free look down on these outsiders as prisoners who are not free. On the other hand, every prison has to guard something, but if the prisoners, being guards, guard themselves, the suspicion could arise that the guards are guarding something other than themselves, which is why the opinion is becoming more and more prevalent that the real purpose of the prison is not to guard the freedom of the prisoners but to guard banking secrecy. Whatever the case may be, the prison is flourishing, and its business is so enmeshed with the business of the outside world that gradually people are beginning to doubt whether the prison still exists at all, that is, whether it hasn't become a phantom prison. In order to prove the prison's and therefore its own reality, the prison administration spends billions of Swiss francs to equip the guards who are their own prisoners with ever more modern weapons that keep getting obsolete and making new weapons necessary, despite the probability that a war would destroy everything the prison administration seeks to defend. The administration indulges in the utopian fantasy that in an increasingly catastrophe-prone technological world, the Nibelungen strategy guarantees an absolute security, instead of realizing that this prison called Switzerland can particularly well afford the bold gesture of getting rid of its guards, trusting that its prisoners are not prisoners but free, which of course would mean that Switzerland would no longer be a prison but part of Europe, one of its regions, for Europe is altogether in danger of disintegrating into its regions, despite the shock of Germany's unification.* Thus the prison has fallen into disrepute. It doubts itself. The prison administration, which tries to regulate everything with laws, claims that the prison is not in a crisis, that

*German unification took place in 1990.

the prisoners are free insofar as they are the kind of prisoners who are genuinely loyal to the prison administration, while many prisoners are of the opinion that the prison is in a crisis because the prisoners are not free but prisoners, an intraprison discussion that creates nothing but confusion, because the prison administration is getting ready to celebrate the alleged founding of the prison seven hundred years ago, even though at that time the prison was not a prison but a widely feared robber's nest. Now we don't know what we are supposed to be celebrating, our prison or our freedom. If we celebrate the prison, the prisoners will feel imprisoned, and if we celebrate freedom, the prison becomes superfluous. But because we don't dare to live without a prison, we will once again celebrate our independence, for no one can tell from outside whether inside the independent prison of our neutrality we are imprisoned or free. Wars and occupations can be weathered, though not without great sacrifice, which I do not wish upon anyone. Your country, and not least you yourself, dear Havel, have proven it, while we Swiss, with a resistance that has not been tested, have proven and continue to prove nothing. A strange feeling overcame me, dear Havel, as I wrote this speech, and it overcomes me now as I am giving it. There is much embarrassment in this feeling, for you could very easily be misused as living proof that our Western world is quite all right, and that there is nothing greater than freedom. We are all too prone to suppress what you wrote in your essay on "Living in Truth":* "It does not look as if the traditional parliamentarian democracies have a prescription to offer against the 'self-propulsion' of technological civilization, of industrial and consumer society. Willy-nilly, they, too, are being dragged along. Only their way of manipulating people is infinitely more subtle and refined than the brutal methods of the post-totalitarian system. But in this whole static complex of petrified mass parties guided by no principle other than political efficacy, governed by professional apparatuses that relieve citizens of any concrete and personal responsibility, in all these complicated structures of secretly manipulative and expansionistic centers of capital accumulation, this omnipresent dictatorship of consumption, of production, of advertising, of commerce, of consumer culture, this endless flood of information—in all this, so frequently described and analyzed, one would be hard put to find anything like a perspective, a path on which man could find the way back to himself." It's worth one's while to commit to memory these sentences about our Western freedom exactly as they stand, especially since they come from the dungeon of dogmatic, really existing socialism. To be

---

Living in Truth, published in 1986, is a collection of essays by, and about, Havel that analyzes modern society.

sure, we boast of our direct democracy; to be sure, we did introduce retirement pensions and widows' and orphans' insurance and finally, to the amazement of the world, even women's suffrage, while privately we are insured against death, illness, theft, and fire: fortunate he whose house burns down. In our country, too, politics has retreated from ideology into economics; its questions are economic questions. Where is it permissible for the state to interfere and where is it not, where are subsidies allowable and where are they not, what can be taxed and what can't? Wages and vacations are determined by negotiation. Peace is threatening to become more dangerous than war. A cruel statement, but not a cynical one. Our streets are battlefields, our atmosphere is exposed to poisonous gases, our oceans are oil spills, our fields are polluted with pesticides, the third world has been plundered, worse than the orient was by the crusaders—no wonder the Middle East is extorting us now. Peace, not war, is the father of all things; war results from conditions of peace that have not been mastered. Peace is the problem we have to solve. One nasty characteristic of peace is that it integrates war. The free market economy is an industrial battlefield, driven by competition, a war for markets. The human race is exploding like the universe we live in; we don't know what it will be like when ten billion people inhabit the earth. The free market economy operates under the primacy of freedom; perhaps, then, a planned economy will operate under the primacy of justice. Maybe the Marxist experiment was premature. What can the individual do? What now? This is your question, too, Václav Havel. The individual is an existential concept; the state, the institutions, the economic systems are general concepts. Politics deals with general, not existential matters, but it must address the individual in order to be effective. Man is more irrational than rational, more powerfully influenced by emotion than by reason. Politics takes advantage of this. There is no other explanation for the triumphal march of the ideologies in our century. Appeals to reason are ineffectual, especially when a totalitarian ideology wears the mask of reason. The individual must distinguish between what is humanly impossible and what is humanly possible. Society can never be just, free, socially responsible, but only more just, more free, more socially responsible. What the individual may demand, and not only may but must demand, is what you too have demanded, Václav Havel: human rights, daily bread for every one, equality before the law, freedom of thought and speech, freedom of assembly, transparency, the abolition of torture, and so forth. These are not utopias, they are self-evident necessities, attributes of man, insignia of his dignity, rights that do not violate the individual but make it possible for him to live together with other individuals, rights as an expression of tolerance—traffic regulations, to put it crudely. Human rights alone are existential rights; every ideological revolution aims at their elimination and demands a new humanity. Where have we not seen examples of that?

Dear Václav Havel, your task as president coincides with Václav Havel's task as a dissident. Mr. President, you are here among Swiss, Swiss men and women have welcomed you, the Swiss president has received you, a senior member of the Swiss Federal Council has given you a eulogy, and I, a Swiss, have also spoken, for we do a lot of talking in Switzerland. What sort of people are we, the Swiss? To be spared by fate is neither a disgrace nor an honor, but it is a kind of handwriting on the wall. Plato, near the end of his *Politeia*, tells us how the soul after death must choose its lot for a new life: "It happened, though, that the shade of Odysseus was last in line to step forward and choose his lot. But since, remembering his previous hardships, he had given up all ambition, he went about for a long time in search of a life of calm retirement, and succeeded at last in finding one that the others had passed by. And when he had discovered it, he said he would have acted likewise if he had been first in line, and that his was a happy choice." I am sure that the lot Odysseus chose for himself was to be a Swiss.

Monster Lecture on Justice and Law, with a Helvetian Interlude

A Minor Dramaturgy of Politics   [1969]

Ladies and Gentlemen,*

To tell you the truth, I feel lost. Led astray by two Swiss professors who work at the University of Mainz's faculty of law, I gave in to a certain patriotism and agreed to give a lecture on justice and law. Patriotism makes people blind. In their blindness, the Swiss lawyers assumed that I, a Swiss writer of comedies, must have something to do with justice and law, and I in my blindness assumed that I was capable of speaking on a subject I have nothing to do with at all. The mistake of the two lawyers is understandable and is conditioned by patriotism only insofar as patriotism lured them into that thoughtlessness that is precisely the essence of patriotism, and that prevented them from discovering their mistake by themselves. This mistake arose from the circumstance that in the materials we playwrights choose for our subject matter, all sorts of possible and impossible crimes take place, murders, chicaneries, adulteries, and so on, a fact that could easily give rise to the supposition that the playwright is concerned with justice and law; but actually the playwright is no more concerned with these than the criminal is; like the criminal, the playwright is content to supply the lawyers with material for thought and classification. Whether a real Mr. X or a make-believe Mr. Oedipus killed his father and slept with his mother is of no interest to an expert in the theory of law; he is interested only in the case itself, and whether it is actual or invented is, to him, a matter of indifference; and for the practicing lawyer, this question is of interest only insofar as he can expect a fee from Mr. X and not from Mr. Oedipus. Therefore, to ask a playwright to supply the legal profession with anything more than material is unjust. After all,

---

*This lecture was in part given before the studium generale of Johannes Gutenberg University, Mainz, and was in part expanded later on the basis of discussions with the students, but there was no reason not to retain the form of a lecture.

one doesn't require a criminal to be conversant with the problem of justice and law; he has the freedom and the right to commit his crimes in complete naïveté, a rule that applies to all criminals except those whose crimes would not be possible without legal expertise: such crimes are of course less frequently committed by playwrights than by members of the legal profession.

But my own error, even after allowing for patriotism as a mitigating circumstance, is more complicated. On the one hand, there is the influence of a feeling of inferiority arising from the fact that after ten semesters of philosophy and without a degree I switched my major to comedy, and on the other hand, there is the influence of a certain megalomania without which no dramatist would be capable of writing plays. My feelings of inferiority in the presence of academicians seduce me into trying for once to show academicians what an academician is, and my megalomania lures me into going ahead and doing that. I would therefore define the position in which I have landed as follows: in dramaturgical terms, pretty much the way Rudi Dutschke would feel if he suddenly had to run the government.* But let's not anticipate ourselves. Tactically, I will have to be comedically academic; that is, as a writer of comedies who uses stories as his basic material, I shall tell my stories in such a complicated fashion that you, as academicians, will feel you are attending an academic lecture. I shall therefore base my lecture on justice and law on two tales from *A Thousand and One Nights*. I shall tell them from memory, not with precision, not scientifically, not newly translated from the Arabic with a commentary; no, I will tell them anew.

The First Story

The prophet Muhammad is sitting on a hill in an isolated region. At the foot of the hill is a well. A rider approaches. While the rider is watering his horse, a money pouch drops from his saddle. The rider leaves without noticing the loss of the money pouch. A second rider arrives, finds the money pouch, and rides away with it. A third rider comes and waters his horse by the well. In the meantime the first rider has noticed the loss of his money pouch and returns. He thinks the third rider has stolen his money, and a fight ensues. The first rider kills the third rider, is taken aback when he finds no money pouch, and gallops away. The prophet on the hill is in despair. "Allah," he cries, "the world is unjust. A thief escapes punishment, and an innocent man is

---

*Rudi Dutschke (1940–1979), outspoken leader of the radical German student movement in 1969, was a founding member of the Green Party in that country.

slain!" Allah, normally silent, replies: "You fool! What do you know about my justice! The first rider had stolen the money from the father of the second rider. The second rider took what belonged to him already. The third rider had raped the wife of the first rider. By slaying the third rider, the first rider avenged his wife." Then Allah falls silent again. The prophet, having heard the voice of Allah, praises his justice.

Ladies and gentlemen! The story I have just told is an ideal, positive story. We find here an observer, an observed course of events, an explainer who provides the observer of the observed event with a perfect explanation; and an amoral story proves to be a moral one.

Now obviously, it's not a matter of indifference *who* is doing the observing. There is no such a thing as an observer "per se"; an observer observes, interprets, or acts according to his nature. The observer in our story is a prophet, and what he observes is an instance of injustice. But to wish to be nothing but an observer requires a certain inhuman hardness of heart, for just a faint stirring of human sympathy would have moved the prophet to call out to the first rider that he had lost his money pouch, in which case the second rider would not have committed a theft and the third rider would have stayed alive; but this would have also brought the machinery of cosmic justice to a momentary and somewhat embarrassed halt, its demonstration by Allah hindered by a small human gesture that all of us can understand. Just a grain of humanity would have cost us tons of divine majesty.

If the observer on the hill were a criminal, he would steal the first rider's money pouch before the second rider's arrival, which would give a new twist to the story and to the role of justice within it: certainly the second rider would have had no opportunity to steal and thereby obtain his rights, and to the unpunished theft committed against the father of the second rider we would have to add the unpunished theft committed by the criminal observer.

But the second part of the balance sheet of cosmic justice is also threatened with a deficit, for as far as the third rider's death is concerned, this retribution for the rape of the first rider's wife is suddenly thrown into question by the possibility of a shift in timing: since the second rider found nothing to steal at the well, he would have had no reason to depart in a hurry. In that case, the first rider upon his return would have found two riders by the well: the second one, still lingering, and the third, who had since arrived. Because of this, the first rider would have accused one of the two or both of them of having stolen his money. If he had accused one of the two other riders, he would have accused the second rider, since the second had arrived at the well before the third. Depending on whom he accused, the first rider would have had to fight with both of the others or with the second rider. In the first variant, the death of the first rider is probable, one against two, and in the second variant, either the first kills the second, or the second kills the first. In both variants, the rape remains unpunished, and in each variant, justice is imperfect. Either the first rider is punished with death for the theft he has committed against the second rider's father, but the second rider does not recover his property; or the second rider loses his life along with his property. Also, statistically, the first rider has less of a chance to survive than the others. Here, too: a considerable increase in cosmic injustice, and once again it is impossible for Allah to prove cosmic justice: this time the tons of divine majesty have been thwarted by a shabby theft on the part of an observer.

We see that when an observer interferes in any way in the event he is observing, the event is altered and so is the result of the event. A different result takes place; indeed, many other results are imaginable, not just as regards the riders, but also as regards the justice and injustice of the world and thus the very structure of the universe. Furthermore, the fragility and the exclusivity of poetic parables are revealed. They attempt to say something special about the world, for in order to say something obvious about the world, there is no need of poetic parables. But an event that says something special about the world is too special not to have been especially invented for that purpose: to the coincidence that at this isolated well no less than three riders meet, who, though they know nothing of each other's existence, are yet so intimately bound to each other, is added the coincidence that they are observed by a prophet, and the even greater coincidence of Allah's speaking. It is the incredibility of this story that makes it useful, and we should really ask ourselves whether a poetic parable proves anything at all, or whether it merely demonstrates what can only be proven by logic; or finally, whether the poetic parable doesn't in fact demonstrate something that cannot be proven but only surmised. By poetic levity.

Let us not be discouraged by these considerations, indeed let us be bolder, let us replace the prophet with a scientist, let's say a behavorial scientist who studies human behavior at isolated wells and as a matter of principle does not intervene in events in order not to falsify the results of his observation. If the scientist thus behaves as the prophet did, the only question is whether he will interpret what he observes in the same way, and whether, should the scientist share the prophet's interpretation of the events as unjust, he too will be enlightened by Allah. Now Allah, when he does speak, does not customarily speak with scientists, precisely because they are scientists and not prophets; but probably the scientist's judgment of the events would be different from that of the prophet.

The coincidental nature of the events does not, in itself, bother the scientist. Coincidence is, for him, a statistically improbable but nevertheless possible occurrence. If it occurs, it occurred despite its improbability. Above all, the scientist regards the events by the well as natural. Each rider behaves in conformity with his character. A man who finds a money pouch by an isolated well and has neither the moral nor the financial resources to disdain it, will take it; and someone who thinks he has found a thief in an isolated region, has a hot temper, and commands the necessary physical strength, will punish the supposed thief by killing him on the spot.

What the scientist rejects, however, is the conclusion drawn by the prophet, that the world is unjust. First of all, the scientist employs the words "justice" and "injustice" only with caution; they sound rather like political or moral or even religious terms, and are therefore scientifically slightly suspect. At most, he will characterize the events at the isolated well as breaches of law—provided the well is not located in a country that is so underdeveloped that the law of the jungle still holds there. Under such prelegal conditions it seems questionable to the scientist to apply any notions of legality at all. Secondly—and this is his main objection—even if he admits justice and injustice as fictions that are, after all, employed by human society, the prophet's conclusion will seem premature to him and therefore logically not possible, for given a global population of three billion, it is not admissible to draw a conclusion about the moral state of this planet's entire population from an observation of the moral state of three riders; we would have to examine the moral state of thousands of people at isolated wells in order to venture a cautious conclusion about the probable moral state of the aggregate. Thirdly, and finally—and this is his second principal objection—the cultural condition and social environment of the three riders he has observed seem to the scientist to be atypical in a world that suffers from overpopulation and reaches for the pill, and to have nothing in common with masses of humanity that are, in part, approximately civilized, and to the extent that they are civilized, rush about in overcrowded streets, are ruled by megalogovernments, live in megalopolises, and work in megalofactories; in short, the scientist questions the validity of our model; he considers it too specific to have any general application.

Our prophet will therefore have to allow us to adapt his model to our world. We will set ourselves the task of modifying his model in such a way that it will be valid both for a citizen of a bourgeois country and for a citizen of a socialist country. This demand seems at first glance impossible to fulfill, but actually we need only to perform a simple manipulation. To find out how to do this, we must ask ourselves what the world of the bourgeois citizen and the world of the socialist citizen have in common.

Let us view the incident by the well with classically bourgeois eyes. For a classical bourgeois, the three riders have acted in an illegal, albeit understandable way. That one man should attack another, that wars break out among human beings, that every person will try to have his way and to increase his wealth and power at the expense of others—all this the classical bourgeois accepts as natural; he is a realist. *Homo homini lupus.** However, in order to prevent the egotistic qualities of human beings from leading to a war of all against all, each wolf has bound itself to certain rules vis-à-vis the other wolves; more precisely: a game has been established among the wolves. But a game among wolves is possible only if security is guaranteed to two elements: the player and the prey that is the game's reward. If the player has no guaranteed security, he may be attacked at any time by another wolf who has had enough of the game, and if the prey is not secured, the wolf will return to hunting in the wild, since the game does not furnish him with prey.

Transposing this from the lupine world to the bourgeois world: the individual citizen and his property are insured in such a way that one citizen may prevail against another only if he obeys the rules of the game, and that a citizen may come into possession of another citizen's property only if he obeys the rules of the game. If, however, the relationships among citizens and the relationships between citizens and the things that constitute their possessions are to be transformed into a game, those things must be converted into something like the chips in a casino. That is why the classical bourgeois is bound to money and capital: money is the counter or chip in the game, and the capital a citizen has at his disposal (either by earning or inheriting it) is the sum of chips available for play, and precisely for this reason the classical bourgeois sees nothing evil in the task his money performs for him in the game: this task is a property that inheres in the chips in the same way that a range of possible moves inheres in the figures on a chessboard. The profit for which the bourgeois stakes his chips is what prey is to the wolf—his loot, which he wins in the game and, thanks to the rules, may insure against loss.

As the originally simple rules become more differentiated, however, the game gets more complicated as well; and the more complicated the game is, the more comprehensive it becomes; and the more comprehensive it is, the

*"Man is a wolf to man."

more those players whose cleverness has gained them a greater sum of playable chips than other players have won are the ones whose turn it is to play; and the more unequally the chips are distributed among the players, the more urgent becomes the question of who is actually in control of the game. It is, of course, in the interest of all players to stick to the rules, but the complexities of the game tempt the craftier players, on the one hand, to cheat, and to cheat so well that the less crafty players don't notice until it's too late, and on the other hand tempt players handicapped by a scarcity of chips to become free wolves again and mug players who are loaded with chips, thus improving their chances in the game by breaking its rules.

The game itself, therefore, necessitates an umpire; not just to supervise the game, but also to introduce the chips into the game. For chips represent things; things can be produced, therefore it must be possible to produce chips as well. Obviously, the direct production of chips can be permitted to no one but the umpire; the players can be permitted only an indirect production of chips, in the form of stocks and bonds, for instance, that can then be wagered as well. But an umpire has to be paid. Each player, therefore, has to render some chips for the umpire's compensation, with the result that soon the salaried umpire starts playing the game himself and, since everyone is paying him, becomes the most powerful player of all. At this stage in the game it is no longer possible to determine whether the umpire exists for the sake of the players or the players exist for the sake of the umpire.

This umpire is the bourgeois state. If we want to modernize our ancient model, therefore, we will have to introduce the power of the state into it. This can be done rather simply: by assigning a policeman to the isolated well. With one restriction, however. We are forced to impose it because we are still only dealing with three riders. If we place a policeman by the well so that he is visible to all three riders, our revised model becomes too ideal. In daily life we hardly ever have a policeman standing next to us, watching every move we make in the game. Certainly the police are there, in part, to prevent cheating or even more serious infractions of the rules, but the effects of this prevention are almost impossible to determine. They may be significant or trivial, we do not know, even though a glance at the world and its dealings might lead one to suspect that the amount of cheating that escapes detection by the police must be enormous. The measurable work of the police, on the other hand, consists in the set of persons who have violated the rules of the game and were apprehended: that is, by the set of arrested and clumsy criminals. The visible effect of the police is an after effect. It consists in the punishment of the arrested offenders. These can either be fined, that is, made to pay a number of chips, or be removed and suspended from the game for a period of time; that is, unreliable players are, under certain conditions, taken to a place where they may no longer participate in the game. They go to jail. Therefore the restriction we need to impose on the policeman if we want to adapt our model to classical bourgeois reality can only take the form of his hiding near the isolated well.

The citizen of a socialist country, however, will interpret the incident at the well in yet another way, presuming that citizen is a socialist, for of course there are citizens of socialist countries who are not socialists but have to be socialists. The voluntarily socialist citizen, then, finds the incident unjust, like the prophet, but for a different reason: it is not the world that is unjust, but the social order; the injustice of this order lies in the money pouch that the first rider owns, lies in his ownership of this money pouch; the world can be put in order only by abolishing property. Now property is not abolished by having it belong to no one; property that belongs to no one is an absurdity. It can only be abolished by having it belong to everyone; only then is the abolition meaningful.

Here the socialist runs into difficulties. If his criticism is directed against property, it is also directed against the game the wolves have set up, the great Wolf Game of bourgeois society. The socialist points out that this game includes amoral moves, that it exploits players who are low on chips and favors players who are loaded with them, that various classes of players have emerged and become established, and finally that the umpire is unfair because his primary function is to safeguard the loot gained by immoral moves.

But whoever wants to abolish the great bourgeois Wolf Game must propose another game, for the bourgeois Wolf Game did not develop out of some lupine play instinct, but out of very specific economic difficulties that were no longer manageable by barter. Man's demiurgic ability to constantly produce new objects and to harness the forces of nature, indeed to reconstruct nature itself, has made his environment so complex and impenetrable, and has woven such a dense web of modes of production and products, that he could only make sense of it by devising a system of order, namely the contrived game board of his Wolf Game, onto which objects and processes can be transposed. By destroying the Wolf Game, the socialist runs the risk of leading mankind back to a condition in which people can no longer live, for it is no longer possible to dispense with an abstract system of relationships among people and between people and the things they produce. There is no way back from the necessity of abstraction. When the socialist comes to power, he must take over the old system of abstract relationships, and whether he wants to or not, propose a new game to be played on the old game board.

For this he needs a different point of departure and a new set of rules. He has to reprogram the wolves into lambs. If the classical bourgeois believes that man is an intelligent wolf, the socialist believes man to be an intelligent lamb. *Homo homini agnus.** The bourgeois, from personal experience and on the basis of religious reminiscence, considers man "innately" guilty; the socialist declares man to be "innately" innocent and merely made guilty by the Wolf Game of bourgeois society, against which the socialist holds up the Good Shepherd Game of socialist society. This game was originally conceived as a game played by lambs among lambs. As in the great Wolf Game, the player's security is guaranteed, but the loot belongs to all, so that the chips created by the production of goods go into a communal kitty. The more goods are produced, the greater is each player's share in the common fund of chips. But this game of lambs is as difficult to implement as it appears to be ideal. The inevitable consequence is that only part of the lamb population, although by far the greater part, may remain lambs, while the rest are forced to play at being wolves; or, to put it in classically bourgeois terms, a part of the wolf population must play the role of lambs, and the rest are allowed to remain wolves. The wolves have the task of administering the lambs' loot and defending it against alien wolves, for as long as alien wolves continue to exist. If one day there aren't any alien wolves left, the lambs that are playing the role of wolves will be allowed to become lambs again, particularly since the lambs who have been allowed to remain lambs, no longer beguiled by alien wolves, will want to remain lambs for good and will then be able to administer their own affairs. The wolves of the Good Shepherd Game are therefore temporary wolves, humanistic wolves, good shepherds. Just as the players in the Wolf Game fall into two groups, the poor in chips and the rich in chips, the players of the Good Shepherd Game fall into two groups as well, the guarded and the guards.

The formal advantage of the Good Shepherd Game consists in its needing no special umpire, since wolves can assume that role. Its disadvantage is that, on the one hand, the lambs who must remain lambs dream of becoming wolves and must therefore be guarded all the more closely, so closely that soon the main task of the wolves as regards the lambs is to prevent them from becoming wolves as well, and that on the other hand, the lambs who are allowed to play at being wolves are determined to remain wolves at all costs and therefore frequently tear each other to pieces in order to establish themselves as wolves once and for all.

*"Man is a lamb to man."

To put it another way: in the Good Shepherd Game, just as in the Wolf Game, the players eventually have only the umpire (the established class of wolves) as their opponent and are therefore at an equally hopeless disadvantage. At this stage of the Good Shepherd Game, both games have converged to such an extent that the umpires are almost indistinguishable, especially as they begin to adopt each other's rules. Suddenly, moves from the Good Shepherd Game are allowed in the Wolf Game, and the Good Shepherd Game permits rules of the Wolf Game: in both games the state has become too powerful.

Applied to our model: we can employ its revised version for both games, since the Wolf Game and the Good Shepherd Game do not illustrate the bourgeois and socialist theories but bourgeois and socialist reality. The social order built by the socialist is, just like the capitalist order, adequately symbolized by a policeman hidden near the isolated well.

Let us return to our hill, let us sit down next to the prophet, let our policeman hide near the solitary well, let the three riders come trotting along, twice, once as bourgeois and once as socialist riders. The results are bewildering.

Now it is true that a money pouch—or let's say a wallet stuffed full of large bills (after all, in our civilized world a money pouch contains only small change)—is a temptation for a policeman as well. A policeman's salary is often quite modest. A policeman can resist or succumb to temptation. If the policeman in our case succumbs to temptation, he will either take off with the stuffed wallet or else remain hidden near the well with the stolen wallet until one of the three riders is killed at the well. Then the policeman will arrest the murderer. If the arrested man is the first rider, then the criminal policeman, needing to cover up his theft, will also accuse him of having fabricated the loss of the wallet, perhaps in order to defraud his insurance company, but it is not these possibilities that are bewildering us.

Let us therefore simply presume that the policeman would resist temptation; generally speaking, we can count on him to do so. There is another factor that is much more confounding, for the question arises: who in a civilized country would come to a solitary well on horseback carrying a wallet stuffed with money? When the poor citizens of a capitalist country or the unpropertied citizens of a people's democracy come to gather wood (presuming they are allowed to), they arrive on foot, and so do the Young Pioneers or members of the Komsomol† combing through some desolate area on a manoeuver,* and besides they don't have wallets, and if they do have wallets,

---

Young Pioneers: Communist youth movement.

they aren't wallets filled with substantial amounts of money. Athletes, too, arrive on foot when training for the marathon, but who would carry a wallet while training? Competitors in an equestrian event? Here, too, the wallet disturbs us. If we want to meet the requirements of our model, there is only one possibility open to us. If previously these were average riders of a time and a country where the natural means of transport was the horse, now our riders belong to exclusive social circles, for in our modern age with its trains, cars, and airplanes the only people at all likely to show up at solitary wells on horseback with wallets full of cash are very rich capitalists or extremely powerful Party members who start their day with a constitutional morning ride.

Our prophet, therefore, suddenly sees himself confronted by a prominent banker, a major industrialist, or a leading politician, if this is a capitalist country, or by a field marshal and two members of the politburo if the country is socialist.* Now the captain of industry might very well steal the bank director's wallet and the banker then murder the leading politician, or the first member of the politburo could deprive the field marshal of his briefcase and the field marshal then kill the second member of the politburo. But how will the policeman behave? As a policeman of the bourgeoisie, he will probably arrest the industrialist and the banker, for his sense of justice is highly stimulated by the sensation his intervention will cause. As a member of the "people's police" he will probably not intervene. He doesn't dare. But these are idle speculations, for to our surprise, no bloody Shakespearean drama takes place. It is improbable that a member of such exclusive society would steal a sum of money that could be contained in a wallet, since the far larger sums he requires are customarily stolen in quite different, legal, and much more effective ways; and it is even more improbable that he would commit murder for such a ridiculous sum, for people in those circles commonly use different, but no less effective means of dealing with their enemies. We need only to insert the names. It is unlikely that Siemens would steal Abs's wallet and that Abs would murder Strauss, or that Brezhnev would pilfer Zhukov's wallet and that Zhukov would kill Kosygin.† These gentlemen have no need of such measures. Nothing would happen by the

---

Politburo: The executive organ of the Communist party.

†Werner von Siemens (1816–1892) was the founder of the great Siemens industrial empire; Hermann Abs (1901–1994), a German banker, was very important for the economic recovery of Germany after World War II; Franz Josef Strauss (1915–1988) was a German politician and statesman; Leonid Brezhnev (1906–1982) was the effective ruler of the USSR from 1964 to 1982; Georgi K. Zhukov (1896–1974), marshal of the USSR, was one of the outstanding commanders of World War II; Alexey N. Kosygin (1904–1980) was premier of the USSR from 1964 to 1980.

solitary well, and the prophet, a little naive, as prophets frequently are, and all the more helpless since we have transported him into our time, would cry out: "Allah, this world is finally just!" But no sooner would the prophet have come to this conclusion, than he would recoil before Allah's mighty voice: "You fool," Allah would thunder, "what you admire as human justice is in truth human injustice, for these three riders need neither steal nor murder, for they wield the levers of human power, which permits them to commit with impunity far more disgraceful wrongs than you in your simplicity can imagine." However—and here we must amend our story—Allah would only proclaim these words in a bourgeois country. He would remain silent in a socialist country, where his freedom of speech is severely restricted.

That is the story of the prophet and the three riders. No matter how we modify it, the prophet always comes to the conclusion, must come to it, that the world is unjust—even if in the last variant Allah himself has to reveal this to him; prophets are radical in their judgments, we know that. We also know that, nonetheless, these radical judgments contain a truth, a bitter one for many of us. The world is a mess, and because it is a mess it is unjust. This statement seems so self-evident that we regard it as true without thinking about it. But actually it is a problematic statement, because justice is problematical. Justice is an idea that presupposes a society of human beings. A man alone on an island can deal justly with his goats, that is all. An idea is thinkable, but the question is whether it can be realized, whether a just social order can be constructed in the same way that a machine can.

Departing from exact concepts, man can construct many things of which he has an exact conception. From exact concepts he develops exact systems and structures for the fields of his thought and environment: numbers, seconds, the meter, money, scientific instruments, machines, and so on. Only man himself cannot be transformed into an exact concept. The concept "man" is a double one. It has a particular and a general meaning. There are of course many concepts that express something particular and something general. The concept "number" can mean a particular number and all numbers, the concept "dog" a particular dog and all dogs. But neither the concept "number" nor the concept "dog" forms concepts, nor do we find, behind our own concepts of number and dog, a number-being and a dog-being that form concepts. Only man forms concepts about himself. The problematic nature of thought arises only where thinking takes place. In his particular concept of himself, man sets himself apart from other men, and in his universal concept, he includes himself among all the others. In his particular concept of himself, he clings to his identity in order not to dissolve into the general concept, and in his general concept he gives up his identity in order to become a function of the general concept. In his particular concept of himself, man sees himself as something unique, subject to a particular fate, aware that he must die, and losing himself in realms of the unconscious that are only partially illuminated by consciousness: he sees himself as an individual. While the particular concept of man is an existential concept, the general concept is a logical one. The existential concept is immediately understandable; in a sense, every human being possesses it unconsciously. One's logical concept of oneself, however, is arrived at indirectly: it must be deduced. By it, a person conceives of himself as one human being among others, and by it a person becomes aware of the problems inherent in having to be one human being among others. By forming two concepts of himself that do not coincide, man becomes paradoxical. The particular concept man has of himself is not included in his general concept of himself. In his general concept, man excludes himself as an individual.

If, therefore, we wish to construct a just social order, there are two possible ways to employ the human material we have at our disposal. We can proceed from the particular concept of man, from the individual, or from the general concept of man, from society. We have to choose. But before choosing, we must have a clear conception of what sort of justice we can realize through a social system. However, just as man forms two concepts of himself, he also possesses two ideas of justice. For the individual, justice is the right to be himself: this right is what we call freedom. It is the particular concept of justice that everyone applies to himself, the existential idea of justice. For society, on the other hand, justice consists in the right to guarantee the freedom of each individual, which can only be done by limiting the freedom of each individual. This right is what we call justice proper, it is the general concept of justice, a logical idea.

Freedom and justice are the two ideas with which politics operates, and political practice succeeds in exercising control over men only to the extent that it takes both ideas into account. When politics ignores one of the two, it loses credibility. Without freedom, politics becomes inhumane, and without justice likewise. Nevertheless the relationship between freedom and justice is problematic. It is a commonplace to define politics as the art of the possible; but if we look more closely, it proves to be the art of the impossible. Freedom and justice are only apparently interdependent. The existential idea of freedom does not exist on the same plane as the logical idea of justice. An existential idea is an emotional given, a logical idea is a product of thought. It is possible to think of a world of absolute freedom and a world of absolute justice. These two worlds would not coincide, they would contradict one another, although each of them would be a hell: the world of absolute freedom a jungle where man is hunted like a wild beast, and the world of absolute justice a prison where man is tortured to death. The impossible art of politics consists in reconciling the emotional idea of freedom with the conceptualized idea of justice; this is only possible on the level of morality and not on the level of logic. To put it differently: politics can never be a pure science.

For the sake of simplicity, we can equate the Wolf Game with the attempt to construct a just society on the basis of individuality, and the Good Shepherd Game with the same project based on collective concepts. If I regard the Wolf Game as just, its justice consists for me in providing insurance for each player and his loot, insofar as he plays by the rules. The freedom of each individual is guaranteed if the rules of the game permit cleverness but not dishonesty. Justice and freedom in the Wolf Game, therefore, coincide only for players who have won many chips, or for those with hopes of playing cleverly enough to win many chips in the future. But for players who are low on chips and have lost hope of winning large numbers of them, or for those who don't know how to play the game cleverly, freedom and justice do not coincide in the Wolf Game. These players are free, to be sure, but they are not in a position to make use of their freedom. Such freedom, to them, seems a bondage, and the justice of the game an injustice. They tend to place their hopes in the Good Shepherd Game, or they begin to play with a disregard for the rules. A judicious player will therefore demand that the umpire conduct the game more fairly, or that he make the game more just for the majority of players. More fairness is achieved when the umpire demands higher taxes on the loot of players who are loaded with chips, and more justice for the majority is achieved when provision is made that players loaded with chips and players who hope to be loaded with chips constitute the majority. If that is impossible, players loaded with chips form a minority. And in order to keep the Wolf Game in operation, they proceed to provide the umpire from their own ranks. At this point, freedom and justice in the Wolf Game become an illusion: players low on chips are dependent on those who have raked in large numbers of them. Justice and freedom are useful only for those to whom they bring profit; morality becomes the privilege of winners. But if the umpire becomes all-powerful by raising taxes on players who are loaded with chips and using their loot to level the playing field and making all the players dependent on him, then the Wolf Game itself becomes illusory, a disguised Good Shepherd Game. Since the Wolf Game constantly runs into these kinds of difficulties, it is forced to employ the idea of a just and free social order, which it had originally intended to realize and which led to an unjust and unfree order, as an argument for the preservation of an unjust social order. The Wolf Game becomes ideological. When a social order is no longer sound, it needs an ideology.

The Good Shepherd Game runs into similar difficulties. It is faced with a problem of distribution. This problem appears to be of a purely technical nature, but it proves difficult nonetheless. For the individual player, it is not a matter of indifference whether the loot he wins in the game belongs to him or to everyone, because loot is what makes the game attractive in the first place. If the loot belongs to all, the game loses its appeal, its intensity dwindles, the players begin to lose interest. The player feels injured in his nature as a player, for the tendency to regard the spoils of the game as one's personal property is a natural one. The player has a moral right to his loot; this moral right is a part of his freedom. The distribution of loot, now declared to be communal property, can therefore not be accomplished without force: it needs to be not only distributed, but exacted as well.

Whoever demands the Good Shepherd Game must, as a tactic, turn to those players in the Wolf Game who are low on chips and whose loot depends on the loot of other players. To these dependent players low on chips the game would seem fairer if their loot represented a part of the communal kitty rather than part of the loot of an individual or a group of individuals.

There are various ways for me to acquire some loot. For example, by creating a product and charging chips for this product, or, if I am loaded with chips, by lending chips to another player and demanding back more than I lent. Producers and buyers or creditors and debtors make up systems of players, or teams, that can be expanded in such a way that, for example, one player along with other players creates a product that is transformed by still other players into a product, and so on until an endgame player tosses the end product directly into the game. The loot of the various team players involved at various stages in the production of the end product is disbursed by the endgame player, who acquires his own loot by the sale of the end product. The more players are involved in a given team, therefore, the smaller their personal loot. Since these players are dependent not only on the team in which they play but also on the endgame player who gambles with the team as a whole, they are dependent and therefore unfree players: workers.

Because the products of present-day technology can only be produced by complicated and at times colossal teams (industry), the unfree player has become the rule and the free endgame player (entrepreneur) the exception: we live in a world of workers. Moreover, it is becoming common for the free endgame player to be replaced by groups of players well endowed with chips who have a shared interest in the endgame loot of a team. Just as dependent players are meshed into teams, individual teams are meshed into still higher team systems; but the endgame players and the groups of players who are rich in chips are also enmeshed in a network that turns the freedom of the individual player into a fiction. Everything is interrelated and interwoven.

Therefore, when the suggestion is made to get rid of the free individual player and to transform the Wolf Game system into a unified Good Shepherd Game system, this demand has already been fulfilled insofar as the Wolf Game has, for the main part, turned into a game played among the various team systems. In many respects, therefore, the Wolf Game represents an evolutionary development that leads to a tempered Good Shepherd Game, while the Good Shepherd Game, if it wants to develop further, runs into a crisis: while trying to assure loot for all, it must retain the various team systems without which products would not be produced. Therefore, as in the Wolf Game, an unfree player in the Good Shepherd Game remains unfree: he is free only to the extent that there are no free players left. Since the Good Shepherd Game must retain the various team systems, it is forced to choose between two alternatives: either to approximate the Wolf Game by introducing free team systems in some form or other, or by coordinating its various team systems into a single unified system. By this last choice, however, it would ultimately fuse into a giant molecule inside which the minutest error in planning could cripple or even paralyze the Good Shepherd Game.

Though the Good Shepherd Game is unable to free the unfree player, it needs to give him the feeling that he is free. The Good Shepherd Game can't do without an ideology, either. Here the question arises: why do people in power, whether they rule as wolves over wolves or as wolves over sheep, have any need at all of an ideology in order to exercise their power, and why do people who strive for power back it up with an ideology? In other words: why does Brezhnev run around as a Communist and Strauss as a Christian, roles for which they could not be more transparently miscast and in which the vaudeville troupe called the world nevertheless accepts them, and why don't the two of them present themselves as what they are: men drawn to power? Ideologies are the cosmetics of power, but why does power need to apply makeup? On the one hand, political ideologies are philosophies designed to perpetuate or transform political circumstances. Politics is enacted on the field of power, philosophy on the field of intellect. An ideology is an attempt to influence power by the application of some philosophy or other. But since power is stronger than the intellect, by which it is only gradually and indirectly transformed, and since it is the dream of humanity that it might be the other way around, power becomes more powerful the more intellectual it pretends to be. Brezhnev as a Communist and Strauss as a Christian become representatives of intellectual principles. Ideologies are excuses for staying in power or pretexts for coming to power. But power can only be maintained or seized by using the instruments of power: by force. Ideologies, therefore, not only justify power, they also glorify force, and subsequently dispose of its victims in the manner of a funeral parlor: they dress up the corpses. On the other hand, the impulse to justify force with ideologies cannot be explained by aesthetics alone. One who wades in blood may like to wear boots, but there must be another reason why man, who makes nature the object of his thought, loses all objectivity when the object is himself and his interests. The reason does not lie solely in man's social organization, it lies in himself.

Ladies and gentlemen, when at the beginning of my lecture I announced that I would base my talk on two stories from *A Thousand and One Nights,* it was surely in part to keep you in suspense about when the second story would finally begin, thereby giving my remarks the same narrative twist that keeps the stories of *A Thousand and One Nights* spinning along. The narrative technique of these stories consists in having a second story develop out of the first, a third out of the second, and so on, each story beginning before the previous story ends, a device that helped Sheherezade to hang on for a thousand and one nights; if for just one night, say the third or the seven hundred and twelfth, King Shahryar had lost his appetite for another story, it would have been all over for Sheherezade the next morning. That Sheherezade was not beheaded after the thousand-and-first night was probably due to the King's having grown used to her; after all, she had borne him three sons in the meantime.

Now, I don't want to claim that I find myself in the same position as Sheherezade, even though I am speaking before an assemblage of students, but my task is to give a lecture on "Justice and Law" and not to write a treatise on the subject. A treatise allows for annotations, it can always be reread, and besides, annotations add a certain air of sagacity; but an annotated lecture is difficult to pull off, its effect has to be immediate. Its ideas, should it contain any, must be instantly clear; or else one must keep them obscure enough so that no one understands them: that is called a profound lecture. But since I am endeavoring to give an intelligible lecture, I cannot avoid making some annotations to several of my ideas that are not self-evident; for a lecture containing only self-evident ideas would be so self-evident that there would be no need to give it; in order, however, to insert these annotations, I have resorted to the narrative technique of *A Thousand and One Nights*, which is to tell stories within stories. Thus I inserted into the story of the prophet at the isolated well the story of the Wolf Game and the Good Shepherd Game, and not only that: I also came up with a story that doesn't sound like a story at all, but more like a philosophy. I told an abstract story: namely, the story about how man forms two different concepts of himself, one particular and existential, the other general and logical. While before I allowed myself a certain poetic levity, now I am indulging in philosophical levity, and I would like to leave open the question of whether poetic levity may not result in philosophy or philosophical levity may not result in poetry. The truth is, I am only concerned with using an intellectual construct to give the ideas of freedom and justice a specific content, which can then be discussed within my intellectual construct. But just as we varied the poetic tale of the prophet by the isolated well, so too the abstract story about the two concepts man forms of himself can be varied. Just as the stories of the great Wolf Game and the Good Shepherd Game served to illustrate two different socioeconomic orders, the variation on the abstract story serves to set up two different socioemotional orders: the first is an existential project, while the second is a logical conception.

Man inclines to broaden the existential, particular concept he has of himself, and to narrow the logical, general concept he derives from himself. If a person did not have this inclination, he would confront the rest of humanity as an asocial, isolated creature, a position generally assumed only by criminals. Man broadens his *I* to a *We* with whom he identifies himself, and reduces humanity, even though he is part of it, to the *Others*, with whom he does not identify himself: on the contrary, he is capable of transforming the *Others*, if he hates them, into the *Enemy*. He sets up emotional realities, the more intimate *We* and the more general *Us*, the more intimate *Enemy* and the more general *Others*. *We* includes wife, family, friends, and so forth; *Us* includes one's own tribe, countrymen, race, and so on. The concept of the *Other* comprises the stranger, the other tribe, the other nation, the other race, all those who under certain conditions can become the *Enemy*, the enemy tribe, the enemy nation, the enemy race. Once this supposition has been accepted, politics employs ideology to transform social institutions, whose functions properly ought to be those of technical administration and arbitration, into emotional realities with which the individual can identify himself. That is why man is perpetually duped by politics. The emotional side of politics is just as powerful as its economic aspect: the state becomes the homeland, the fatherland.

Applied to the great Wolf Game: the individual wolf instinctively forms a *We* with his pack, which is always headed by a lead wolf who represents not only the pack but also the individual wolf, who, in turn, is able to identify himself with the lead wolf. The individual lead wolves, if they cooperate, lead a grand pack, an *Us*, with which the lead wolves and the individual wolves identify themselves. If the *Us* is led jointly by the lead wolves, the result is a democratic wolf community; if the individual wolves are dominated by a lead wolf or by a clique of lead wolves, a lupine dictatorship is the outcome. For the ordinary individual wolf, the grand pack, regardless of its organization, represents a suprapersonal, or, to stay with our metaphor, a supralupine being, with which he identifies himself: the more powerful this superwolf is, the more powerful the individual wolf feels himself to be. Transposed back into the human world: the state becomes the beloved fatherland, for which one kills and is willing to be killed: gladly, even in the throes of death.

Nevertheless, the state has a weak spot once it passes itself off as the emotional reality called fatherland: the individual wolf identifies himself with it only in a state of emotion. When this emotion is lacking, the superwolf becomes a mere institution again, a more or less fair umpire, whom the individual wolves, caught up as they are in the Wolf Game, sometimes criticize and at other times curse—what player ever accepts an umpire's ruling without protest! That puts the superwolf in a serious pickle; his ideology is no longer believed, an *Us* becomes the *Other,* or even the *Enemy.* The superwolf's problem is peace. During a time of peace he must prove that he is needed; not so when there is danger, which usually means a crisis or a war. Then emotions are unleashed that transform the state into a fatherland.

War, however, is never in serious danger of degenerating into genuine peace. The Wolf Game is always in a state of war. During peacetime, too, the superwolves fight each other, the lead wolves mangle each other, the individual wolves maul each other economically. Add to this the human tendency, even in peacetime, to construct a *We* with whom the individual wolf gladly identifies himself, and an *Enemy* by whom he feels threatened. One such *We* is the international jet set, whose ideological function within the Wolf Game is to demonstrate how far an individual wolf can go once he is loaded with chips; he can allow himself what a Wolf Game player who is low on chips can not allow himself: everything. Each individual in these circles is proof that the great Wolf Game has opportunities to offer, that it is possible to hit the jackpot. That is why this society is international: it is the great, intimate *We* of all wolves who are somewhat low on chips, who, like untalented but impassioned chess players, supported by a powerful illusion industry (the press, the movies), dream of becoming world champions someday. In addition to this more intimate *We* there is also a more general *Us* that the wolves are proud of and which transforms their state into a fatherland: the Germans, for instance, speak of "our soccer team," "our Goethe," "our Schiller" and we Swiss stand behind "our watch industry," believe in "our Pestalozzi," revere "our Gottfried Keller."* This *We* and this *Us* stand opposed to the *Others* and the *Enemy*. For the Wolf Game player, the *Enemy* was originally the Good Shepherd Game player, just as, for the Good Shepherd Game player, the Wolf Game player was the *Enemy*. But in times of peace, the *Enemy*, too, is not the same as in war: in war, the *Enemy* develops out of the *Other;* in peace, out of the *Us.* Just as for Allah and for the Devil the *Enemy* is neither the Devil nor Allah, but the atheist, who believes neither in the Devil nor in Allah, so in both games the intellectuals have become the *Enemy*. The two forms of society that we see today, mere systems of organized power, have so thoroughly betrayed the ideologies to which they hold fast that rebellion against them can only be in the right, which is not to say that rebellion always does what is right.

Beginning of the Helvetian Interlude

Given that, in the Wolf Game, the emotional realities of the *We*, the *Us*, the *Others,* and the *Enemy* combine into fatherlands whose ideologies infuse them with particular political meanings, we shall proceed, ladies and gentlemen—as a matter of courtesy, since I speak to you as a Swiss citizen—to examine Switzerland as one example of Wolf Game politics and of the contradictions in which such politics become entangled. Every nation has an ideology that is the result of its economic, international, historical,

---

*Johann H. Pestalozzi (1746–1827) was a Swiss educationist and follower of Jean-Jacques Rousseau; Gottfried Keller (1819–1890) was one of the most famous Swiss poets and novelists of the nineteenth century.

and emotional structure. Switzerland's ideology consists in our country's pretense of passivity. Switzerland is a superwolf that, by proclaiming its neutrality, declares itself a superlamb. In other words: Switzerland is a superwolf that announces that it harbors no aggressive intentions toward the other superwolves. This disguise is extraordinarily successful: not even the superwolf Hitler gobbled up the Swiss superwolf in lamb's clothing.

Nevertheless, the ideological claim to lambhood leads Switzerland into a dilemma, because a Swiss is a wolf like any other wolf, which compels the definition of Switzerland as a nation of wolves protected by a superlamb. The absurdity of this notion is obvious: it's the idea of "intellectual national defense,"* a peculiar phenomenon, because if there is anything that cannot be defended intellectually, it is a state.

A state, it is true, has more to do with the intellect than many people think. As an institution, it has to be administered, an activity which, contrary to the opinion of many civil servants, does require the use of the mind; furthermore, if a state does not want its continued existence to be meaningless, two intellectual faculties must remain active within it: the ability to preserve and the ability to plan ahead. But a state's existence needs no justification; if it collapses, it no longer exists, and no longer needs to be justified, either.

Whoever seeks to defend himself intellectually must either be afraid or have a bad conscience. Both are true of Switzerland. It has a bad conscience because it pretends to be a lamb, making appeals to the humanity of wolves and trying to be useful to them by maintaining an all-night pharmacy, the Red Cross; it is afraid because in reality it is a wolf after all, albeit a small one, so small that it lives in constant fear of being torn to shreds by other wolves and therefore instinctively bares its teeth. But having little confidence in its own bite, it returns to the tactics of intellectual national defense. Intellectual national defense is the thread on an endless screw.

To be sure, a country does not need to mobilize a spiritual national defense unless it finds itself seriously threatened by the international situation. But since spiritual national defense, if it is to work in a real emergency, requires drilling and training like any other national defense, the international

---

*Translator's note: For the translation of "*geistige Landesverteidigung*," a choice had to be made between "spiritual" and "intellectual" national defense. I have chosen to use "intellectual" here, to accommodate F. D.'s remarks in the immediately following passages, and "spiritual" later on, where the term's emotive and anti-intellectual meaning is discussed.

situation is always serious for Switzerland. Not that such a view is entirely mistaken, but still, there is no denying that Switzerland is one of those countries that, in order to defend themselves spiritually, thrive on the cold war. But the gravity of the international situation is not a sufficient reason for a nation to defend itself spiritually: the nation itself must be worthy of defense. Thus the question arises: what qualities of the Swiss people make their country worth defending? If the Swiss had no special qualities, the country's economy could be annexed to southern Germany's, and its hotel business to that of Tyrol; our great banks and arms factories, too, are more easily explained on an economic than on an intellectual basis. Therefore the country's spiritual defense program must declare Switzerland to be an exceptional, divinely ordained superwolf, a notable metaphysical entity, a shrine. The effect is a Switzerland elevated, as it were, beyond the reach of the Swiss. Therefore a Swiss citizen who wants to engage in spiritual self-defense must himself be like that high and holy place: he must be a wolf of particularly noble breed, a noble wolf whose qualities can be deduced from the premises of his Wolf Game: he must be free, obedient, capitalistic, socially concerned, democratic, federalistic, religious, anti-intellectual, and prepared to take up arms. These qualities call for some specification.

Free and obedient: like other Wolf Games, the Swiss version is founded on individualism and holds high the idea of freedom, though at the same time this freedom is restricted in order for the game to work. The individual is required to be free and obedient. This dichotomy in particular leads to the creation of the superwolf called the state, which has all the freedoms that an individual wolf caught up in the Wolf Game no longer has, though he imagines he has them. The fact, for example, that to the Swiss citizen, Switzerland appears to be independent, leads him to believe that he is free. For him, as an inveterate Wolf Game player, freedom is identical with independence. The independence of a nation, however, does not necessarily entail the freedom of its citizens. Independence is certainly a prerequisite of freedom as long as there are other superwolves around, but no more than a prerequisite. Independence makes freedom possible, but does not guarantee it. Spiritual national defense, however, clings to the equation Independence = Freedom; if it didn't, our prototypical Swiss would start thinking about his personal freedom and become suspect as a citizen. For then he might not automatically accept the equation Freedom = Obedience, which spiritual national defense derives from the first equation, since its tactic, after all, is to sacrifice the freedom of the Swiss to the independence of Switzerland. This wipes out Switzerland as a reality to make room for Switzerland as an ideology, or, to stay with our metaphor: the Swiss citizen is required to be a wolf in lamb's clothing if he wants to be a good Helvetian.

Capitalistic and socially concerned: in or out of lamb's clothing, a wolf is a wolf, and the only game he can believe in is the Wolf Game, for no other game can give an individual wolf who has been forced to disguise himself as a lamb the assurance that he is still a wolf. One problem, however, remains unsolved: players low on chips are dependent on players who are loaded with chips. This supports the tendency of the players low on chips to introduce the Good Shepherd Game; that is, not to rest content with being wolves in disguise but to become real lambs. We have already indicated the impossibility of a pure Wolf Game. Just as there is a revisionist socialism, so there is a revisionist capitalism that has to pretend to be socially concerned in order to give the country's basic capitalist structure an alibi for remaining capitalist; at the same time, it gives the Good Shepherd Game players an alibi for howling with the wolves. All in all, a tendency that is aesthetically compatible with spiritual national defense: a socialist Switzerland sounds bad, a socially concerned Switzerland sounds progressive.

Democratic and federalistic: democracy is one of the great political ideas of mankind. Rudimentary forms of it exist in Switzerland, even though a democracy without women's suffrage is incomplete.* Democracy is an attempt to allow as many people as possible to share political power: the majority rules over the minority.

But the more complex a nation becomes, the more complicated the implementation of democracy is; Switzerland, which still retains some possibilities of direct democracy, is no exception. A nation must not only be governed, it must also be administered. Resolutions must not only be made, they must also be implemented: politics consists of politicians who make policies and civil servants who carry them out.

Now, the more complex the total political apparatus of a nation becomes, the more normal it is for politicians to become civil servants and vice versa. Our present-day parliament consists primarily of civil servants and functionaries, a trend that is further supported by the tendency of the Wolf Game and the Good Shepherd Game to weave society into one impenetrable mesh of power relations. It is only in an ideological sense that parliament represents the people; in reality, it represents only itself. The structure of modern society, in which everyone is in some fashion an employee, works

*Women were granted the vote in Switzerland in 1971.

against democracy. Everyone is used to being supervised. But democracy presupposes criticism and the habit of keeping an eye on government. A parliament consisting entirely of civil servants and functionaries, however, is soon tempted to dictate how people should behave, and like that Zürich police chief who, on national television, expressed annoyance at teenage hairstyles, our politicians demand a standardized spiritual haircut: the one called spiritual national defense. We are to be obedient democrats. Spiritual national defense would have us believe that a democracy that is no longer functioning is a functioning democracy: we are supposed to call ourselves democrats without being permitted to be that. Its approach to federalism is the same. The spiritual national defense people like to refer to the nation as "our homeland," which sentimentalizes the matter: the Swiss citizen should not be defending a nation, but his valley.

Religious and anti-intellectual: spiritual national defense, strictly speaking, presupposes a belief in an emotional reality that does not, in reality, "exist in and of itself." The state is not an emotional but rather a constructed reality, not unlike a work of art. Its function is to make it easier for people to live together. A function must be open to critical review. It presupposes critical discourse, for, if it does not function, its premises need to be examined, a process in which the distinction between destructive and constructive criticism is as meaningless as that between positive and negative art. Either a critique is correct, in which case it is justified, or it is not correct, in which case it is not a critique. But a thing that can be critically examined cannot be believed in. For those people, therefore, who ask us to believe in a function, any criticism is not criticism but unbelief: whoever criticizes is a communist or a nihilist, depending on the political climate. But whoever believes in a fatherland as an objective entity and does not see through it as an emotional reality will avail himself of whatever other belief he may hold, especially a belief in humanism or Christianity: he will act as if there really were such a thing as a humanistic or even a Christian Switzerland. But here the Swiss spiritual defense program reveals itself to be a state religion, because if there is one thing that cannot be humanistic or Christian, it is the state, no matter whether it adopts the name fatherland or homeland. Only people can be Christian or humane, not institutions.

Prepared to take up arms: here the spiritual defense program turns out to be a comedy. Even though the Swiss citizen is a wolf in lamb's clothing, he must always make it clear to the world that he is a wolf after all. That is the reason why a wolf in lamb's clothing who claims to be a lamb is punished, even if it turns out that he truly is a lamb and not a wolf. The Swiss citizen is supposed to believe in the ideology he is proffered, but not to take it seriously. It is no coincidence that those who busy themselves with spiritual national defense in Switzerland are demanding atom bombs along with spirit; good old Helvetia would look pretty awkward standing there with a dreadful weapon in her hands, yet blinded by motes of spirit dust she had managed to sprinkle in her own eyes.

End of the Helvetian Interlude

Ladies and gentlemen, at this point a personal comment is necessary. I am not at all embarrassed to be Swiss, any more than I would be embarrassed to be French, German, Italian, and so on. I am even Swiss with something of a passion. I like living in Switzerland. I like to speak Swiss German. I love the Swiss and I love having it out with them. I would find it hard to imagine working anywhere else.

I know that I am bound to Switzerland for emotional reasons, but I also know that Switzerland is only a nation and nothing more, that its constitution, its social and economic structure, and the people that comprise it exhibit certain defects; and finally, I know that many things for which other nations admire us are not true; for instance, that people who speak different languages live together there. They don't live together, they live alongside one another. It may be that human beings cannot manage without emotion, but that does not mean that we can manage without thought.

I love Switzerland and think objectively about it. Good things can of course be said about it as well: it is, among other things, a small nation, and I consider small nations to be a much happier political invention than large ones, if only because small munitions depots are less dangerous than large ones in the event of an explosion. I am not ashamed either of having taken no part in the war, or of having been spared by it. I am thankful that I did not have to be a hero, because I do not know whether I could have been one, and I am conscious of the fact that I owe this good fortune more to the smallness of my country than to Hitler's fear of it, for a functioning Switzerland was more useful to Greater Germany than a conquered one.

As for the rest, I am an obedient citizen where obedience to the state is appropriate; I abide by the laws, pay my taxes, and in the use of my car and my dealings with fellow citizens I comport myself as correctly as possible. It's true that I no longer serve in the militia. However, I do not owe this fortunate circumstance to a free decision; I did not subject myself to any voluntary martyrdom, I owe it solely to my body, which plays other tricks on me instead; on the contrary, just as I have nothing against the Swiss state, I have nothing against the Swiss army. It is a popular element and just for that reason an important political instrument, a piece of folklore, a fraternity that holds the Swiss together, but that is precisely why Switzerland could afford to do what it refuses to do: make provision for its conscientious objectors: those who are lazy and clever enough will dodge military service anyway, but a man who openly refuses to serve shows courage: why on earth should a brave man be forced into military service, particularly since he is asking to perform a civilian service that is no less demanding?

My view that an army is generally superfluous for a small nation is based on tactical considerations. The issue for a small nation is not winning a war, but surviving it. Denmark did not defend itself in World War II, and I don't consider the Swiss better than the Danes any more than I consider the Danes better than the Swiss. For small nations, what is decisive is internal resistance, not the deployment of armies; even Czechoslovakia still has a chance, in my opinion: small nations have a way of going under and coming up again and again.

Therefore, when I deduce the notion of fascism from the attempt to defend Switzerland intellectually, it is not in order to offend Switzerland or characterize it as fascist—I do not see a fascist in every one of our spiritual national defenders; what I am concerned with is to define fascism politically and remove its nimbus of demonic potency. Fascism is something you slide into, not something you fall under the spell of, like the devil: someone who thinks he's possessed by the devil feels all too guiltless once his devil has been exorcized. My intention in pointing out prefascist traits in Switzerland and not in Germany is not to exculpate the Germans, but to absolve neither the Germans nor the Swiss, for fascism arises out of the Wolf Game, out of the individualistic concept man has of himself, out of the idea of freedom.

Only by this paradox can fascism be explained. Its dangerousness resides in the altogether emotional nature of its politics. Only emotional realities make fascism possible: they bring it about by assuming total dominance. The *We* becomes the absolute fatherland, the *Us* the master race with which every individual belonging to this *Us* can identify. The *Other* becomes the absolute *Enemy*: the Jew, the Bolshevik, the *Untermensch*, and so on.* The freedom of the individual is sacrificed to the independence of the fatherland.

Untermensch: "Subhuman."

The equation Freedom = Independence is made absolute. There is no other freedom than that of the fatherland. The individual's natural conflict with the state is decided in the state's favor. Fascism is the Wolf Game played to its conclusion, its checkmate. All the individual wolves fall prey to one su-perwolf, the state. That is why Switzerland, too, shows fascist traits; in the attempt to defend itself intellectually, Switzerland becomes a total, emo-tional concept that eliminates the human being whose defense is supposed to be at issue.

Another example is the ideology of the ideologues of separatism. The "Jurassic people" as such is an emotional construct. There are people living in the Jura region, some of them speaking French, some German, but there is no special people to whom the Jura region belongs, which does not pre-clude me from considering a separate Jura canton to be necessary;* it means only that it is a matter of complete indifference to me whether I happen to be in the canton of Bern or in the canton of Jura.

It is no coincidence that every variety of fascism is associated with a "blood and soil" literature. Emotionalism and cultism go together. Just as nowadays we make a distinction between a hot art that appeals more to the emotions and a cool art that mainly addresses the mind, we can also speak of hot and cool politics. Fascism, like all emotionalism, holds out the tempta-tion of a hot politics. The individual is lured into an identification with an emotional reality; indeed all his emotions are set free, the positive and the negative ones, love, faith, loyalty, hate, aggression, and so forth; feelings that, in combination with a purely emotional, hot politics, become destruc-tive, even suicidal.

Before we discuss the ideology of the Good Shepherd Game, there is some-thing I need to make clear: if in this lecture I have talked a great deal about wolves and lambs, it is not because I have anything against wolves and lambs. On the contrary. I consider it an honor that we human beings may still com-pare ourselves to wolves and lambs.

As for the Good Shepherd Game, the reason it is not easy to talk about it is that it represents an ideology with a second and even a third ideology piled on top of it; so that actually we are dealing with an ideological com-plex, where faith in the various possible ideological paths leads to battles over the true faith, very much like those that Christianity used to fight and still does. Whereas the various forms of the Wolf Game are differentiated into power blocs, the various forms of the Good Shepherd Game split over

*Jura: A region in northwest Switzerland; the canton of Jura was established in 1977.

questions of faith; and battles over questions of faith tend to be even more ruthless than battles for power.

The Good Shepherd Game originates in a general, logical definition of man. Its point of departure is not man as he is, but as he ought to be: a reasonable lamb, not a ravenous wolf. The Good Shepherd Game is a fiction. From a collective point of view, it conceives of man as a reasonable creature, an idea that certainly honors man but does not correspond to him—any more than does the Wolf Game fiction that man, viewed existentially, is a reasonable wolf.

But the Good Shepherd Game leads to a difficulty that is unknown in the other game: even the most unreasonable wolf constructs his emotional realities on an existential foundation; even though they are, like himself, unreasonable, they are nonetheless products of instinct. It appears impossible, however, to start out from general, logical premises and arrive at an existential *We* and *Us*, at emotional realities with which the existential *I* is able to identify itself. Even though man, defined in general terms, falls under the primacy of justice, nevertheless the contradiction between the two different ways he conceives of himself forces him to produce emotional realities. The Good Shepherd Game is therefore forced to construct an existential, logical concept, a particular universal.

The genius Karl Marx came up with the concept of classes. The human race is divided into two classes: an exploiting and an exploited class. The exploiting class represents mankind, from the point of view of the individual, as a free but unjust community of wolves; the exploited class represents mankind, from a collective viewpoint, as unfree and unjustly treated, while the reason for this exploitation lies in the exploiting class. Since the exploited class appears in the passive tense, as it were, it becomes, if not quite an intimate *We*, at least a more general *Us*, with which all unfree and unjustly treated people can identify.

The Marxist dialectic, therefore, is a dialectic between the existential and the logical notions man forms about himself. Its political form is the class struggle, by means of which the exploiting class becomes the *Enemy*, and the goal of the class struggle is the classless society. But this dialectic, too, is problematic. The Good Shepherd Game must demand of each player that he see it as the only fair game. This demand could be accepted by the individual in three ways: rationally through insight, understandably through hope, and unwillingly in submission to force. Acceptance through insight takes place when the individual realizes that his fate depends on the fate of all men; through hope when the individual is unable to change his situation by himself; by force when some authority uses violent means to set up the

Good Shepherd Game. Insight and hope join together with state power to change the world, a dubious alliance that revolutionaries have tried to legitimate by demanding the dictatorship of the proletariat, suggesting that the hope of the masses for a change in their situation and the insight that such a change is necessary must be allied with violence, which alone can bring about such a change.

The proposal to establish the dictatorship of the proletariat serves the tactical function of establishing a communist party that equates the existential with the logical concept of man. This Party can be compared only with the Church. Like the equation of God and man in Christ, the equation of the existential with the logical concept of man is a dogma that cannot be proved but only believed, and from which further dogmas can be deduced.

If by dogma we understand a construct made up of logical and existential or of logical and theological concepts (which may very well contain truths), then Marxism is not a science but a dogmatics. Communist politics is a politics that has become "theology" and is therefore conspicuous for its cultic forms and perpetual avowals of commitment to the purity of the doctrine, a form of lip service that is incomprehensible to noncommunists. Its dogma has the advantage, however, of reducing the more general, logical concept of the exploited class, the *Us* construct, to a more intimate, logical *We*, the Party, which fights for the victory of the exploited class, and it has the further advantage of making a distinction between the more general *Others*, namely those members of the exploited class who don't know yet that they are exploited, and the construct of the more intimate *Enemy*, who was supposed to be represented by big business. Supposed to. But like every Church, the communist Church is constructed of dogmas and hence a paradox, a mind-made vessel into which the most contradictory streams of belief can flow. As a dogmatic construct it runs the danger of assimilating every emotional reality; and in fact, communism has now reappropriated such concepts as "state," "fatherland," "the people," even "race."

As in the Wolf Game, the true *Enemy* is not the capitalist, who has become the *Other* with whom coexistence is possible, but the heretical communist. The communist also demands of his noble lambs qualities rather like those demanded of noble Swiss wolves by the spiritual national defense program. The noble lamb, too, is required to see his freedom in the independence of his fatherland; he must be obedient, democratic, a federalist, a socialist, a true believer, anti-intellectual, and ready to take up arms, indeed in his own way capitalistic, since he has to believe that Marxist economic policy will enable him to achieve a higher living standard than is possible under capitalism. A Marxist need not be better than a capitalist, but he must live better—a reproach leveled against him with the utmost sharpness by the Marxist Konrad Farner. Contemporary communism is therefore in many ways a logically camouflaged fascism, a fascist state with a socialist structure. It is a national communism that should really be called national socialism if Hitler hadn't already usurped the term, and the question as to how things could come to this pass is answered by the history of the last several decades. The present course of world events is sad proof of the impossibility of appealing solely to man's reason; people want an emotional, hot politics to warm their hands by.

Having played through the economic and emotional structure of the present world, we are faced with a rather grave conclusion. Because both the Wolf Game and the Good Shepherd Game are beset by emotions from which they cannot free themselves, they need ideologies to keep control over their players. That is why, in the social systems with which we are familiar, freedom and justice—the ideas in whose name injustice is committed—are mere ideologies; the difference being that the Wolf Game is more inclined to use freedom as an excuse and the Good Shepherd Game is more inclined to use justice.

Applied to our question concerning a just social order: because of their emotions, social orders are in and of themselves misconstructions, not only in terms of justice but also of freedom; or, to put it another way, social orders are unjust and unfree orders that we are forced to establish if we are to have any order at all, because the contradictions of human nature render us incapable of a purely rational politics. Putting it even more nastily: there is no such thing as a just social order, because if man seeks justice, he is justified in finding every social order unjust, and if he seeks freedom, he is justified in finding every social order unfree.

There seems to be only one logical possibility. Since it turns out that in both games an institution emerges as the big winner, with the result that man comes under the domination of other men who are in charge of that institution, we have no choice but to separate the existential concept of man, an ungovernable creature, from the logical concept of man, a quantifiable entity, and to govern the determinable part with computers.

A computer is a prosthetic appendage to the human brain. It is a machine. What the animal accomplishes by means of an evolution that takes millions of years, like the gradual changes in the bone structure of, say, the reptile, which allowed it over time to live in the water, on land, and in the air, man accomplishes, thanks to his machines, in a much more efficient manner than the reptile ever could. We speed along in cars, fly in airplanes and rockets, swim in ships. Without technology, man would be no longer able to live. The more perfectly we build our machines, the more capable they are of performing all our tasks, including that of governing us. It seems that man can be governed objectively only by machines; he has no choice but to entrust himself to them. Only by complete automation can he liberate himself from the struggle for existence, only machines can set him free. Man becomes the total consumer, the consumer who does not need to work for what he consumes.

What will such a person find important? Works of art? Will there be an explosion of Sunday painters? Will there still be politics, or will politics become a farce? A ceremony? Solemn protest marches demonstrating against a computer's irrevocable decisions that make sense only to other computers? Will sects arise, new religions, because man, his physical sustenance assured, will be interested only in metaphysics? Will bloody religious wars sweep across a planet administered by computers? Will the clean-shaven be exterminated by the bearded or the bearded by the clean-shaven? Will soccer become so vitally important that fans of different teams will tear each other to pieces? Will a new priesthood rule over humanity, will a handful of technicians servicing the computers seize command over the earth? Will a humanity ruled by computers unleash a revolution against the machines? Will man become a lake dweller again?

Once we enter the realm of total freedom, everything becomes possible, the sublime and the ridiculous, the humane and the horrible, the survival and the destruction of the human race. Man undergoes his own Last Judgment, he has to endure himself. An evolution in this direction puts everything into question.

Is this the only way? Or do we no longer have a choice, have we boarded a train that is now running so fast that we can no longer jump off? Have we described the future or are we describing the present? Hasn't modern society long since led to a civilized wilderness to which man reacts like a Neanderthal?

He does not comprehend the forces of nature that control him. He uses the telephone, radio, television, stereo, electricity, medicine, computers, airplanes, cars, and so on, without really understanding them; the scientists and technicians who do know something about them appear to him like medicine men, possessors of a secret knowledge with which they control his world. Modern man has become inured to the barbarism of his civilization. He settles himself into this wilderness like a primitive farmer tilling his field. He sits in his office or works in a factory. He earns his bread by whatever means of livelihood the civilized wilderness offers him, without understanding this wilderness as a whole, often without understanding the full effects of his own occupation.

Outside his sphere, a new breed of humanity is emerging. This new man uses the civilized wilderness like a nomad, riding a motorcycle instead of a horse. He does not live in civilization, he travels through it, from job to job, from one ramshackle house to another. Today's bikers are, in their own way, the first people to have liberated themselves from modern civilization, who no longer ask about its meaning, who no longer experience it as a prison, but as nature. They protest against those people who feel that they live in a prison but don't revolt against it. The bikers shock the philistines who have surrendered themselves to their fate and accepted it as immutable.

But let us turn once again to our story, to our prophet, to the three riders, to Allah. In his first answer—we have not forgotten it—Allah proved the justice of his world. Let's be honest, he had it easy, given the range of his vision, and later, when things got more difficult, he remained silent, unfortunately; it was just in these more perplexing cases that we had hoped for his answer. Maybe he was silent on purpose. He sees us as an exact, not as a paradoxical concept. It may be that from his point of view we offer a sight as astonishing as the one the Andromeda nebula presents to us from a distance of two million light years; it may be that from Allah's viewpoint even the catastrophes in the world of men, the famines, the wars, the extermination camps, have a meaning. We do not know. Allah does not expound on the subject. He does not want to offer us cheap consolation, for we are not outside of ourselves, and even as observers we are enmeshed with the observed, incapable of interpreting ourselves completely: he does not want to console us at all. For Allah establishes his justice by establishing our injustice; his first and his second answer do not contradict each other. Through our injustice, the world is justly unjust, and the world could only be justly just if we ourselves were just. From the point of view of Allah, of the Absolute— no matter whether we believe in him or hypothesize him—the justice of the world is dependent on human conduct. The world is as man makes it. Allah in his justice merely judges it. *Mene, mene, tekel upharsin.** The Allah of our story is implacable; he is not the good Lord our love of comfort would like to believe in, the one whose business it is to practice mercy and turn a blind eye

*From Daniel 5:27: "Thou art weighed in the balances, and art found wanting."

on our bungling. Before the Allah of our story, there can be no change in human society without a change in man.

Ladies and gentlemen, I think dramaturgically. That is, my intellectual method as a dramatist consists in transforming the social reality of man into theater, and then using this transformed reality to investigate matters further. By playing out the world, I think the world through. The result of this thought process is not a new reality, but a comedic gestalt in which reality encounters itself in analyzed form, or more precisely, in which the audience encounters itself in analyzed form. This analysis is governed by imagination, by experimental thought, by playfulness; so it is not strictly scientific, it is in many ways frivolous, but useful precisely for that reason. The great Wolf Game and the Good Shepherd Game are therefore not meant to represent this or that liberal theory or Marxism, they are comedic repetitions of political structures in which we and others live.

Dramaturgical thought examines reality by exploring its internal tensions. The more paradoxically reality can be depicted, the more suitable it is as dramatic material. Dramaturgical thought is dialectical, but not in the sense of a political ideology. Dialectical materialism, for instance, is forced, willy-nilly, to give a positive twist to its system. Dialectics comes to a halt, and the belief in a more reasonable world of the future sets in: a lovely trait, but not without fatal consequences. The system must not end up as a paradox, because the system is supposed to make logically positive action possible. So it comes with a moral: he who acts in the spirit of the system is revolutionary and progressive, while he who does not act in the spirit of the system is reactionary; he who profits from the system is a shareholder in it, he who deviates from the system is a traitor. And because the course of history must be positive, every conceivable crime committed within the system can be positively construed as a politically necessary act. The consequence of this way of thinking is that even the Russians still consider themselves revolutionary. Dramaturgically dialectical thought need not fear the paradoxical; it can afford to issue in paradox, even though of course it, too, is not able to be purely dialectical: a story told in dialectical fashion must also come to an end. While political dialectics tries to set up a doctrine of how white wins in a chess game, dramaturgical dialectics represents a description of chess in which it doesn't matter whether white or black wins, or whether the game results in mate or in a draw; it is the game alone that matters, the theme set up by the opening, the drama of the endgame: dramaturgical thought, applied to politics, tries to get at its rules, not its content. To some people, admittedly, this may not seem very exciting: the rules by which *Hamlet* is constructed are simple, but what a play!

But this fact could make dramaturgical thought useful for politics. It is a corrective. It puts political reality into a different light, into the limelight, into the glaring light of satire. Dramaturgical thought points to the contradiction between human thought and human action. It is a manual for thinking about reality in a playfully critical fashion, a proposal for a way in which politics, too, should perhaps occasionally reflect on reality: without ideology and with imagination—which, after all, is the gift of foresight. Dramaturgical thought could prevent politics from making absolutes of its criteria, its goals, and its adversaries. Possibly. It could lead people to understand ideologies as mere working hypotheses that might be more easily replaced by other working hypotheses, should that prove necessary; just a minor linguistic adjustment, to be sure, but prisons and forced labor camps might be less densely populated for the sake of a working hypothesis than for the sake of an ideology. In the same way, the word "fatherland" could be replaced with "administration": who would think it sweet to die for an administration! (Though I'll grant that in our retrogade epoch there are constellations vis-à-vis the superpowers that make the word "fatherland" meaningful again.) Politics could function more critically and more freely in many ways. All too often, it still functions ideologically and therefore obstinately or simply cynically. We need only think of Vietnam. For the ideologues, there are only the guilty and the innocent. Either the Americans are guilty and the Russians and the Chinese are innocent, or the Americans are innocent and the Russians and the Chinese are guilty, or, say, the Americans and the Russians are guilty and the Chinese are innocent. But to a dramaturge, the ideological struggle between the three superpowers might seem like an enormous shadowboxing match, with both the South and the North Vietnamese as its victims. The dramaturgical imagination suspects that, if peace were brought about, the Americans would fear an alliance of the Russians and the Chinese, the Russians would fear an alliance of the Chinese and the Americans, and the Chinese finally would fear an alliance of the Americans and the Russians. Ideological thought depicts a struggle as necessary; dramaturgical thought seeks for the actual reasons, which lie not only in economics and power politics, but also in the realm of emotion. Dramaturgical thought does not try to justify any given policy, it tries to see through it.

That would be lovely and worth wishing for. But wishing is not political action. He who seeks paradox, becomes paradoxical himself. It's not just that all of a sudden the writer of comedies feels the need to be taken seriously. As a dramatist I can depict politics only when I think dramaturgically; but as a political animal, which like every thinking person I also am, I must act politically. This seems to be a contradiction. It is a contradiction.

As a dramatist, I depict the world as a questionable thing; as a political creature, I am part of this questionable world and therefore questionable myself. As a dramatist, I may legitimately use murder and mayhem to set a plot in motion or bring it to a conclusion; as a political man, I abhor murder and mayhem. On principle, I consider wars to be crimes, and I think the same of many other things that many people do not consider to be crimes.

I have nothing against social orders that are at least partially rational, I just refuse to canonize them and to accept their huge remainder of unreason and taboo as divinely ordained; I consider halfway rational social orders worth improving.

I agree with Socrates that human greatness lies in the ability to bear whatever injustice befalls us, but so much greatness is needed for this that I consider it my political duty to do everything I can to prevent someone from being forced to muster the greatness it takes to bear such injustice.

I often consider revolutions to be sensible, and often I consider them senseless. In South America, for example, I can imagine perfectly sensible revolutions, whereas in a highly industrialized nation with a huge administrative apparatus, a tightly woven economy, and a high living standard, revolution is probably senseless. Senseless because it would be a revolution only in appearance; the administrative apparatus would have to be adopted, indeed reorganized as an even more grotesque contrivance, and the inescapable compromises would be such that the revolution would ultimately prove worthwhile, not to the masses but only to the brains of the revolutionaries: to their fantasy of having made a revolution.

What can we do? The question remains. Protest. Certainly. Against Vietnam, against the atom bomb, against the dictatorship in Greece, against writers' being put on trial, against . . . the possibilities are limitless. But is our protest meaningful? Do we accomplish anything by it, or are we easing our conscience with the illusion that something has been accomplished?

Whoever tries to act politically, acts in large measure emotionally. He acts in the belief that he is doing something meaningful, even useful. We jump into the water to save a drowning person (if we can swim) without first analyzing whether his rescue makes sense. If the drowning person is a determined suicide, then as soon as we have saved him he will throw himself under the next train. Our act of rescue proves to have been meaningless, and yet we could not have acted differently. We have to believe that rescuing is meaningful if we are to do any rescuing at all. An investigation as to whether a drowning person is worth saving leads to his death, because our attempt at rescue, if indeed it is made on the basis of the established worthwhileness of rescue, will come too late. Our political actions often fare similarly. In our world, causes and effects are so intertwined that we are unable to determine precisely what it is we are accomplishing. Even exact calculations yield uncertain results. It is not the individual who changes reality, reality is changed by everyone. Reality is all of us, and we are always only individuals. One of the difficulties of politics is expressed in this dramaturgical axiom.

Even though my comedic meditations represent no more than a rough sketch of political reality, the sketch does allow us to draw certain conclusions about political reality. Of course, in arriving at these conclusions, we must take account of the extent to which political reality is constantly changing.

If we compare the planet we live on—and despite space travel it is still the only planet we have at our disposal—if we compare the earth with a ship, I am perfectly able to give a description of the conditions that prevail in its first, second, and third class quarters and to indicate the various rules that govern the mutual relations of passengers; for example, the social necessity of wearing black tie for dinner in first class.

This description, however, is put into question when the number of passengers changes. The class distinctions and hence their description are definite only if the number of passengers remains essentially the same; if the number of passengers diminishes or increases, the regulations prevailing in the various classes and the description of those regulations become questionable. If the first class consists of single cabins, the second of doubles, and the third of ten-man cabins, this arrangement becomes meaningless when there are only two passengers occupying each class. Each passenger then has a cabin, with the largest reserved for third class; also, sheer boredom will forge a bond among the six passengers, and the wearing of formal attire will become a nuisance in the absence of formal occasions: why should two people squeeze themselves into tuxedos when the other four run around with their collars unbuttoned? If the ship is overcrowded, the class system breaks down as well.

On a normally booked ship, the governing principle for first-class passengers is freedom. Each passenger has a cabin to himself and is to be left as free and undisturbed as possible. Second- and especially third-class passengers are more largely governed by the principle of justice. But if the number of passengers increases, single cabins can eventually no longer be granted, and from sheer necessity, stricter regulations concerning the social life of passengers have to be introduced. Both the single cabin and the tuxedo become a privilege that grows increasingly offensive as the number of passengers swells. The imperative of justice, therefore, depends on the number of passengers; the larger that number, the less freedom there is for the individual, until finally, with everyone penned into their respective classes, the only freedom left him is that of the mind.

Applied to our planet: the larger its population, the more crucial justice becomes, the more inescapable is its primacy. The population explosion leads to the Good Shepherd Game, to socialism; man can no longer afford the Wolf Game. The problems posed by the Good Shepherd Game become the important ones, humanity slides off to the left.

But an increase in population entails several other aspects. Whereas until now, human beings were divided into rich and poor, powerful and weak, and politics received its impulse from these polarities, another polarity becomes noticeable as the population increases.

The economic, political, and social systems that make up a nation can be regarded as an organization. If the population grows, the organization grows as well. The result is the formation of ever more powerful organizations. But the more powerful, complex, and labyrinthine an organization becomes, the more it expends its powers in preserving its balance, the more inflexible it becomes, the more its purpose is exclusively in itself, and the more difficult it becomes for the organized to examine the usefulness of the organization and to change it if it proves to be irrational. The organization becomes a given, an established order, and develops for its members some very unpleasant traits. But no human organization can live on its own substance; it is bound up with man, with his mortality, it needs fresh talent, a new generation that can be educated in the ways of the organization. But this very education forces the successors to think about the organization they will be taking over. And to think about something is to examine it.

Students, who must learn to think because today's world can only be mastered by thinking, and who, because they must learn to think, cannot be prevented from thinking about politics, are the weak spot in our current established orders. They are in the privileged position of being able to think about the organization with which they are confronted, because they have not yet been fully incorporated into it. Their demands, however, come not only from the intellect, but also from the emotions. As young people, they instinctively resist the established order, and as thinking people, they consciously oppose that order when it is false. That is why, when the established order is a false order, the student movement is so potent—and where do we have a genuine order nowadays!

But this privileged position isolates the students. They are not a social class like workers, or not yet: they are being trained to be a class, their freedom consists in their not yet being what they are supposed to be. Workers, as a class, are fitted into the existing order, they are accustomed to being organized, so they know how to organize themselves. Their rights derive from their function as a class. Students do not yet have a real function, they are merely expected to become functionaries. Their right resides only in the rightness of their thinking. Either they are intellectuals or they not, either they are scientists or they are not; they can legitimize themselves only by being intellectuals and scientists, only then can they take on a function, only then are they more than an expression of the generation gap. Their right, then, is founded on the absurd fact that our society uses knowledge like a whore instead of being guided by it. But if the students slip off into romantic, utopian byways, if they lose themselves in ideological hair-splitting, which only serves to invent new adversaries, new windmills to joust against, if finally they mistake the necessary transformation of reality for a gigantic hoopla, they will miss their political chance as well.

Tactics are important, and so is an analysis of the situation in which we find ourselves. We are not only prisoners and beneficiaries of a civilization that deforms us all, because it digests even the revolutionaries and anarchists; we are at the same time members of a human race, two thirds of which vegetate in such lamentable conditions that my talk would be incomprehensible to them. The paths we must pursue, and therefore the methods we must employ, are various. We cannot exchange one field of battle for another; each one of us must take up his position where he stands. But we are all called upon to take the political reality with which we are confronted at its word, to judge it by what it claims to be, to demand democracy from democracy, socialism from socialism, and yes, Christianity from the Christians, because the way some people run around posing as Christians is beginning to border on the obscene.

We find, then, that the world, whether we like it or not, is irrevocably sliding to the left; that is its trend. Fine, there is a kind of duty to be a Marxist—not by reciting a Marxist catechism, but by reexamining the legacy of Marx. It is to Marxism, above all, that we must address our demand for intellectual freedom. This demand is anything but harmless. Freedom of the mind is the only freedom that is still possible for mankind. It entails risks, like every freedom. By its exercise, political praxis is tested again and again by the individual. It draws political freedom in its wake and ultimately raises the question of who is at the controls of power. The chess game does not change its rules when better players sit down at the board. A political system without an opposition is inhuman, it calcifies in its own institutions. Only by means of an opposition can politics retain the character of a game, without which it ceases to be politics. Marxism becomes a farce when it does not allow new political freedoms to be based upon it, or when it stifles all free discussion of what is to be done. That is why the Russians intervened in Czechoslovakia: so that Marxism could remain a farce.

Konrad Farner is certainly right, the issue is not how to live better but how to be better.* But in a social order that degrades human dignity, most people are already better than the lives they live, because they live miserably. Therefore Konrad Farner's demand is valid only for a social order that dignifies human existence. Only there does the commandment to be better rather than live better become meaningful.

Returning to the fable from *A Thousand and One Nights,* there is only one more thing I can say, politically and as a man: I take off my hat to our prophet. He is right. He has convinced us, like all great men. The world is unjust, and we have tried to draw our conclusions from that. Nevertheless, I would have called out to the first rider: "Hey, you dropped your money pouch." Without a doubt, justice is something grand and unattainable, and yet, on the other hand, just a simple, self-evident action. Which is, of course, no consolation. But the hope remains that the development of the human race and its increasingly desperate predicament will force man to be rational. The confounded part of it, though, is that we may have damned little time left.

On this note, ladies and gentlemen, I would gladly close my lecture. However, I cannot permit myself to do so, and this not in order to emulate Goethe's "That you cannot end is what makes you great," but because I am speaking not only before students, but before jurists. My topic is not only justice, but also law, and therefore, strictly speaking, I'm only done with the first half of my lecture. Now, I could, like the homicidal rapist Moosbrugger in Musil's *Man Without Qualities,* cry out: "My right is my law" and with that definition, which does bespeak a certain genius, forgo any further discussion, but that would not be right either, because even jurists have a right to come into their own. Besides, I am somewhat embarrassed in their

*Konrad Farner (1903–1974), Swiss Marxist art historian.

presence. I feel like a physicist who is always telling electricians about electricity instead of making occasional mention of the lovely uses electricians make of electricity, of excellent street lighting and superb electric motors, of electric stoves and irons, or, to use a more negative example, I feel like a chemist who expatiates before a group of distillers, at length and in detail, about the chemical composition of alcohol, instead of saying a word or two about the harmful effects whiskey has on human society.

I will therefore in all haste take refuge in a second story, which, due to the advanced hour, takes place at night and is moreover so easily interpreted by jurists and nonjurists that it requires no further commentary. My story deals with the usefulness of law, especially when it is administered by an elevated social class, but it is also instructive for the lower classes, an urgent warning not to give free rein to their carnal instincts. You may think it strange that I thus conclude with a story instead of with a moral, but first of all, my story does have a moral, and secondly, I can appeal to no less an authority than Aristotle, who is said to have illustrated his principal and unfortunately lost works with odd and unusual stories, making it all the more fitting for me, who am not a philosopher, to emulate that great thinker at least in this respect.

The Second Story

The Caliph Harun al Rashid and his Grand Vizier were hard pressed by the Christians, whose consumption of alcoholic beverages before battle gave them a slight advantage in that it enabled them, during the battle, to rouse themselves into a frenzy. The Caliph and his Grand Vizier decided to get at the root of the matter scientifically, and they obtained permission from the holy Imam, a great scholar of the Koran, to drink several captured bottles of Châteauneuf du Pape for research purposes. After drinking three bottles of Châteauneuf du Pape and drilling themselves thoroughly in Christian war tactics, they began, without quite knowing why, to speak of women. The Grand Vizier owned a beautiful slave girl, whom the Caliph demanded he give him as a present. The Grand Vizier swore by the beard of the Prophet that he would not give the slave girl away. The Caliph offered to buy her. The Grand Vizier, strangely stubborn, which wasn't usually his way at all, swore by the beard of the Prophet that he would not sell the slave girl. After two more bottles of Châteauneuf du Pape the Caliph likewise swore by the beard of the Prophet that the Grand Vizier's slave girl would be his personal property that very night. No sooner had this oath been uttered than the two men stared at each other in alarm: each had sworn by the beard of the Prophet the opposite of what the other had sworn. They summoned the holy Imam, who came reeling and lurching and half asleep, for he had permitted himself, as well, to take home a bottle of Châteauneuf du Pape for research purposes. The Caliph and the Grand Vizier explained their dilemma to the holy man. The Imam yawned. "Great Caliph," he said, "the problem is easily solved. The Grand Vizier shall sell you half his slave and give you the other half as a present. That way he will not have broken his vow, for what he swore by the beard of the Prophet was neither to give away nor to sell the entire slave." The Imam was rewarded with a hundred pieces of gold and went back home, the Caliph and the Grand Vizier drank another bottle of Châteauneuf du Pape, and the slave girl was led in. She was so beautiful that the caliph swore, unfortunately once again by the beard of the Prophet, that he would sleep with her that very night. The Grand Vizier turned pale, uncorked another bottle of Châteauneuf du Pape for the sake of science, and mumbled thickly: "Mighty Caliph, you have sworn another impossibility by the beard of the Prophet, for this slave is still a virgin, and according to the law of the Koran you may sleep with her only after rites that last several days." Dismayed, the Caliph summoned the Imam. The holy lawyer, awakened for the second time, took in the unfortunate news. "Great Caliph," he said, "this is child's play. Have a male slave brought in." The slave was called and stood shivering at attention before the Caliph. "Give the girl to this slave for a wife," the Imam commanded. The Caliph obeyed. "Now let the slave express his desire," the holy man continued, "to be allowed to divorce the girl. You shall perform the divorce, and according to the law of the Koran you may sleep with a divorced woman at any time." But the girl was so beautiful that the slave refused to divorce her. The Caliph offered him a piece of gold, ten pieces of gold, in vain; the slave remained obstinate. The great Imam shook his head. "Great Caliph," he yawned sadly, "how meager is your knowledge; nothing can impede the law of the Koran. There are still two possibilities. Hang the slave, you can take his widow to bed any time you please, the widow of a hanged man is without honor." "And the second possibility?" the Caliph asked. "Make a free woman of the slave girl," the Imam calmly commanded. "She is a free woman," said the Caliph. "You see," the Imam observed, "now you can divorce her from the slave against his will, for she is a free woman and he is a slave, and the marriage between a free man and a slave woman or between a free woman and a slave can be dissolved at any time, thank heaven—I shudder to think what would become of our social order if it were not so. But now I must really get some sleep." The great lawyer was awarded ten thousand pieces of gold, took his leave and departed. By now the Grand Vizier had fallen asleep. He was carried to his palace, the slave was hanged anyway, and the Caliph Harun al Rashid was alone with the beautiful freed slave girl and the last bottle of Châteauneuf du Pape.

Ladies and gentlemen, I thank you for your attention.

Afterword

In this lecture, no attempt is made to delineate the entire political reality of this world, but only to indicate some of its laws. Just as in Kepler's laws only a limited aspect of the universe becomes visible,* a lecture can only illuminate a limited, one-sided aspect of politics, and even that aspect only in part. A dramaturgical characterization of what is happening in China today, for example, would probably demand a dramaturgy as different from ours as does Chinese theater itself.

---

*Johannes Kepler (1571–1630), German astronomer, chiefly famous for his discovery of the laws of planetary motion.

Sentences from America

1. When we flew to New York, a windstorm over the Atlantic forced the plane to veer so far to the right that Greenland suddenly lay beneath us, an immense country—a continent, really. Snow-covered mountains, one massif after another, wild jagged crags against the horizon, between them icy rivers, everything golden in the sunlight. On the coasts the glaciers dissolved into thousands of icebergs drifting south like sailboats, and among them, seemingly motionless, a single, black ship.

2. Switzerland is almost as small as one imagines it to be and considerably larger than one thinks. Arrived at JFK airport, we circumvented New York by way of a mile-long suspension bridge, the plans for which its creator, Ammann, had shown me when I met him for the last time in 1959.*

3. In Philadelphia, Temple University is considered progressive. I imagined I would have conversations with black students and professors, but I didn't meet any. The university is in the middle of the black part of town, and it is unpopular because it keeps getting bigger, displacing blacks from the area. But blacks are withdrawing from whites more and more altogether. Instead of moving closer to each other, the two races are polarizing. The whites do what whites do, the blacks do what blacks do. My presence at Temple University was of interest to whites, and the blacks took no notice of it.

4. A professor of Buddhism at the theological faculty reported that the American Indian has set himself completely apart in the United States and

*The Verrazano-Narrows Bridge.

is sending people to the universities only to have them trained as lawyers, but that these are so good at their job that Indians win every lawsuit against the United States. It seems, therefore, that we belong to a race with which Indians make contact only through lawyers.

5. The theater group of Temple University performed my *Meteor*.* In the theater group, there were two professional actors, the rest were students. I expected something amateurish and went there with not a little trepidation. I was wrong. After Zürich and Warsaw, this was the third performance I was happy with. The director—and this is a rare thing these days—didn't come up with any superfluous ideas.

6. Many people told us they had stopped going to the theater in New York, not because of the high price of admission but because of the impossibility of finding a taxi in New York. Traffic, they say, is choking the city, public transportation is insufficient, and the night hours are feared because of crime. Going to the theater is getting to be too much trouble.

7. The crucial question is not how and whether theater is still possible, but *where;* a no less difficult question, for nowadays theater is often possible only in places where it can serve as an excuse, and impossible where it hopes for new impulses: the idea of street theater is a beautiful thing, but where is the traffic that could still make it possible?

8. University theater: a symptom of the tendency of the theater to withdraw into the laboratories in order to become a science. From this hiding place, however, there is no way out; one can only go a step deeper: philological theater, theater as a doctoral dissertation: there are precedents for this already.

9. We went to Fort Lauderdale in Florida, and while we stayed in a houseboat there, two Americans visited the moon for the second time.† The event did not cause a great stir, the sensation of the century had already become a routine operation. Every once in a while, on TV, at intervals between old movies, among advertisements for soap, candy, tires, cheese, toys, credit cards, and cigarettes, a few blurred images could be seen; then came the landing on Earth. The reception was noticeably cooler than the first time,

---

*A tragicomedy (1965) about an immoral artist condemned to immortality.
†The Apollo 12 mission launched on November 12, 1969.

there was no singing president, indeed no president at all; it was purely ceremonial. The difference from earlier voyages of discovery became apparent. On the one hand, the two American lunar expeditions were subject to the same compulsion as any other expedition: once it was declared to be possible, it had to happen. But in the past, possibility was a vague and all but impossible thing, while today, degrees of possibility can be predicted and the possible is only attempted when it is very probably possible: adventures have become too possible to still be adventures. That is precisely the reason why a trip to the moon is not an adventure, neither the first nor the second one, nor a flight to Mars.

10. What we noticed in Philadelphia was also the case in Florida. This subtropical state is tempting more and more affluent or retired whites to live there, and the Cubans, too, are starting to displace the Negroes. The Negroes move north, where, multiplying faster than whites, they populate the large cities. Already the opinion is spreading that the south will solve the race problem before the north does. If there is a race war, it is difficult to say which of the two groups would be trapped. While the blacks could take over the northern cities, the whites control the suburbs.

11. The Black Panthers are making a mistake, in my view, by applying the tactics of the class struggle to the race struggle.* A people can be conditioned by constant terror to accept communism, but no amount of terror can turn a white into a black: the radicality of the Black Panthers is radicalizing the whites. The sense that no solution is possible is spreading on both sides, and both sides are armed.

12. On the last Thursday of November, "Thanksgiving Day" was celebrated. As with any historical event, there are various reports concerning its origin. In the Brockhaus Encyclopedia, Thanksgiving is described as a general celebration of peace and thanksgiving for the harvest, dating back to 1621, when the Pilgrim fathers brought in their first crop. We, however, were told that the feast commemorates the time when the Pilgrim fathers were saved from starvation because the Indians gave them turkeys. While Americans now slaughter millions of turkeys a year in retrospective celebration of this rescue, the Indians, who should properly be remembered as rescuers, were slaughtered long ago; indeed there was a time when a white

---

*The Black Panther Party, founded in October 1966 by Huey P. Newton and Bobby Seale, was a black nationalist political party.

man could get a very decent price for an Indian scalp. A hundred dollars for the scalp of a warrior and ten dollars for the scalp of a child under ten years of age.

13. Americans believe that anything can be learned. Consequently there are schools for everything in the United States. Even schools for orators. I visited one such school in Fort Lauderdale. Before the meeting, everyone prayed. People were always praying in the United States. Then the American flag was saluted. People were always saluting the American flag in the United States. The ideal of an American orator is to appear as confident as possible, to speak without halting or stumbling, and to express so many positive thoughts that no one has to implement them. A master orator is called a toastmaster. The greatest toastmaster I saw was Billy Graham.* He is God's toastmaster. On three evenings, his "Crusade" to southern California was televised in color from the football stadium in Anaheim, near Los Angeles. It was the only television show that was not interrupted by commercials. Consequently this TV show cost God's toastmaster a million dollars. First the white-clad Crusade Choir sang, then a converted opera singer sang with a bass voice, then Billy Graham preached. Each time in sporty attire, each time in a different suit, modest red checks, modest green checks, modest blue checks, each time with a different tie, a top sales manager disposing of his goods. And sure enough, mass conversions took place on each occasion. Instantaneous conversions. God's hand seemed to be reaching into people's hearts directly through Billy Graham. America became Christian on the television screen. Everyone was deeply moved. Only then did the ads for soap, deodorants, detergents, and cars reappear. Later we saw Bob Hope. Also in color. He wasn't talking to thousands of Christians but to thousands of soldiers in Vietnam. All of them young, with likable faces. Some of the GIs appeared to be drunk, many were exuberant, only a few looked thoughtful. After every joke, whistles, laughter, shouts. Bob Hope, not as modestly dressed as Billy Graham, showed up at every performance wearing the uniform of the military branch whose soldiers he was addressing, and holding a golf club. Instead of the Crusade Choir, Miss World 1969 made an appearance, a black girl danced, Bob Hope told old jokes with a stony poker face, a white girl sang "Silent Night, Holy Night," the soldiers sang along, some of them wept, there were tanks standing all around, helicopters, bare hills. Again everyone was deeply

*Popular American evangelist (b. 1918).

moved. Then came a Japanese horror film in which people turned into mushrooms.

14. In a falsely structured society, piety remains ineffectual.

15. A sin of omission: Arthur Miller sent me a telegram urging me to protest against the Russian Writers' Union's treatment of Solzhenitzyn.* I protested. In Russia the people are made stupid by the Party, in the United States they are stupefied by television. That is something neither Arthur Miller nor I protest against.

16. Since the brain structure of dolphins, according to Professor G. Pilleri, is supposed to have reached a degree of centralization that far exceeds that of human brains, I can say that the dolphins I saw in Miami are the most carefree Americans; they perform the most unbelievable stunts, and we never had the impression that they had been trained. It all seemed to be pure playfulness. I was especially impressed by a dolphin who would snap fish from the hand of a man who called the dolphin's name while holding the fish high above the water. The man was standing on a stepladder on top of a springboard that was six feet high. Thus the dolphin had to leap at least twelve feet high in order to get the fish. The impressive part of it was that the other dolphins would crowd together in the middle of the pool to allow the dolphin whose name had been called to swim around the pool in faster and faster circles, until he reached the speed he needed for his giant leap.

17. We saw a second, considerably more negative creation by an emigrant Swiss: the ruins of the Mayan cities of Uxmal, Kabah, and Chichen-Itza in Yucatan. The Hasburg Emperor Carl V. had arranged to have the peninsula conquered, destroyed, and converted.

18. Mayans still exist; they are quiet, friendly, extremely small people. Two-year-old children look as if they are eight months old, exceptionally beautiful babies romping about. The beggars know how to fold up their bodies in such a way that a tiny heap of body holds up a large head, with a hollow hand jutting out beneath it. If you look closer, you notice that they are begging in

*Aleksandr Isayevich Solzhenitsyn (b. 1918), Russian novelist, winner of the Nobel Prize for Literature of 1970.

their sleep. The women wear skirts of a blinding whiteness, with colorful lacework sewn on. The men seem constantly to be slightly anesthetized. Knowledge of herbal poisons is widespread. The Mayans evince highly developed cheekbones and picture the rain god as a stylized elephant, which suggests that they might be of Asian ancestry. They were once great astronomers and mathematicians; their calendar was more accurate than the Gregorian calendar. The written form of their language, which covers their ancient palaces and temples, can no longer be read by anyone. Like in the old days, when they erected mighty buildings, ballparks, and observatories for their gods, kings, and priests, they still live in round, reed-thatched mud cottages. I do not believe that under the Spaniards—provided they weren't slaughtered or didn't die of the European diseases—their lives were any worse than under their own regents; life may even have been a little better, but due to their conquerors' senseless obsession with religious conversion, their poverty, their suffering, and their temples alike lost their meaning. Introverted and patient, they seem to be waiting for a new meaning.

19. Archeology reveals the absurdity of history. Archeology reconstructs what history has destroyed. While in Yucatan the Spanish colonial cathedrals stand around like rotted, ghostly ruins, scientists are excavating the old Mayan cities from jungles where the jaguar and the black panther are still being hunted; a colossal undertaking. But once the colossal deed has been done, once the cities have been excavated, the archeologists will set about reconstructing the Spanish cathedrals.

20. The absurdity of history is countered by the hope that history has a meaning: this brings me to the third Swiss whose work occupied my mind throughout our voyage: Konrad Farner and his new book *Theology of Communism?* published by the Protestant Stimme-Verlag. Konrad Farner is a non-Christian and a Marxist who wholeheartedly loves a type of man he cannot be because he regards him as his brother: the true Christian. Farner declares that there would be more true communists if there were more true Christians; he sees in communism the last chance for Christians and in Christian love the last chance for communists to change the world, and he clings with unshakeable faith to the great hope that man will someday through insight become what he should be, while my incorrigible pessimism fears that man, if he does not want to perish, will only through dire necessity become what he should be.

21. Two old Americans lived in our hotel. In the afternoon they sat by the swimming pool reading the newspaper, in the evening they sat in mutual and friendly silence in the lobby. Sometimes I joined them, and we talked. One of them told me that Hemingway, O'Neill, and Traven had frequently stayed in this hotel.* The last always under a different pseudonym. The second American was a more than eighty-year-old Jew who for years had been coming to this hotel in December to spend the winter. He came from Riga, the old Capital of Latvia. His life had been adventurous. He had made his way to America via Berlin and had become rich. He spoke English with us but reverted more and more to Yiddish, the language of his childhood. He told me that if I spent just a week speaking only English with him, I would be speaking better English than an American, because he still spoke real English. I tried it. I spoke to him only in English, but he answered me only in Yiddish. When I pointed this out to him, he was surprised. He had been speaking Yiddish unconsciously. He was as concerned about us as a father. When we left the hotel in Merida on a Sunday at seven a.m. to fly from Jamaica to Yucatan, the old man was standing in the lobby and warned us not to stop off in Puerto Rico.

22. In Jamaica we took a three-hour taxi ride from Kingston to a hotel that an American woman in Fort Lauderdale had recommended to us. The hotel was in the middle of the jungle, and by the open verandah outside the open dining hall hung mighty bundles of bananas. Unfortunately the entire hotel was wide open. Even in the lobby some of the outer walls were missing, and it was raining and storming. For three days. Plus the palms were rustling. The rustling of palms is not pleasant. From the open bar we had a view to the Caribbean Sea, which, nastily enough, was always sunlit. The manager said this was the first time it had rained in November. It was the middle of December. The manager's wife predicted beautiful weather in January. One guest praised the month of March, and when, soaked to the bone, we asked the black gardener his opinion, he replied with a sepulchral voice that it was always raining there, that we were in a rain forest, since the hotel had been built by the side of a mountain that blocked the clouds. There must have been something true in what he said, for every morning, from our room, we could hear the voices of guests arriving in the rain and remarking how "beautiful," "marvelous," and "lovely" the hotel

---

*"B. Traven" was the pseudonym under which the enigmatic author of *The Treasure of the Sierra Madre*, among other works, published his novels; his identity is still the subject of speculation.

was, but driving on immediately, leaving behind an increasingly depressed manager who seemed to have no recourse except to sigh "Oh, my God."

23. In Jamaica people pray: "Give us this day our daily bananas."

24. In Jamaica, by the side of the rain-swept swimming pool, I got into a conversation with a black man. He told me in his English that he had visited his aged grandmother. Since my English was far poorer than his, I mistook "meet" for "eat" and thought he was telling me he had eaten his aged grandmother, whereupon I was overjoyed at having met my first cannibal. When the misunderstanding was cleared up, my sympathy for the man was undiminished, but he had sunk a bit in my estimation: I felt equal to him.

25. Rain anywhere, and especially in the tropics, makes people in hotels move closer together. I often talked with an old man who looked like Socrates and was a painter or a writer and was apparently influenced by the far East, for occasionally he danced alone in the rain beneath the palms in front of the swimming pool. He spoke a very rapid English and talked about art. I also talked about art. He didn't understand me and I didn't understand him. Deeper conversations about art have probably rarely been conducted.

26. Since it was still raining on the fourth day, we took our leave under the pretext of coming back in January. The manager looked at us mildly, visibly disbelieving our words, murmured "Oh, my God" and for thirty dollars drove us back to Kingston, where the weather was splendid.

27. In Kingston we moved into a large hotel recommended by a Swiss who runs a clock store in the city. The hotel consisted of interconnected two-story buildings that formed a mighty rectangle enclosing a large swimming pool. Unfortunately this large hotel was expanding, like every other large hotel on the Caribbean islands: since large hotels are less profitable than small ones, they are constantly expanding, which makes them even less profitable. Thus everything was already being dwarfed by a huge, already half-completed skyscraper on whose scaffoldings black men with colorful hats were climbing about, gazing down at the swimming, sunbathing, and lounging whites, so that I constantly felt watched.

28. During the day, my wife went swimming while I sat under a coconut palm and wrote, after first making sure that the coconuts had already been cut. Coconuts can weigh five kilos, and the palm was a good fifteen feet

high. After dinner we went to the bar. Alleged natives played allegedly native music. Well-built Negroes with golden watches stood leaning casually against the bar, for hours, motionless, with the patience of lambs, before them a glass of Coca-Cola with whiskey, which they never touched, waiting to be coupled with older American women. Most of the American women were on drugs. The pimp in charge of this business was an extremely dignified, tall, slender, white-haired gentleman with a deeply intellectual face, who, when you saw him wearing a bathing suit during the day, was carrying a belly in front of him like that of a pregnant woman. Since our criminological curiosity had, unfortunately, been aroused, we selected the Sheraton Hotel in San Juan, Puerto Rico, on the recommendation of our hotel in Kingston, and thus found ourselves flying after all to the island that the old Jew in Merida had warned us against.

29. Since the writer's profession consists of inventing stories, Brecht's "five difficulties in writing the truth" are annulled by the difficulty of getting people to believe you. Even if the writer writes the truth, it will be considered a fiction. This circumstance will make many of my experiences in America unbelievable as well.

30. The day after arriving in San Juan, I sat in the garden of the Sheraton Hotel (also under a coconut palm) writing a new novel, *The Pensioner*. The novel is about a police commissioner of the city of Bern who, immediately after retiring, visits all the criminals he has allowed to escape out of kindness and knowledge of the inadequacy of human justice. Just when, in my manuscript, I was having the commissioner tell an occasional thief that what separates a true professional from an amateur is simplicity and speed of action as well as his well-planned collaboration with accomplices, someone removed from my wife's beach bag her watch, her money, and a key to the safe of the Sheraton Hotel. As a seasoned writer of crime novels I naturally discovered the theft within twenty minutes and immediately had the locked safe opened, but the money deposited there was already gone. There we stood, penniless. The German-speaking executive assistant manager of the Sheraton, whom we were finally able to reach, solved the case with aplomb: he declared it to be impossible.

31. When I told the assistant manager that he apparently considered us swindlers, adding that we, therefore, considered him a crook, he laughed. When the police finally arrived, they, too, laughed.

32. There was another fellow who used an even simpler device. He put on a white smock, planted himself in front of the Suisse Chalet restaurant where we were spending New Year's Eve, gratefully accepted a tip and the car keys of a freshly arrived American who took him for a valet of the Suisse Chalet, thanked the man as he entered the Suisse Chalet with his family, wishing him a happy new year, got into the Cadillac, and drove away, never to be seen again.

33. The Swiss honorary consul in Puerto Rico took up our cause with great energy. He put us up in another hotel in San Juan. I began to continue my novel, even though it was going to include a murder and a suicide. But when several days later the owner of the Sheraton took his life and when it turned out that the personnel of our present hotel, who were demanding higher and higher salaries and sabotaging the business more and more, were organized by the union of the notorious Hoffa, against which the hotel management was waging a life-and-death struggle, I stopped writing:* less out of fear than out of the gloomy feeling that it's actually difficult *not* to tell the truth.

34. Since the money that had been stolen from us included the sum given us by Temple University to cover our round trip to Philadelphia, I can say with a good conscience that I not only earned my honorary doctorate, but that I also paid for it.

35. In several long rides in his car, the Swiss honorary consul took us on a crisscross tour of Puerto Rico. The island is hilly. Since the honorary consul and I both come from the Emmental, the landscape looked to us like a somewhat tropically altered Emmental. We were both proud. Not of Puerto Rico, but of the Emmental.

36. Together with the Swiss general consul we visited the biggest hotel in Puerto Rico, El Conquistador. It stands on a cliff by the sea. It consists of many white, interconnected buildings, and the immense ballroom is crowned with a mighty flat dome, which gives the whole thing a volcano-like appearance. The huge swimming pool lies three hundred feet deeper, but still above the beach. You descend to the beach by aerial trams built by a Swiss company; one of them was still under construction. A stream of curious visitors slowly flowed through the endless corridors of the hotel; only a

*James R. "Jimmy" Hoffa (1913–1975), U.S. labor leader.

few guests were to be seen. On the side facing the land lies the landing site for helicopters bringing guests from San Juan, and an immense golf course with a few golfers rolling about in its vastness in golf carts, stopping, getting out, whacking their golf balls, and driving on. That this mammoth hotel, new parts of which are constantly being added, doesn't bring in any profit because it needs more employees than it can control, which more or less paralyzes the whole establishment, is a well-known fact; what remains obscure is where all the millions come from that keep this absurdity going. Consequently this enterprise is generally referred to as the Mafia Hotel.

37. Nowadays the difference between Russia and the United States consists mainly in the fact that in Russia everyone considers everyone else an informant and in the United States everyone considers everyone else a crook.

38. The particular bad luck of the United States consists in the fact that the capitalists have led capitalism and the unions have led socialism *ad absurdum.*

39. Shortly before my departure, when I called the assistant manager of the Sheraton once again, in the vague hope of still recovering my money, the voice of the assistant manager sounded depressed. He had been robbed by burglars.

40. In front of the hotel there was a round wall enclosing a heap of dirt on which a palm tree had been planted. There were always hippies under the palm tree and on the wall, new ones every day. One night, when we returned to the hotel at around four, the hippies were sitting and lying in the soft easy chairs and couches in the hotel lobby.

41. In Puerto Rico I saw on television a new, indescribably crude sport. On an oval track, two teams on roller skates tried to prevent each other from breaking away and thereby gaining points. The teams were mixed. They consisted of men and women, and any method was allowed. Especially one fat, blond Texan woman stood out for her brutality. During time-outs, there were interviews with the players, who shouted each other down and beat each other up. But this was already sport as a spectacle, a phenomenon we are acquainted with in Europe as well. The Americans, however, turn other kinds of sport into a cult, which is most evident in the great golf tournaments one sees on TV: the golf players resemble our great violinists or

pianists. Accompanied by a devout throng of acolytes, they execute their strokes like sacred acts.

42. Cuba will soon lose its reputation as the best tobacco island: the cigars rolled by exiled Cubans in Puerto Rico with locally grown tobacco are comparable in quality to the kind Fidel Castro smokes.

43. Americans have their own Potemkin villages.* The road from the airport to San Juan passes a slum. Before Kennedy visited Puerto Rico, the facades facing the street were newly painted so as not to shock the president.

44. From Puerto Rico we flew to Santa Cruz. The island lies southeast of Puerto Rico and used to be Danish, which is why the two little towns on it are called Christiansted and Frederichsted. No doubt the many windmills that stand around the island as much admired ruins also date back to the Danish period. The island is part of the Virgin Islands and is now called St. Croix.

45. While in the interior of Puerto Rico people still grow sugar cane, the ears of which, from a distance, create the impression that between the tropical hills there is frost, the sugarcane fields on St. Croix are devastated. The United States used to import sugar from Cuba; now they produce too much sugar themselves. The former sugarcane island of Santa Cruz is now dependent on tourism. The foreigners are white, and those who serve the whites and build the hotels are black.

46. The hotel where we stayed on St. Croix consisted of bungalows, which gave it the character of a village. Every morning we were awakened at nine thirty by a black man from Martinique. He spoke French and brought us our breakfast, which we consumed on the terrace of our bungalow, right in the middle of a noisy building site: an eighty-four-bedroom hotel was being constructed next door. We were surrounded by various machines, trucks, cranes, and by Negroes who were covering vast walls with white paint, using rollers. Once a large Buick came along, stopped, and an old American stepped out and watched the men at work. Then he came to us. He said that for seven years he had spent his vacations in our bungalow. He called it his

---

*Defined by the *American Heritage Dictionary* as "something that appears elaborate and impressive but in actual fact lacks substance," Potemkin villages take their name from Grigori Aleksandrovich Potemkin, who had elaborate fake villages constructed for Catherine the Great's tours of the Ukraine and Crimea.

bungalow. From here he had seen the sea and now—"horrible," he exclaimed, with a deprecating gesture in the direction of the new building. When he heard that we were Swiss, he shook his head: "Swiss? You're Swiss and capitalists just like us? I have two sons in Vietnam. Crazy."

47. The personnel manager in the hotel, a young Swiss, told us about a Negro who had dropped a large stack of porcelain tableware and just laughed, saying it was nothing to get upset about, it was just the hotel owner's china, whereupon he deliberately dropped a second stack of china. The logic of the have-nots stands opposed to the logic of the haves.

48. In the United States, the whites speak well but think ill of the blacks, while the blacks speak and think ill of the whites! The whites are afraid of Negroes because they have a bad conscience, and the Negroes hate the whites because they don't need to have a bad conscience.

49. It gave me great pleasure to observe the Southern Cross, which thousands of years ago must have been visible in our part of the world as well. I discovered it only once: at three a.m., deep down in the south. But since there were clouds of mist over the Caribbean Sea, it was nowhere near as impressive as I had expected. Sometimes even the heavens disappoint.

50. On January 19, we flew back to New York from St. Croix. It was evening when we landed at Kennedy airport, and night by the time we got to the city. From the hotel, we walked to the apartment of a friend who was giving a party. Bitter cold, the streets almost empty. For the first time, we experienced this winter as winter. At the party, a doctor from Boston complained that he had owned a breed of twelve hundred hamsters and had carefully marked each animal, sorting the families by generation, an incalculably valuable resource for science; but some teenagers had eliminated six hundred of these hamsters by killing some and releasing others, whereupon he had been forced to destroy the remaining six hundred hamsters, because as soon as Nixon had come to power, the government, to cut costs, had refused him a research grant. The police arrested the teenagers. They were punished, the government wasn't.

51. The next morning we looked out on the frozen Central Park through our hotel windows. Bare trees. In the distance, ice skaters, then the front of a row of skyscrapers made of metal and glass. When we stepped outside, the streets between the skyscrapers lay before us like canyons. People came along in fur

coats that reached almost down to the ground, and wearing fur hats. We did-n't feel like exploring the depths of New York once again, so we withdrew back into our hotel. We had only a few hours left. New York looked like Moscow.

52. The United States is a giant with which I have only a superficial ac-quaintance. I could compare it with Switzerland, which I know better. But such a comparison would be unsound—comparing something well known with something less well known. It is better, therefore, to compare the giant United States with the giant Soviet Union, since I know both of them only from visits. This comparison would result in a more superficial but just for that reason more accurate picture.

53. I visited the two empires in different ways. In the empire of the red Czars, I was only permitted to move along the main traffic arteries and to look at the official holy sites: the Hermitage in Leningrad, a few renowned and renovated churches, Lenin's dead body, and, from a distance of approx-imately thirty feet, the still living politburo. In the United States I moved freely, but only in the parks and outlying districts, under certain weather conditions. In each empire, I got to know a specialty: in Russia, it was Ar-menia, and in the United States, Puerto Rico.

54. My main sources of information in both empires were not observations so much as personal conversations. About the ones I had in Russia I cannot say anything, for fear of getting my interlocutors into trouble, indeed I fear that even this hint will get them into trouble. In the United States, my in-terlocutors are not in any danger. Also, in America one is far better in-formed of events by television and by the newspapers.

55. The United States is an incomparably more complex system than the Soviet Union, but paradoxically, this makes the two empires comparable. The factor of insecurity produced by lack of information about a relatively simple system is counterbalanced by the factor of insecurity produced by the greater possibilities inherent in a more complex system.

56. In St. Croix, during a conversation with a banker about the structure of the great economic empires, one of which is the Mafia, I noticed the simi-larity between the Soviet Union and these giant firms. They are all hierar-chies and hence subject to the laws of hierarchy.

57. A hierarchy can be compared to a pyramid. The taller a pyramid, the broader its base. The top of the pyramid consists either of an individual, or, in the case of a blunted pyramid, several individuals.

58. The laws of hierarchy are simple. An office worker doesn't become an office supervisor until the office supervisor has become department manager, the department manager a director, and so on. But this struggle takes place not only on the vertical but also on the horizontal levels of the pyramid. A person who gets pushed to the top of a vertical level or to the edge of a horizontal level is out in the open. His possibilities are exhausted. Eventually he either gets put on ice or he falls down the pyramid.

59. Within a hierarchy, groups struggle against groups. Individuals look around for help. Also, those closer to the top of the pyramid find it easier to rise, since there are few above them, while those closer to the base of the pyramid have a harder time. Most of the pyramid's weight rests upon them. Therefore changes at the base are difficult to recognize; it's the changes at the top that meet the eye.

60. Compared with the prototype of a hierarchy, the Soviet Union does not represent a uniformly pyramidal structure. In a way it resembles the blunted Mayan pyramids I saw. The Mayans would eventually build a new pyramid around an old one, and so on all the way to the outermost pyramid, which encloses the others like a coat. The Soviet Union's outermost pyramid is the Party; the blunt top of the pyramid is the politburo; the inner pyramids, successively from the outside in, are the bureaucracy, the army, the scientists, the intellectuals, and finally the people. In sheer volume, the people make up by far the greatest part of the pyramid, but encased by all those coats, they have no say at all.

61. The struggles within the pyramid are fought with dogged persistence, the changes are gradual; thus, the Soviet Union represents a relatively stable hierarchy. Sometimes a boss is replaced by another; sometimes, from the inside of the pyramid, one hears some muted thuds of protest, and that is all.

62. In St. Croix a floodlight was placed on the ground in front of each bungalow. At night large toads, often entire families, would sit in front of the floodlights, obstinately, motionless, as if mesmerized. This wasn't a cult, though, they weren't worshiping floodlights; their interest was in the insects that were attracted by the light. Thus, the animals were able to gobble

up their food, which happened so quickly that the movement was almost imperceptible.

63. The Soviet empire is more powerful than its citizens. It instills in them a feeling of being confronted with something immutable, an incomprehensible presence. The citizens content themselves with whatever prey the system dishes out to them. Usually these are rather modest helpings; bigger ones are rare. They take advantage of the situation as it presents itself, and they consider it pointless to attack the status quo. They have capitulated. Not all of them, but most of them. But the few who have not capitulated are perhaps not few.

64. The United States is an unstable formation. It can't be compared with a pyramid. It is like a landscape convulsed by eruptions and covered by streams of lava. Next to the main crater, volcanic cones shoot forth and secondary craters open up. Everything is sliding over and into everything else.

65. The similarity between the Soviet Union and the United States seems to consist in the fact that both empires present themselves as a union of different states. The Soviet Union is a union of different peoples and races; the various American states differ as to their laws, and so forth. But here we can already perceive differences. In the Soviet Union, with the exception of the Jews, who are denied, each people has, as a rule, a state of its own—which has an advantageous effect on the race problem. Except for its obnoxious anti-Semitism, the Soviet Union does not seem to have any racial problems. In the United States, people of different races and nationalities are scattered together. This leads to tensions. Also, the Soviet Union, with the help of its Communist Party, imposes a hierarchy that allows its various states to exist more in theory than in fact; their existence is mainly folkloric. The United States, on the other hand, establishes its unity by taxation. The lion's share of the taxes goes to the federal government, a smaller part goes to the various states, and a very small part goes to the local governments. Thus, the counties and municipalities are poor. The mayor of a city has to ask the governor of his state for money, and the governor must turn to the federal government for financial aid.

66. Since the United States is a commercial empire, it finds itself facing other commercial empires on its own territory: the economic empires, the financial empires, the unions, the Mafia. In the Soviet Union, society exists for the state; in the United States, the state exists for society. But if a state for

which a society exists is amoral, then the state that exists for society is as moral as its citizens are: the United States, therefore, reflects the moral condition of its citizens. If in the Soviet Union the head rules the body, in the United States the body rules the head, which is confused and paralyzed by the often mutually exclusive special interests of private enterprise.

67. The banker on St. Croix with whom I discussed these matters told me he had such a large income that he hadn't had to pay any taxes for years. As a financial layman I didn't quite understand this; even he thought it was unfair.

68. Because of its structure, the United States gets embroiled in contradictions. Thus, the government will attack drugs while at the same time enabling their distribution by pretending to be powerless against the Mafia and, to cover up this feigned helplessness, accusing the Swiss banks (which is not to say that Swiss banks are paragons of virtue). A person who voluntarily enlists for active duty in Vietnam only has to serve in the army for a year; after a brief period of training, he is sent straight off to the war, while a man who does not enlist has to serve for several years (depending on which branch of the army he is drafted into, and presuming he is not sent to Vietnam anyway). The effect: intelligent fellows who don't want to waste time with their studies are seduced into going to Vietnam, despite the chance that they may die there. However, a man who takes drugs won't be accepted in the army, which in turn inspires young people to take the drugs offered them by the Mafia, against which the state must pretend to be powerless because it is permeated by the Mafia, and so on. But a man who goes to Vietnam, that is, who neither takes drugs nor refuses to go to war, has much easier access to drugs in Vietnam than in the United States, and succumbs to them all the more readily, as he is exposed to fear of the enemy.

69. In the area of social welfare, there are often grotesque developments: for example, a mother who is unable to identify the father of her child receives fifty dollars a month, a sum that is tax free. Therefore, black women often join together to raise an enormous swarm of children whose fathers are allegedly unknown to them. The funds they receive for the support of their brood often enable them to live better than many married women whose husbands have to pay taxes. This law is expected to be repealed. Not because it is felt to be immoral, which it isn't, but in order to slow down the growth of the black population.

70. President Johnson tried to swim against the stream and was swept away by the stream. President Nixon swims with the stream from the start.

71. The United States thinks economically. That is why it has difficulty thinking in terms of power politics; the Soviet Union thinks in terms of power politics. That is why it thinks uneconomically.

72. The two empires have different political dramaturgies. In the Soviet Union, everything happens against an oppressed society; in the United States, everything happens for a chaotic society. Take the example of military defense: for the Russian people it is obviously very costly; it renders all luxuries unaffordable and produces a lack of consumer goods, while in the United States, defense is an economic regulator. Private enterprise is so powerful and satisfies the desires of consumers so completely, but has moved so close to the limit of the market's capacity, that the state, in order to make better use of private industry and to prevent unemployment, must give the private sector contracts for the production of wares that do not compete with the consumer market: weapons. After all, who is going to drive around in a private tank! Thus, paradoxically, the defense industry in the United States represents a social service on the part of the state. It creates jobs that private enterprise can no longer supply without government subsidies.

73. Unfortunately it is a matter of indifference for the victims whether they are killed by weapons manufactured for reasons of private enterprise or by weapons that were produced for reasons of power politics.

74. What is true of armaments is also true of trips to the moon. What is shot out to the moon is a heap of scrap metal; the money it cost to build the rocket remains on the earth. Therefore, when the United States limits its space program, this does not necessarily mean that the government wants to organize its social services more sensibly in other areas or even to increase them. On the contrary, the government is starting to cut costs in the area of social services as well, which in the United States are always in a slightly bad odor of being only there for malingerers. The money saved by cutting back on space travel goes toward the defense industry: NASA has done its duty; it can do no more than be the first on the moon, and Mars is already less attractive, just as for Europe the discovery of America was more important than that of the more distant Australia. The true mission of space travel, which it shared with the armaments industry—to create work and,

with its adventurous goal, inspire men to make new inventions—now once again devolves upon the armaments industry.

75. Thanks to its mighty industrial capacity, easily able to foot the additional bills for an arms race, a Vietnam war, and a lunar expedition, the United States has become a world power and must practice a global politics, power politics. But its power politics, too, is conditioned by commercial thinking; the United States is convinced that the world can be bought. There is a widespread opinion that after the withdrawal of the United States, South Vietnam will not become communist, because the South Vietnamese will be economically better off than the North Vietnamese, and the question never arises: which South Vietnamese? Political thinking in the United States never reckons with those beneath the upper ten thousand. Hence the many miscalculations.

76. Commercial though the mentality of the United States is, nowhere else but in Russia have I encountered such jingoism and such a feeling of being ungratefully and unjustly treated by the outside world. The United States affords itself a patriotism and finds it comical when other nations presume to have one as well. Basically, the United States grants only the Russians the right to patriotism.

77. I am afraid that the Russians, too, grant only the Americans the right to be patriotic. It is rare to find Soviet citizens who have any objections to Russian foreign policy; if the occupation of Czechoslovakia produced some signs of discontent, there were no such signs with regard to Beijing. Absurd horror stories are told about experiences with black Africans. Someone in Moscow informed me that the Egyptians supposedly still had slaves, two for each foreman and one for each worker, and that in addition, Russian engineers were forbidden to drive these slaves to work in their cars; but when I asked why the Soviet Union supports Egypt, he said it was because the Jews were fascists.

78. In the United States, the state lured society into the Vietnam War and society lured the state into chaos.

79. A diagnosis for the Soviet Union is easy to make: arteriosclerosis. An arteriosclerotic is incapable of recognizing either an innovation or the need to introduce innovations. He lives in the past. Thus, the Russians consider themselves to be revolutionary for the sole reason that they once carried out a revolution, just as many Swiss still consider themselves heroes because

some of their ancestors won a battle at Morgarten in 1315. An arteriosclerotic considers everyone who is different from himself an enemy. Unfortunately he considers himself healthy and capable of thinking. He has fixed ideas and can become a menace to the rest of the world.

80. The United States is more difficult to diagnose. The symptoms are contradictory, and their vast number is confusing. The overall impression is that of a battle, organ against organ, cell against cell. There is evidence of tumors.

81. This could indicate cancer, but fear of this diagnosis leads the United States to take each symptom for a separate disease and combat it independently of the other symptoms.

82. A diagnosis is a conclusion I draw from reality. The validity of a diagnosis depends entirely on whether one's comprehension of reality has been accurate or not. I would not dare to answer this question in the affirmative, either with regard to the Soviet Union or to the United States. I was much too dependent on evidence that I evaluated purely on the basis of feeling and that I had neither the time nor the means to verify. My diagnoses, therefore, are impressions. This is even more true of my prognoses. A prognosis is a conclusion drawn from a diagnosis. A prognosis bets on a possible development of the reality one has comprehended. The more imprecisely a reality has been comprehended, the more arbitrary the prognosis will be. Most prognoses are shots we send off into the future, without any assurance of their hitting the mark, because we don't see the future until it has become the present.

83. Seen from a distance, the United States could be compared with imperial Rome when it had become a world power but found itself embroiled in increasingly difficult domestic problems, while the Soviet Union is looking more and more like the Eastern Roman Empire, which was a totalistic state and installed Christianity as an ideology. The Soviet Union is a Marxist Byzantium.

84. The United States seems to have entered a stage in its history when a nearly three-hundred-year evolution could be supplanted by a revolution. There is a general ferment, the disorder is growing. But it is unclear what the revolution would aim at if it took place. The call for a strong government cannot be overheard. But the country is running the danger of attacking

those minorities that it regards as the cause of its disease, like the hippies or the Negroes, for example. Also, the fires of nationalism are being fanned, since the country is heading for a defeat in Vietnam. The United States is therefore increasingly susceptible to every kind of fascism.

85. In today's world, the United States represents one of the most incalculable factors. When we called it an unstable formation, we were thinking of those unstable stars we know from astronomy. We still lack sufficient experience and knowledge to make exact predictions. A sun can grow, can contract, but it can also with unimaginable force turn into a supernova, hurling its matter into space and destroying everything.

86. These are, of course, gloomy prognoses. However, in both empires there are rays of light. In the Soviet Union, the people have been educated, and it could happen that some day they will break their dogmatic chains. The trend toward self-criticism in the United States is unmistakable. The intellectuals are alarmed, the young people are starting to think, the political murders have shaken up the nation. Unfortunately only on its surface.

87. In both empires, tradition is important. In Russia, it was the state that was held high and holy; in the United States, unrestrained freedom. This has not changed. Russia won its empire by a tenacious conquest of the Mongols and the Turkic peoples, until it eventually encircled China; the United States conquered a continent by the might-makes-right practices of its trappers and industrial pioneers. The ideals of a nation revenged themselves; models like Ivan the Terrible and Rockefeller cannot, any more than Bonnie and Clyde, be emulated with impunity. Thus, in Russia the government is humbly endured, and in the United States people still believe in the self-made man, without giving any thought to whether he earned his immense fortune legally or illegally. This question is only addressed by Hollywood movies, always with the assurance that the characters are freely invented. The only thing that counts is success. That is why the gangster, though feared, is basically a popular figure, because he embodies unrestrained freedom. One gives him credit for his struggle against the police, much as if he were engaged in an athletic contest. Thus, it is hard to say whether the structures of both empires are capable of change or whether the Soviet Union will settle into terminal paralysis and the United States will explode. It is a question of time and of our planet's political development, just as everything since the invention of the atomic and hydrogen bombs has

become a question of the time we still have left. Atlantis can sink again, this is probable, but it can also rise again, this is possible.

88. When we flew back from New York to Geneva it was night. The wind was in our back, so we didn't have to fly over Greenland. The airplane zoomed across the Atlantic at six hundred miles an hour, on the border between boundless cloudbanks and a deep black sky. Through the porthole, only two bright stars could be seen. They stood close to each other, apparently planets. Probably Saturn and Mars, the god who devoured his own children and the god of war.

89. Looking back, what were my strongest impressions? In Miami I saw the so-called killer whale. It was probably a sword whale, part of the dolphin family and considered to be the most dangerous predator in the sea. This powerful animal was about seven yards long. It was very beautiful, its dorsal area deep black with large white spots, its belly white. The pool in which it was lying diagonally seemed too small for its size. The animal eats enormous quantities of fish every day, and I was told that tranquilizers were constantly mixed into the water to keep the whale calm. If it became conscious of its strength, it would destroy its prison. But then the animal would be asphyxiated by its own weight.

90. In Kabah on the Yucatan peninsula I stared for a long time at a bizarre stone sculpture on the steps of a destroyed Mayan temple. The stone sculpture suddenly moved. It was an iguana.

91. Incidentally, I have just been told that for some time now an alligator has been swimming past the houseboat where we lived, in the middle of the teeming town of Fort Lauderdale.

Theater Problems [1954]

In the arts as they are practiced today, there is a conspicuous drive toward purity. The artist strives for the purely poetic, the purely lyrical, the purely epic, the purely dramatic. Purely painterly paintings, purely musical music are, for a painter or musician, a consummation devoutly to be wished, and I have already been told by a man of the radio that pure radio is a synthesis between Dionysus and Logos. But what is even more remarkable for our time, which is not otherwise distinguished by its purity, is that everyone imagines himself to have found his own and the only true purity; there appear to be as many varieties of chastity as there are vestals of the arts. That is why modern theories of the drama, of the purely theatrical, the purely tragic, the purely comic, are almost impossible to count; each playwright has three or four of them at hand, and for this reason, if for no other, I am a little embarrassed to come along with one of my own.

I want to ask you also not to regard me as a representative of any particular movement in the theater, or any particular dramatic technique, and I am certainly not knocking on your door as the traveling salesman of one of the philosophies that are in vogue in the theater these days—as an existentialist, a nihilist, an expressionist, or an ironist, or whatever labels get stuck on the jars in which literary critics keep their preserves. For me, the stage is not a field for theories, philosophies, and declarations, but an instrument, the possibilities of which I seek to know by playing with it. Naturally there are characters in my plays who have a belief or a *weltanschauung*—a play populated only by dimwits wouldn't be interesting—but the play is not there for the sake of their pronouncements, the pronouncements are there because my plays deal with people, and because thinking, believing, and philosophizing are, to a degree, part of human nature. But the problems I face as a playwright are practical, working problems that present themselves not before, but while I am working, or usually afterward, to be exact, when I get curious to know how I did what I did. I would like to say something about these problems, even at the risk of failing to satisfy the general longing for profundity and sounding more like a tailor than an artist. But actually I have no idea how anyone can talk about art in an untailorlike fashion, and so I can only speak to those who fall asleep when listening to Heidegger.

What I am concerned with are empirical rules, the possibilities of the theater, but since we live in a time when literary scholarship and criticism flourish, I cannot entirely resist the temptation of casting a few sideward glances at dramaturgical theory. The artist, of course, does not need scholarship. Scholarship derives its laws from something already given, otherwise it would not be scholarship, but the laws found in this manner are useless for an artist even if they are correct. He cannot adopt a law that he has not discovered for himself; if he does not find one, the one found by scholarship is of no use to him, and if he has found one, he doesn't care whether scholarship has discovered it or not. But scholarship, repudiated, stands behind him like a menacing ghost, and shows up whenever he wants to talk about art. Right now, for instance. There is no getting around it, to speak of the problems of the theater is to take up the challenge of literary scholarship. But I begin my endeavor with some misgivings. To literary scholarship, the theater is an object; to a playwright, it is never something purely objective, separate from himself. He is a participant. It is true that his activity turns drama into something objective (that's what his work is about), but he then destroys this object he has created, he forgets, disowns, despises, overestimates it, in order to make room for something new. Scholarship sees only the result: the playwright cannot forget the process that led to this result. What he says must be taken with a grain of salt. What he thinks about his art changes constantly as he creates it and is always subject to the mood of the moment. The only thing that counts for him is what he is doing at the moment; for its sake he can betray whatever he has done before. So he would do better not to talk, but once he's talking, it may be worth one's while to hear him out. A theory of literature that has no notion of the difficulties of writing and of the hidden reefs that deflect the stream of art in frequently unexpected directions runs the danger of winding up as an exercise in mere assertion, obstinately proclaiming laws that aren't laws at all.

There is no doubt, for instance, that the unities of place, time, and action, long believed to have been derived by Aristotle from the practice of classical tragedy, represent the ideal of dramatic action. From a logical and hence aesthetic point of view, this thesis is incontestable, so incontestable that we have to ask ourselves whether it doesn't once and for all establish the framework within which every playwright must orient himself. Aristotle's unities demand the greatest precision, the greatest economy, and the greatest simplicity in the treatment of dramatic material. When you get right down to it, the unities of place, time, and action ought to be imposed on playwrights as an absolute standard by the literary scholars, a standard that they do not impose for the sole reason that no one has obeyed Aristotle's unities for ages; nor can they be obeyed, for reasons that best illustrate the relationship of the art of writing plays to theories about that art.

For the unities of place, time, and action in the main presuppose Greek tragedy as their prerequisite. It is not Aristotle's unities that make Greek tragedy possible, it is Greek tragedy that makes Aristotle's unities possible. No matter how abstract an aesthetic rule may appear to be, the work of art from which it was derived is contained within it. If I set about writing a dramatic action that is to unfold, say, within a span of two hours in a single place, then this action must have a backstory, and the fewer characters I have at my disposal, the more extensive this backstory will have to be. That is an experience of theater in practice, an empirical rule. By "backstory" I mean the story preceding the action on the stage, a story without which that action would be impossible. The backstory of Hamlet, for instance, is the story of his father's murder; the drama, then, lies in the exposure of this murder. Also, the action on the stage is as a rule briefer than the events it depicts. Frequently it starts in the middle of those events, and often near the end of them: before Sophocles' play can begin, Oedipus must have already killed his father and married his mother, actions that require a certain amount of time. The stage action will compress an event to the degree in which the action corresponds to Aristotle's unities; therefore, the closer a playwright adheres to Aristotle's unities, the greater will be the importance of the backstory.

Naturally it is possible to invent a backstory and hence an action that would seem particularly favorable for Aristotle's unities, but here a general rule obtains: the more invented a plot is or the more unknown it is to the audience, the more careful must be its exposition, the development of the backstory. Now, Greek tragedy had the advantage of not having to invent a backstory, because it already had one: the spectators knew the myths that were enacted on the stage, and the fact that these myths were public, a given, a part of religion, made possible the audacious and unequaled feats of the Greek tragedians: their abbreviations, their directness, their stichomythia, and their choruses, and therefore also Aristotle's unities. The audience knew what the play was about, its curiosity was not focused on the story so much as on its treatment. Since the unities presuppose a general familiarity with the subject matter—one brilliant exception is Kleist's *Broken Jug**—and hence a religious, mythic theater, the Aristotelian unities had to be reinterpreted or dropped as soon as the theater lost its religious, mythical significance. An audience encountering an unfamiliar story pays more attention to the story than to its treatment; of necessity, then, such a play must be richer in detail and circumstances than one with a well-known story line. In both cases audacious risks may be taken, but they are not the same risks. Each art exploits only the opportunities offered by its time, and a time without opportunities is an unlikely event. Like every other art, drama creates its own world, but not every world can be created in the same way. That is the natural limitation of every aesthetic rule, no matter how self-evident that rule may appear to be. But this does not mean that Aristotle's unities are obsolete: what was once a rule now becomes an exception, a case that may occur again at any time. The one-act play still obeys the unities, though under different conditions. Here, instead of a backstory, it is the situation that dominates the plot, which makes the unities possible again.

But what is true of Aristotle's dramaturgy—that it depends on a particular world and is therefore only relatively valid—is true of every other dramaturgy. Brecht is consistent only when he incorporates into his dramaturgy that *Weltanschauung* to which, in his view, he belongs—communism—even though in doing so this poet is cutting into his own flesh. Thus his plays seem at times to be saying the opposite of what they claim to be saying, but this misunderstanding cannot always be blamed on the capitalist audience; frequently what is going on is simply that Brecht the poet has broken loose from Brecht the dramatic theorist, a perfectly legitimate occurrence that becomes ominous only when it no longer takes place.

Let us speak plainly here. My introducing the audience as a factor may very well seem strange to many: but just as a theater without an audience is not possible, it also doesn't make sense to consider and treat a play as a sort of ode for alternating voices in a vacuum. A play comes to life in the theater, where it can be seen, heard, felt, and thus directly experienced. This immediacy is one of the most important aspects of the theater, a fact that is frequently overlooked in those sacred halls where a play by Hofmannsthal counts for more than one by Nestroy,† and a Richard Strauss opera is

---

The Broken Jug is a tragicomedy by Heinrich von Kleist (1777–1811).

† Johann Nestroy (1801–1862), Austrian actor and prolific playwright famous for his bitingly satirical comedies.

preferred to one by Offenbach. A play is something that happens. In drama, everything has to be transformed into visible, sensuous immediacy, with the addendum, obviously justified in these times, that not everything can be translated into sensuousness and immediacy: not Kafka, for instance, which is why he really does not belong on the stage. The bread one is served here provides no nourishment, it remains undigested in the cast-iron stomachs of theatergoers and subscribers. Fortunately, though, many of them interpret the resultant queasiness not as a stomachache, but as the nightmarish pressure exerted by Kafka's true works, and so things are set right after all, by a misunderstanding.

The immediacy to which every play aspires, the spectacle into which it would be transformed, presupposes the audience, the theater, the stage. So we are well advised to examine the theater for which we have to write. We are all acquainted with these impecunious institutions. Like many contemporary establishments, they can only be justified on idealistic grounds: actually even that is no longer the case. Their architecture—their seating arrangements and their stages—evolved from the court theater, or rather, remained stuck there. For this reason alone, contemporary theater is not contemporary. In contrast to the primitive wooden platform of Shakespeare's time, to this "scaffold" where, to quote Goethe, "one saw little, and everything was but an indication," the court theater strove to satisfy a craving for naturalness, even though the result was a much greater unnaturalness. People were no longer willing to imagine the King's chamber behind a "green curtain," but instead set about finding ways to show that chamber. The hallmark of this theater is its tendency to separate audience and stage, by means of the curtain and by having the spectators sit in the dark facing an illuminated stage, surely the most harmful innovation, since it alone made possible the solemn atmosphere in which our theaters are suffocating. The stage became a peepshow. Inventions were made, better and better lighting, the revolving stage—and I've heard they've invented a revolving auditorium as well. The courts went, but the court theater stayed. True, our age has found its own form of theater, the movies. However much we emphasize the differences, and important though it is to emphasize them, it must still be pointed out that film grew out of the theater, and that it is able to accomplish precisely what the court theater with its machineries, revolving stages, and other effects only dreamed of: the simulation of reality.

Movies are nothing more or less than the democratic form of the court theater. They amplify intimacy to such an immense degree that they run the danger of becoming the essentially pornographic art, forcing the viewer to be a voyeur, and the popularity of film stars consists merely in the fact that everyone who has seen them on the screen has the feeling of having slept with them—that's how well they are photographed. A close-up is in and of itself indecent.

But what is contemporary theater? If film can be considered the modern form of the old court theater, what is theater besides? There is no denying that to a large degree it has become a museum where the art treasures of bygone theater epochs are on display. There is no way of changing that. It is only too natural in an age that looks toward the past and seems to have everything except a present. In Goethe's time the ancients were rarely performed, Schiller once in a while, but mainly Kotzebue and whatever their names were.* I want to point out emphatically here that the movies have relieved the theater of the Kotzebues and the Birch-Pfeiffers. There is no telling what sort of plays would have to be put on these days if film had not been invented and if the screenwriters were writing plays.

If today's theater is in part a museum, this has a certain effect on the actors who work there. They have become civil servants, quite often with a retirement plan, provided their film activities still permit them to perform on the stage. The members of this once despised estate—a human advance, but artistically dubious—have long since moved into the bourgeoisie, and now hold a rank somewhere between doctors and small industrialists; within the arts they are surpassed only by Nobel Prize winners, pianists, and conductors. Some actors are visiting professors or freelance scholars of sorts, who take turns appearing in the museums or arranging exhibitions. The management takes this into account, arranging its repertoire more and more according to the guest star's schedule: what plays should one put on when this or that authority in this or that field is available at this or that time? Furthermore, the actors are forced to perform in the most various styles, one day baroque, classical the next, then again naturalistically, and tomorrow Claudel, which is something an actor in, say, Molière's time didn't have to do.† The director has become more important, more dominant than ever before, like the conductor in the field of music. Historical works demand, and ought to demand, correct interpretation, but theaters have not yet advanced to the kind of fidelity that some conductors aspire to as a matter of course.

---

*August von Kotzebue (1762–1819), prolific German playwright and novelist murdered in 1819 by a student. His plays were immensely popular in the United States during the nineteenth century.

† Paul Claudel (1868–1955), French playwright, poet, and diplomat.

All too often, the classics are not interpreted but executed; the curtain falls on a mutilated corpse. But there's no real danger, for always there comes to the rescue the convention by which all things classical are accepted as perfect, a sort of cultural gold standard, consisting of the opinion that everything that glitters in deluxe editions must be gold. The theatergoing public streams to the classics, no matter whether they are played badly or well, applause is assured, indeed it is an educated person's duty, and in a legitimate way you are relieved of the compulsion to think and to form a judgment that might differ from the one that was drummed into you in school.

And yet there is one good thing about the many styles the contemporary theater has to master. This good thing at first appears to be something negative. Every great era in the history of the theater was made possible by the discovery of a particular form, a particular style, in which and by means of which plays were written. This can be observed in the development of the English and Spanish stage, or in the Wiener Volkstheater, that most marvelous phenomenon of all the varieties of theater in the German tongue. How else to explain, say, the great number of plays Lope de Vega was able to write? A play was no problem for him stylistically. But to the same degree that we no longer have and no longer can have a uniform style, the writing of plays becomes problematic and therefore more difficult. Contemporary theater is, therefore, two things at once: a museum, but also a field for experimentation, and this to such a degree that each play presents its author with new problems, new questions of style. Style, today, is no longer a common property; it has become a personal matter, indeed a unique decision from case to case. There is no style, there are only styles—a statement that characterizes contemporary art altogether, for art in our day consists of experiments, no more and no less, like today's world itself.

If there are only styles, then there is no dramaturgy either, but only dramaturgies: Brecht's dramaturgy, Eliot's, Claudel's, Frisch's, Hochwälder's, a different dramaturgy in each case:* nevertheless, a single dramaturgy may still be conceivable, one that would apply to all possible cases, just as there exists a geometry that comprises all possible dimensions. In this dramaturgy, Aristotle's theory of drama would merely be one of the possible dramaturgies. This one dramaturgy would have to investigate the

*T. S. Eliot (1888–1965), American poet resident in London; Max Frisch (1911–1981), Swiss dramatist whose most famous work is *The Firebugs*; Fritz Hochwälder (1911–1986), Swiss dramatist.

possibilities, not of a particular stage, but of *the* stage, a dramaturgy of experimentation.

What, finally, can we say about the audience, without which no theater is possible, as we pointed out earlier? It has become anonymous, just "the public," and that's worse news than may be apparent at first glance. The modern author no longer knows a particular public, unless he wants to write for village theaters or for the drama festival at Caux, which wouldn't be much fun, either. He invents his audience, but in truth that audience is himself, a dangerous situation that can neither be changed nor circumvented. The dubious, worn-out meanings that attach themselves to the concepts of a "people" or a "society," to say nothing of a "community," and that are so easily misused for political purposes, have unavoidably crept into the theater as well. How does a playwright make his points now? How does he find his subjects, arrive at his solutions? Questions for which we may find an answer once we take stock of the possibilities that the theater still offers.

When I undertake to write a play, my first step is to make clear to myself where it is to take place. At first glance this does not look like an important question. A play takes place in London or Berlin, a mountainous region, a hospital, or a battlefield, wherever the action demands. But this is not quite accurate. A play takes place on a stage that must represent London or a mountainous region or a battlefield. This is a distinction that need not, but can be made. It depends how much an author takes the stage into account, how strongly he wants the illusion without which no theater can get by, and whether he wants it smeared on thickly like gobs of paint heaped upon a canvas or applied as a glaze, translucent and fragile. A playwright can be in dead earnest about the scene of the action, making it Madrid, or the Rütli, or the Russian steppe, or he can think of it as a stage, as the world, or as his world.*

Representing a particular place on the stage is the set designer's job. Scenic design is a form of painting, and the developments that have taken place in painting cannot have passed it by. Even though abstraction in scenic design has essentially failed—because the theater can abstract neither man nor language, which is simultaneously abstract and concrete, and because no matter how abstract a stage set pretends to be, it always must represent something concrete to make sense—the theater has nonetheless returned to the green curtain behind which the spectator is required to imagine the

---

***The Rütli:* Rütli Meadow is the legendary site of the founding of the Swiss Confederation in 1291.

King's chamber. Stage practitioners remembered the fact that no matter how detailed, how convincingly lifelike a stage set may be, the dramatic place is not on the stage, it has to be brought into being by the performance. A word, and we are in Venice; a word, and we are in the Tower. The audience's imagination needs only slight support. The stage set wants to suggest, signify, intensify, not describe. It has become transparent, dematerialized. But the dramatic place represented by the sets can also be dematerialized.

The two plays of recent years that most clearly exemplify the possibility I would like to call the dematerialization of the scenery and the dematerialization of the dramatic place are Wilder's *Our Town* and *The Skin of Our Teeth*. The stage in *Our Town* is dematerialized as follows: it is empty, except for a few objects needed for rehearsal, chairs, tables, ladders, and so forth, and out of these everyday objects the locale is created, the dramatic place, the town, and all this is done through the word, the play, which awakens the spectator's imagination. In his other play, this great fanatic of the theater dematerializes the dramatic place: where the Antrobus family really lives, in what period and what stage of civilization, is never quite clear: we're in the ice age at one moment, next we're in a world war. This experiment is found quite frequently in the work of modern playwrights: it is uncertain, for example, where Max Frisch's uncanny Count Öderland lives; no one knows where Mr. Godot is being awaited, and in *The Marriage of Mr. Mississippi* I expressed the indefiniteness of the locale (in order to suspend the play on the hook of wit, of comedy) by having one window of a room look out upon a northern landscape with a Gothic cathedral and an apple tree, while another window of the same room offers a view of a southern landscape with an ancient ruin, a bit of sea, and a cypress. The decisive point is that, to quote Max Frisch, the playwright's imagination works *with* the stage, a possibility that has always engaged my interest, and that is one of the reasons, if not the main reason, why I write plays. After all, plays have always been made not only on the stage but with it; I'm thinking, for instance, of Aristophanes' comedies or Nestroy's comic plays.

But let us return to our main topic. What are the particular problems that I, for example—to cite an author with whom I am more or less familiar, though I don't comprehend him entirely—have had to face? In *The Blind Man*, my intention was to juxtapose the dramatic place and the word, to turn the word against the scene. The blind duke believes he is living in his well-preserved castle but actually lives in a ruin, he thinks he is humbling himself before Wallenstein but sinks to his knees before a Negro. The dramatic place is one and the same, but through the pretense that is carried out before the blind man it is doubled, it becomes a place seen by the audience and a place in which the blind man believes himself to be. And when in my comedy *An Angel Comes to Babylon* I chose for a locale the city in which the great tower was built, essentially I had to solve two problems: in the first place, the stage had to express the fact that in this comedy there are two places: Heaven and the city of Babylon. Heaven as the mysterious point of origin of the action and Babylon as the locale where the action unfolds.

Now, Heaven could simply be represented by a dark background to suggest its infinity, but since the idea of Heaven in my comedy is not one of infinity but of something radically incomprehensible, altogether different, my directions are that the stage background, the sky above the city of Babylon, should be occupied by an image of the Great Nebula in the Andromeda galaxy as we might see it in the mirror of the observatory on Mount Palomar. What I am trying to achieve is to give tangible presence, stage presence, to Heaven—to the sky, that is—as the incomprehensible, the inscrutable. The device also brings out the idea of Heaven approaching Earth, a rapprochement that is expressed in the action by having an angel visit Babylon. It is also a way to construct a world in which the result of the action, the building of the tower of Babel, becomes possible.

In the second place I had to think of how Babylon, the place where the action unfolds, was to be represented on the stage. What attracted me about Babylon was its modernity, its Cyclopean character as a sort of New York with skyscrapers and slums, and by having the first two acts take place on a quay by the Euphrates, there's a bit of Paris in it as well: Babylon stands for the idea of metropolis. It is a Babylon of the imagination, so it needs some typically Babylonian features, but in a modernized, parodied form, just as certain modern properties, like a street lamp, are parodied in Babylonian style. Naturally the execution, the construction of this stage, is a task for the stage designer, but the playwright has to think about what kind of stage he wants.

I love a colorful stage set, a colorful theater, the stage of Teo Otto, to mention one revered name.* I have little use for theater in front of black draperies, as was fashionable a long time ago, or for the tendency to exude an air of poverty, which some set designers find irresistible. Certainly it is the word above all that matters on the stage, but take note: above all. After the word, there are

*Teo Otto (1904–1968), renowned German stage designer who emigrated to Zürich in 1933. At Zürich's Schauspielhaus he designed the sets for a production of Dürrenmatt's *The Visit* in 1959.

many other things that belong to the theater; a certain levity for instance, and if someone with a deep mind were to ask me whether I really believe in the feasibility of a four-dimensional theater, because in my *Mississippi* a person enters the stage through a grandfather clock, I can only say that I wasn't thinking of Einstein. In my daily life it would give me great pleasure to go to a social gathering and astonish everyone by entering the room through a grandfather clock or floating in through a window. Surely, no one should deny us playwrights the chance to indulge such desires now and then, at least on the stage, where they can be fulfilled. The old argument about which came first, the chicken or the egg, could, in art, be varied as follows: which is the worthier subject, the chicken or the egg, the world as potential or as plenitude? Artists might then be divided into those who favor the egg and those who favor the chicken. There really is such a debate. Alfred Polgar once said to me that he found it peculiar that while in contemporary Anglo-Saxon drama everything happens through dialogue, in my plays much too much happens on the stage, and that some day he would like to see a simple Dürrenmatt. Behind this truth lies only my refusal to give the egg precedence over the chicken, and my prejudice of loving the chicken more than the egg. It is my not always happy passion to want to put on the stage the abundance, the diversity of the world. As a result, my theater tends to be ambiguous, with many possible meanings, and seems to have a confusing effect. Also, misunderstandings creep in when people desperately search the chicken coop of my plays for the egg of explanation, which I obstinately refuse to lay.

But a play is not only bound to a place, it also renders a time. Just as the stage represents a place, so it also represents time, the time the action takes (and the time in which it takes place). If Aristotle had really demanded a unity of time, place, and action, he would have equated the duration of a tragedy with the time it takes for the action to be performed (which the Greek tragedians approximately achieve), in which case everything would have to be concentrated upon that action. Time would thus be "naturalistically" rendered as a seamless succession, one thing after the other. But this need not always be the case. Generally, the actions on the stage do follow one another, but in Nestroy's magical farce *Death on the Wedding-Day* (*Der Tod am Hochzeitstag*), for instance, two acts take place simultaneously, and this illusion of simultaneity is cleverly suggested by having the action of the second act serve as background noise for the first and the action of the first act as background noise for the second. Other examples of the use of time as a dramatic possibility would not be difficult to come up with. Time can be shortened, slowed down, intensified, arrested, repeated. Like Joshua, the playwright can call out to his theater sun: Stand thou still upon Gibeon; and thou, theater moon, in the valley of Ajalon.*

It may be noted further that Aristotle's unities were not perfectly kept in Greek tragedy, either. The action is interrupted by the choruses; in effect, the choruses divide time into sections. The chorus interrupts the action and is, with respect to time and not at all profoundly—here's tailor-talk for you—what the curtain is for us today. By means of the curtain, the time of an action is cut into separate parts. Nothing wrong with this venerable device. The curtain has the virtue of clearly bringing an act to an end, it clears the deck. Also, psychologically, it is often all too necessary to give the exhausted and frightened audience a rest. But now, playwrights have developed a new way of connecting language and time.

If I refer to Wilder's *Our Town* once again, it is because I can assume that this lovely play is widely known. Everyone knows that in it several characters turn to the audience and talk about the troubles and cares of the small town. Because of this device, Wilder can dispense with a curtain. The curtain has been replaced by the direct address to the audience. An epic element has been added to the drama: description. That is why this form of theater is called epic theater.

But if we look closely, we find that Shakespeare or, say, Goethe's *Götz von Berlichingen,* are in a certain sense epic theater. But in a different, more covert manner. Since Shakespeare's histories often extend over long periods of time, this time span is again divided into different actions, different episodes, each of which receives its own separate dramatic treatment. *Henry IV* consists of nineteen episodes, *Götz* has no less than forty-one by the end of act 4. I stopped counting after that. If one looks at the way the plot as a whole is constructed, it comes close to being an epic play as far as the treatment of time is concerned, like a film that is run too slowly, so that the separate frames become visible, for the concentration of all the action into a particular time has been given up in favor of an episodic form of drama.

Now, when the author in certain modern plays addresses the audience, it is an attempt to give the play more continuity than is otherwise possible in an episodic drama. The idea is to eliminate the emptiness between acts, to bridge gaps in time by the word instead of by a pause, by describing what has happened in the meantime, or by having a new character introduce himself. The expositions are worked out in an epic manner, not the actions to which the expositions lead. Here the word has made an advance in the theater, the

*Joshua 10:12: "Sun, stand thou still at Gibeon, and thou Moon in the valley of Ai'jalon."

word is attempting to reconquer territory that was lost long ago. Attempting, I say, for often these days the device of addressing the audience serves only to explain the play, a perfectly pointless undertaking: if the audience is swept away by a story, it doesn't have to follow it, and if it is not swept away, it won't go along with you no matter how well it follows.

In contrast to the epic, which is able to describe human beings as they are, dramatic art imposes an unavoidable limit that stylizes their representation on the stage. The limitation is due to the art form itself. Man in the theater is a creature of words: that is his limitation; and the purpose of the action is to force him to speak in a particular way. The action is the crucible in which man becomes language, and cannot do otherwise. But this means that in a play, I have to put people in situations that force them to speak. If I show two people drinking coffee and talking about the weather, politics, or fashion, it doesn't matter how clever they are, their situation is not yet dramatic and neither is their dialogue. Something else has to come in, something that would make their talk uncommon, dramatic, double-edged. For example, if the viewer knows there is poison in one of the coffee cups, or even in both, which makes for a conversation between two poisoners, then this little device turns the drinking of coffee into a dramatic situation, out of which and on the basis of which dramatic dialogue can develop. Without the addition of some special tension, some special situation, there is no dramatic dialogue.

Just as dialogue has to emerge from a situation, it must also lead to a situation, a different one of course. Dramatic dialogue brings about: an action, an affliction, a new situation, out of which a new dialogue develops, and so forth.

Now, man is more than a creature of words. The fact that a person thinks, or at least should think, that he feels, indeed and above all feels, and that he does not always want to reveal his thoughts and feelings to others, has led to the use of another artistic device, the monologue. It's true, of course, that a person talking to himself out loud on the stage is not behaving naturally; the same thing can, with even more justification, be said of the operatic aria. But the monologue (like the aria) proves that a gimmick, which really ought to be avoided, can achieve an unexpected effect, and that audiences are, with good reason, taken in by this trick again and again, so much so that Hamlet's "To be or not to be" and Faust's monologue are probably the most beloved and most famous moments in the theater.

But not everything that sounds like a monologue is a monologue. The purpose of dialogue is not only to get a person to act or suffer the effects of an action; occasionally it also moves him to give a great speech, an explanation of his point of view. Many people have lost the feeling for rhetoric, ever since, according to Hilpert, an actor unsure of his lines invented naturalism.* That is a pity. There is no other theatrical device that can reach an audience more effectively than a speech. But the critics no longer have much use for it either. A contemporary author who dares to use a speech will suffer the same fate as the peasant Dicaeopolis:[†] he will have to lay his head on the executioner's block; except that unlike Aristophanes' Acharnians, most critics will wield the ax readily: it's the most normal thing in the world. The busiest decapitators have no heads of their own.

Moreover, the drama has always involved narration; it's not just found in epic theater. For instance, a backstory may have to be told, or an event announced in the form of a messenger's report. Narration on the stage is not without its dangers, because it does not have the same palpable life as an action taking place on the stage. Writers have frequently tried to make up for this lack by dramatizing the messenger: by having him enter at an exciting moment, for instance, or by making him a blockhead from whom the report can only be elicited with difficulty. But there is a rhetorical element that must accompany any narration on the stage. A stage narrative cannot get by without exaggeration. Consider how Shakespeare exaggerates Plutarch's description of Cleopatra's barge. This exaggeration is not just a characteristic of baroque style but a means of launching Cleopatra's barge on the stage, of making it visible. The language of the stage cannot get by without exaggeration; but of course one needs to know where to exaggerate, and above all: how.

Furthermore: just as the characters on the stage can suffer a particular fate, so can their language: the angel who comes to Babylon, for instance, grows more and more enthusiastic from act to act about the beauty of the earth; his language must express this mounting enthusiasm, until it exults as a veritable hymn. The beggar Akki in the same comedy tells the story of his life in a series of *makamat*, a prose form containing rhymes that comes from the Arabic. In this way I try to express the Arabic character of this personage, his pleasure in making up stories, in repartee and wordplay, but without dropping into some other form, like, say, the chanson. Akki's *makamat* are nothing less than the ultimate reach of his language, and hence an intensification of his character. In these passages, Akki becomes pure language, and this is something a playwright must always strive for: to have moments in his theater when the characters he has written become language and are nothing but language.

---

*Heinz Hilpert (1890–1967), German actor and director.
[†] A character in Aristophanes' play *The Acharnians*.

Here, of course, there lurks a danger. Language can be seductive. The joy of suddenly being able to write, of possessing language, an experience that came over me while I was working on *The Blind Man*, for example, can persuade an author to flee his subject and escape, as it were, into language. Keeping close to the subject is a great art, which is only achieved when there is an opposing drive that needs to be kept in check. Dialogues, too, can seduce an author with wordplay that unexpectedly drives him away from his subject. But again and again, new ideas crop up that should not be resisted, not even if they threaten to make a shambles of a carefully laid-out plan. A cautious resistance to sudden inspirations is important, but so is the courage to expose oneself to them.

All these elements and problems of place, time, and action, merely hinted at here, densely interwoven, belong to the elements, devices, and tools of the playwright's craft. Now, I cannot conceal the fact that I am at war with the concept of playwriting as a craft. The idea that art can ultimately be learned by anyone who applies himself to its production with enough diligence and perseverance is a notion we thought discarded long ago, but evidently it can still be found in critical judgments concerning the art of writing plays. This art is presumed to be a solid, worthy, upstanding sort of business. A playwright's relationship with his art is considered to be a marriage in which everything is perfectly legal, blessed with the sacraments of aesthetics. That is probably the reason why critics frequently refer to the theater, more than to any other art, as a craft that, depending on the particular case, has been mastered or not; but if one investigates closely what exactly they mean by "the craft" of the drama, it turns out to be nothing more than the sum of their prejudices. There is no such craft, there is only the mastery of one's material through language and the stage; or to be more exact, it is an overpowering of the material, for every act of writing is a passage at arms with its victories, defeats, and undecided battles. Perfect plays do not exist except as a fiction of aesthetics, which rather resemble the movies, that last refuge of perfect heroes. No playwright has ever left the battlefield without a wound, and each has his Achilles' heel. Also, the antagonist, one's subject matter, never fights fairly. This cunning foe often refuses to be lured out of his fortress, and he can set the most secret and dastardly traps. This forces the playwright to fight with every legitimate and illegitimate means, no matter what the master craftsmen and their venerable guild may proffer in the way of sage admonitions, maxims, and rules. Fair and soft goes far in a day, but not in the theater; it won't even get you around the block. The difficulties in writing plays lie where no one suspects them; frequently in just having two people say hello, or in writing the opening sentence. What is now considered to be the craft of the drama can easily be learned in half an hour. But how difficult it is to divide one's material into, say, five acts, and how few subjects there are that allow this, and how nearly impossible it is to write in iambic pentameters any more, is least understood by those tinkering craftsmen who can give any subject a five-act treatment and have always written in iambs with ease and still do. They really do choose their subjects and their language the way the critics imagine it is done; they don't sound like tailors when they talk about art, but they certainly ply their craft like tailors. No matter what their material, they always produce the same nightgown. In this garment, no audience will catch a cold, and everyone stays sound asleep. There is nothing more idiotic than the opinion that only a genius does not have to abide by the rules prescribed for writers of talent. In that case I might as well consider myself a genius. I can't say it emphatically enough: the art of writing plays does not necessarily start out with the planning of a particular brainchild, or however a eunuch thinks love is made; it starts out with lovemaking, of which the eunuch is incapable. However, the difficulties, the pains, but also the joy of writing do not lie within the scope of what we mean to talk about, or even can talk about. We can only talk about a craft of the drama that exists solely where there is talk about drama, but not in the making of it. The craft of the drama is an optical illusion. To talk about plays, about art, is a much more utopian undertaking than is realized by those who do most of the talking.

With this nonexistent craft, then, and a particular subject or story that attracts us, we set about writing a play. It usually has a center, the hero. Dramaturgical theory makes a distinction between a tragic hero, the hero of tragedy, and a comic hero, the hero of comedy. The qualities proper to a tragic hero are well known. He must be capable of arousing our pity. His guilt and his innocence, his virtues and his vices must be very delicately and pleasantly mixed and apportioned according to precise rules; for instance, if I choose a villain as my hero, I must endow him with an amount of intelligence proportionate to his villainy, a rule that has made the devil himself the most appealing character on the German stage. The rule still obtains. The only thing that has changed is the social status of those who awaken our pity.

In Greek tragedy and in Shakespeare the hero is a member of the highest social class, the nobility. The audience witnesses the suffering, the actions, the ravings of a hero who holds a higher social position than its own. Audiences today still find this extremely impressive.

Now when Lessing and Schiller introduce the bourgeois drama, the audience sees itself as the suffering hero on the stage. Subsequent writers went even further. Büchner's Woyzeck is a primitive proletarian who represents less, from a social point of view, than the average theatergoer.* The audience is now invited to see itself, its humanity, in this last, most miserable form of existence.

Here finally we must mention Pirandello,† who was the first, as far as I know, to render the hero, the character on the stage, in a dematerialized, transparent form, just as Wilder did the dramatic place. The audience faced with these specters finds itself attending its own dissection, its own psychoanalysis, and the stage becomes an internal space, the inner space of the world.

Now the theater has never dealt exclusively with kings and generals, there was always, in comedy, the peasant, the beggar, the commoner as hero—but in comedy only. Nowhere in Shakespeare does a comic king appear; in his time, a ruler could be shown as a bloodcurdling monster but never as a fool. His comical characters are fawning courtiers, artisans, laborers. Thus, in the development of the tragic hero, we see a movement in the direction of comedy. The same can be observed in the history of the fool, who becomes more and more of a tragic figure. This fact is not without significance. The hero of a play not only propels an action forward, not only suffers a particular fate, he also represents a world. We must therefore ask ourselves how our precarious world ought to be presented, and with what sort of heroes, and how the mirrors that reflect this world should be ground.

To pose the question concretely: can today's world be dramatically treated by Schiller's methods, as some writers claim, since Schiller still captivates modern audiences? To be sure, in art everything is possible if the art itself is valid, but the question is whether an art that was valid for its time is still possible today. Art is not repeatable; if it were, it would be foolish not simply to write according to Schiller's rules.

Schiller wrote the way he wrote because the world in which he lived could still be mirrored in the world he wrote, the world he fashioned for his own uses as a historian. Just barely. After all, Napoleon was probably the last hero in the old sense. But it would be virtually impossible to take the measure of today's world, as it appears to us, through a historical drama in Schiller's manner, if only because we no longer have tragic heroes, only tragedies

*Woyzeck is the eponymous antihero of the play by Georg Büchner (1813–1837).
†Luigi Pirandello (1867–1936), Italian dramatist.

staged by world-butchers and produced by meat-grinders. Hitler and Stalin can no longer be made into Wallensteins.* Their power is so enormous that they themselves are nothing but incidental, superficial, easily replaced expressions of this power, and the misfortune associated especially with the former and to a considerable extent with the latter is too far-reaching, too confounding, too cruel, too mechanical, and often simply too senseless. Wallenstein's power is still a visible power, while power in our time is almost entirely hidden, like an iceberg; that is, all but a minuscule part of it is submerged in anonymity and abstraction. Schiller's drama presupposes a visible world, an honest-to-goodness affair of state, as does Greek tragedy. Only a surveyable reality can be made visible in art. But the modern state has become unsurveyable, anonymous, bureaucratic, and this not just in Moscow or Washington, but by now in Bern as well, and today's affairs of state are satiric comedies staged in the wake of tragedies that have been previously enacted in secret. There are no true representatives, and the tragic heroes are nameless. Any small-time crook or chancery clerk or policeman is a better stand-in for today's world than a senator or a prime minister. Art, if it touches people at all, may communicate with the victims, but it no longer reaches the powerful. Creon's secretaries close Antigone's case.† The state has lost its visible form, and just as physics can no longer interpret the world except in mathematical formulas, so the state can only be represented in statistics. Power in our time becomes visible, concrete, only when it explodes, in the atom bomb, in this marvelous mushroom that rises and spreads, immaculate as the sun, uniting mass murder and beauty. Now that the atom bomb can be manufactured, it can no longer be depicted. Art as a human creation fails in the face of this reality, for the bomb is itself a creation of man. Two mirrors reflecting each other remain empty.

But the task of art, insofar as art can have a task at all, and hence the task of drama today, is to create form, concrete presence. Comedy is particularly good at this. Tragedy, the severest artistic genre, presupposes an already formed world. Comedy—except for a comedy of manners like Molière's—presupposes an unformed world, a world in embryo or in collapse, a world that is packing its bags, as ours is. *Tragedy overcomes distance*. It brings time-shrouded myths into the living present of the Athenian audience. *Comedy creates distance*. It transforms the Athenians' attempt to gain a foothold in Sicily

---

*Albrecht von Wallenstein was a Bohemian general in the Thirty Years' War, whose life and death were dramatized by Friedrich von Schiller (1759–1805).

† *Antigone:* Eponymous heroine of the drama by Sophocles.

into the birds' attempt to establish an empire before which gods and men will capitulate. How comedy works can be seen in the most primitive humor, the dirty joke, an admittedly questionable subject, which I only mention because it provides the clearest illustration of what I mean by creating distance. Its topic is sex pure and simple, a domain not conducive to either form or distance, but if it wants to assume a form, it will become a dirty joke. The dirty joke, therefore, is an ur-comedy, a transposition of the sexual to the level of the comical, the only decent way to talk about sex ever since the Van de Veldes arrived on the scene.* The dirty joke shows clearly that the comic genius consists in shaping the shapeless, giving form to chaos.

Now the means by which comedy creates distance is the humorous conceit. There are no conceits in tragedy. For that reason, there are few tragedies whose subjects are invented. I am not saying that the classical tragedians were incapable of original invention, as is sometimes the case today; no, their incomparable art was blessed in having no need for invention. That makes a difference. Aristophanes, on the other hand, lives by conceits. His subjects are not myths but invented stories, which take place not in the past but in the present. They fall into the world like missiles, digging up large craters, rendering the present comical, and in the process visible as well. This is not to say that a contemporary play can only be comical. Tragedy and comedy are formal concepts, dramaturgical stances, rhetorical figures of aesthetic theory that can refer to one and the same thing. Only the conditions under which each is created are different, and these conditions are only in small part artistic in nature.

Tragedy presupposes guilt, adversity, measure, a surveyable world, and responsibility. In the muddle and mess of our century, in this last waltz of the white race, no one is guilty any longer and no one is responsible, either. No one can help it and no one wanted it. Everything happens without anyone's doing. Everyone is swept along and gets caught in the meshes somewhere. We are too collectively guilty, too collectively embedded in the sins of our fathers and forefathers. We are nothing but great-grandchildren. That is our bad luck, not our fault: guilt today exists only as a personal achievement, as a religious act. Comedy alone can still get to us. Our world has led to the grotesque and to the atom bomb, both, just as Hieronymus Bosch's apocalyptic paintings are also grotesque. But the grotesque is only a tangible expression, a tangible paradox, the shape of the shapeless, the face of a faceless world,

---

*Theodoor Hendrik van de Velde (1873–1937), Dutch physician and gynecologist, famous for his book *Ideal Marriage, Its Physiology and Technique* (1926).

and just as our thinking seems no longer able to get by without the concept of the paradoxical, so also art and our world, which continues to exist only because the atom bomb exists: out of fear of the bomb.

But the tragic is still possible even if pure tragedy is not. We can approach it through comedy, we can bring it forth as a terrifying moment, as the yawning of an abyss; many of Shakespeare's tragedies, for instance, are comedies out of which the tragic arises.

Now the conclusion might easily be drawn that comedy is the expression of despair, but this conclusion is not a necessary one. To be sure, whoever sees the senselessness, the hopelessness of this world might well despair, but this despair is not a consequence of this world but an answer to it, and a different answer would be not to despair, it would be the decision to endure the world, in which we frequently live like Gulliver among the giants. He too achieves distance, he too steps back to take an opponent's measure, who prepares to fight that opponent or to escape him. It is still possible to portray man as a courageous being.

This, then, is one of my main concerns. The blind man, Romulus, Übelohe, Akki, are men of courage. The lost world order is restored in their hearts—universality escapes my grasp. I refuse to find the universal in a doctrine, I accept it as chaos. The world (and hence the stage, which represents this world) is for me a monstrosity, an enigma of calamity that has to be accepted, but to which there must be no surrender. The world is bigger than man; of necessity, therefore, it assumes such a menacing countenance. Viewed from outside, it would look less threatening, but I have neither the right nor the ability to place myself outside the world. The solace of literature is often all too cheap; it is probably more honest to maintain a human point of view. The thesis Brecht develops in his *Street Scene*—presenting the world as an accident and then showing how this accident came about—may make for superb theater, as Brecht indeed proved, but this proof requires the suppression of most of the evidence: Brecht's thinking is inexorable because he inexorably avoids thinking about many things.

Lastly: only free invention, only comedy with its conceits makes it possible for the anonymous audience to become a public—a reality that must be reckoned with, but which can also be calculated upon. A humorous conceit easily turns the crowd of theatergoers into a mass that can then be attacked, seduced, beguiled to listen to things it would otherwise not so readily listen to. Comedy is a mousetrap in which the public is easily caught and in which it will get caught again and again. Tragedy, on the other hand, presupposes a community, the existence of which cannot always be presumed without embarrassing results: there is nothing more comical, for instance, than to sit and watch the mystery plays of the Anthroposophists as an outsider.*

Granted all this, there is still one more question to ask: is it permissible to argue from a generality to a particular art form, as I just did when I declared that the world is formless and concluded that comedy, therefore, is a possible form for our time? I rather doubt it. Art is a personal matter, and no personal matter should be explained with generalities. The value of an art form does not depend on whether we can find more or less good reasons for it. That is why I have steered clear of certain problems, for instance the current debate as to whether plays ought to be written in verse or in prose. My answer consists simply in writing prose, without thereby claiming to decide the issue. One has to choose a path, after all, but why should one path be worse than another? As for the way I describe comedy, I believe that here, too, personal reasons are more important than general ones, which, after all, can be refuted—show me a logic in matters of art that cannot be refuted! The best way to talk about art is by talking about one's own art. One's choice of an art form is an expression of freedom, without which art cannot exist, and at the same time an expression of necessity, without which art cannot exist either. The artist always depicts the world and himself. Though there was a time when philosophy taught us that the particular can be derived from the general, I can no longer construct a drama as Schiller did, whose point of departure was always a general proposition, since I very much doubt that the particular can ever be reached by way of the general. My doubt is my own, however, and not that of a Catholic, for instance, for whom drama holds possibilities that are, undeniably, closed to non-Catholics, though if he takes his faith seriously, he is barred from other possibilities that are open to everyone else; and this thesis is dangerous only in that there are always artists who will convert for the sake of some general idea to believe in, a step that is all the more remarkable for the sad fact that it doesn't do anyone any good. The difficulties a Protestant has with the art of the drama are precisely those he has with his faith. And so it is my way to mistrust what is called the construction of the drama, and to approach my plays by way of the particular, by way of a radical invention or conceit, and not to start out from a general idea or a plan. For me it is necessary to write my way into the unknown, as I like to put it—my way of

---

*The anthroposophists, followers of the spiritual movement begun by Rudolf Steiner (1861–1925), wrote four modern mystery plays, which were performed in 1910, 1911, 1912, and 1913.

tossing a bone to the critics. They pick it up often enough without any sense of what it means.

But all of this is my personal business, so it is not necessary to invoke the whole world and to claim that this business of mine is the business of art in general, the way Kleist's village judge Adam invokes the devil to explain the origin of a wig that is, in fact, his own.* The maxim holds here as everywhere, and not just in the fields of art: no excuses, please.

Nevertheless the fact remains (keeping in mind the qualification we have made) that we have developed a different relationship to what we call subject matter. One characteristic of our unformed, shapeless present is that we are surrounded by figures and forms that reduce our time to a mere result, and even less, to a stage of transition, and that give preponderance to the past as a time of completion and to the future as the sphere of possibility. This remark could easily be applied to politics as well, but in relation to art it means that the artist is not only surrounded by opinions about art and by demands based not on himself but on something historical, something already given; he is surrounded as well by subjects that are no longer subject matter—that is, possibilities—but by readymade, preformed characters. Caesar is no longer pure subject matter for us, he is a Caesar whom scholarship has made the object of its research. There is no getting around the fact that scholarship, having thrown itself with increasing vigor not only upon nature but upon intellectual culture and art as well—developing intellectual history, literary scholarship, philology, and who knows what else—has produced facts that can no longer be ignored (for there can be no conscious naïveté that could ignore the results of scholarship), thus depriving the artist of his subject-matter by doing what should have been the artist's task. The mastery of Richard Feller's *History of Berne*, for instance, precludes the possibility of writing a historical drama about Bern; the history of Bern has already been formed before literature has touched it, but it is a scholarly form (not mythical, which would still admit of a tragic treatment), a form that narrows the scope of art, leaving to art only psychology, which by now has become a science as well. A dramatic version of the history of Bern would be a tautology, a repetition by means that are inadequate to the task, a mere illustration of scholarly findings: precisely the view science has of literature. Shakespeare's *Caesar* was made possible by Plutarch, who was not yet a historian in our sense of the word but a storyteller, an author of biographical sketches. If Shakespeare had possessed our knowledge of Rome he

---

*Adam: A corrupt judge, the central character in Kleist's *The Broken Jug*.

would not have written his Caesar, because at that moment he would of necessity have lost his sovereign command of his materials. This holds true even for the Greek myths, which to us, who no longer experience but instead evaluate and examine them, recognizing them to be myths and thereby destroying them, have become mummies; and these, bedecked with philosophy and theology, are all too often substituted for what is alive.

That is why, if the artist wants to make use of the fully formed characters he runs into at every turn, if he wants to transform them into subject matter again, he will have to reduce them and hope that he will succeed: he parodies them, that is he consciously puts them in contrast with what they have become. But by this act of parody he recovers his freedom and with it his material, which is now no longer found but invented, for all parody presupposes invention. The dramaturgy of given materials is replaced by the dramaturgy of invented materials. In laughter, man's freedom is manifested, in tears, his necessity; our task today is to demonstrate freedom. The tyrants of this planet are not moved by the works of poets, they yawn at their lamentations. Heroic epics are fairy tales to them. Religious poems put them to sleep. They fear only one thing: our ridicule. That is why parody has crept into every genre, into the novel, into drama, into lyric poetry. Much of painting, of music, has been conquered by parody, and in its wake, over night, often in disguise, the grotesque has made its appearance as well: it is simply suddenly there.

But even that is no match for this hard-boiled age of ours, its bastions are unassailable. Our time has educated the public to see art as a solemn, pathetical, hallowed thing. The comic is considered inferior, dubious, unseemly, unless it allows us to leave the theater glutted with cannibalistic contentment. But as soon as comedy is recognized as a dangerous, muckraking, challenging, moral force, it gets dropped like a hot potato, for art is allowed to be anything it wants, so long as it doesn't disturb.

We writers often hear the reproach that our art is nihilistic. Now of course there really is nihilistic art in our time, but art that looks nihilistic isn't always the genuine item: truly nihilistic art doesn't look nihilistic at all, it is usually considered highly humane, recommended reading for mature youth. A nihilist would have to be quite a bungler for the world to recognize him as such. "Nihilistic," in its common usage, is tantamount to "disturbing." The artist's job now is to make art, not to talk, people say; to create, not to preach. Certainly. But it is getting harder and harder to create purely, however people imagine this is done. Today's humanity resembles a driver at the wheel of his car. He is driving faster and faster, more and more recklessly.

But he doesn't like it when the dismayed passengers shout: "Watch out!" and "There's a stop sign!" "Slow down!" or even "Don't run over that child!" He hates it when someone asks who paid for the car and who provided the gas and oil for this mad race, or even asks to see his driver's license. Unpleasant facts might come to light. What if the car was stolen from a relative, what if gas and oil were squeezed from the passengers themselves, what if it's not gas and oil at all but the blood and sweat of us all, and what if the driver doesn't even have a license; who knows, it might even turn out that he's never driven a car before. That would of course be embarrassing, asking such intrusive questions. So our driver prefers to hear his passengers praise the beauty of the landscape through which he is driving, the silver sheen of a river or the glow of a glacier in the distance, and he loves amusing stories as well, preferably whispered in his ear. But whispering these stories and praising the beautiful landscape is something a writer of our time can no longer do with an easy conscience. Unfortunately he can't get out of the car either, to meet the demand for pure poetry that is being voiced by all the nonpoets. Fear, worry, and above all anger force him to speak.

It would be very nice to close on this emphatic note, a halfway secure exit within the bounds of the not entirely impossible. But it would be dishonest not to ask ourselves if any of this still makes sense, if it wouldn't be much better for us if we practiced the art of silence. I have shown that the theater today is in part a museum—in the best sense of the word, to be sure—and in part a field of experimentation, and I have also tried to give some impression of what these experiments consist of. Now, is the theater capable of fulfilling this second mission? Just as the writing of plays has become more difficult, so has the performing, the rehearsing of these plays. Lack of time alone prevents anything more than, at best, a decent attempt, an initial probe, an advance in some definite direction, perhaps a good one. A play that is more than a conventional effort, that aspires to be an experiment, can no longer be worked out like a theorem at one's desk. Giraudoux's good fortune was Jouvet.* Unfortunately that is an almost unique case. Our repertory theaters are less and less capable of experimentation, less and less able to afford it. The play has to come out as quickly as possible. The museum carries too much weight. Theater, culture, live on the interest of the well-invested intellect, to which nothing can happen any more and for which no royalties need to be

---

*Jean Giraudoux (1882–1944), French dramatist; Louis Jouvet (1887–1951), outstanding French actor and director of the twentieth century, who began his collaboration with Giraudoux in 1928.

paid. With the knowledge of having a Goethe, a Schiller, a Sophocles on their side, the theaters and their public show themselves receptive to modern plays. Preferably only for a premiere. Having heroically discharged one's responsibility, one takes in the next Shakespeare play with a sigh of relief. Nothing to be said against it. All you can do is clear the stage. Make room for the classics. The world of museums is growing, bursting with treasures. The cultures of the cave dwellers haven't been fully explored yet. Let the custodians of future centuries take an interest in our art, when our turn comes around. So it doesn't really matter whether something new is added, something new is written. The demands made of the artist by aesthetics are growing from day to day, nothing but perfection is wanted, the perfection that is read into the classics—a mere hint of retrogression, and the artist is dropped. Thus a climate is created in which literature can only be studied but no longer made. How does the artist survive in an educated world, the world of the literate? A question that depresses me, and to which I do not have an answer. Perhaps by writing mystery novels, by making art where no one expects it. Literature must become so light that it will weigh nothing on the scale of today's literary criticism: that is the only way it will regain its true weight.

Automobile and Railroad Nations

Political systems differ primarily depending on whether they are subject to the patronage of freedom or of justice. A political system that upholds freedom as its supreme principle is comparable to a social order that grew out of the evolution of street traffic. In the beginning, this happy pedestrian society enjoyed unlimited freedom; everyone left his house whenever he wanted and wandered off wherever he wished; not even roads were needed, footpaths were sufficient; to bridge a stream, a tree was cut down, and where a river could not be forded, ropes were strung tightly from bank to bank. It was not until coaches were developed that roads and bridges became necessary, but agreement could still be reached by means of simple calls. Time flowed at a leisurely pace, multiple collisions were virtually unheard of. Then the railroad was invented, tracks traversed the land. Railroad owners were now in charge, regulating the times of departure and arrival, setting the fares. And then the automobile was invented, the symbol of freedom. It rattled up and down dusty roads, killing flocks of chickens; the farmers threw stones after it, but already the roads were being widened and paved and the chickens stopped crossing the road. Highways were built. The railroad degenerated into a poor man's substitute for a car and eventually went to ruin. Grass grew over the tracks, the last railroad baron hanged himself from a signal light, his monocle fell on a railroad tie and shattered. But automobile traffic was producing its own problems. The accident rate had risen to a frightening degree. The men running the Traffic Bureau, still a ramshackle barrack, were gradually forced to consider introducing some kind of traffic code, even though, as a result, freedom would be put in jeopardy. The still-youthful director of the Traffic Bureau earnestly argued that the ordinance requiring drivers to stay in the right lane and pass on the left was merely a voluntary agreement among free human beings, that it was merely a regulation, not a law, that it

could just as well be reversed—driving on the left, passing on the right—
that each person entering into this agreement was doing so for his or her own
security, that it wasn't a moral and certainly not a religious program that
might offend persons of a different faith, that a traffic accident didn't happen
because one person's driving was evil and another one's good or both of their
driving was evil, or because one person drove like a Christian and the other
like a heathen, but because one or both of them had made a wrong turn, or
because one or both of them had lost control of a vehicle. Nor, he continued,
did the traffic code determine a traffic user's status except in purely quanti-
tative terms. A driver had to be qualified to drive; that is, he had to be of a certain age and in possession of certain physical abilities; an infant and a blind
person were intrinsically incapable of driving a car, but the character traits of
any given individual were not at issue. Reasonable though his explanations
were, the protests from all sectors of the freedom-loving population set off a
political crisis. The Union of Nursing Mothers pointed out that driving a car
was easier than walking, and the Lighthouse for the Blind argued that blind
people, too, could steer a car if specially trained dogs were seated next to
them. The traffic code was overturned by a plebiscite. Traffic accidents multiplied, whereupon two parties developed, one that consistently drove on the
right side of the road, and another one that stubbornly drove on the left side.
The left-side drivers were secretly enthusiastic about railroad trains, since
these, too, drove on the left. The two parties collided in a thunderous head-
on crash, a huge and bloody mess, all in all. Inevitably, the point of view that
prevailed in the end was that freedom did not consist in being able to drive as
one wished, but in being allowed to drive if one owned a car. The left-side
drivers acquiesced, gritting their teeth. Freedom fell back upon ownership.
He who owned the best and fastest car was now the freest of the free, and so
everyone wanted to become freer. But a person to whom freedom means
owning a car will tend continually to get into conflict with the traffic code.
He will accept it intellectually, but emotionally he will reject it. A person who
owns a car that can speed along at a hundred and sixty miles an hour cannot
see why he shouldn't pass a car that can only make a hundred and twenty-five,
and so he passes that car in a curve, and promptly meets with an onrushing
truck. The man or woman at the steering wheel is an incalculable element in
any system of traffic regulation. This person relishes his freedom, and finds
perfect freedom only when he is in his car, his foot on the pedal, zooming
away. The Traffic Bureau, relocated to an office at Traffic Police Headquarters, tried to tighten the traffic code by introducing the stop sign, a measure
that succeeded only when drivers were informed that noncompliance would
force the Bureau to augment the Traffic Police Corps, a measure they were

eventually forced to take anyway, for despite the stop sign, the slaughter on the road was mounting to the count of tens of thousands of dead and hundreds of thousands of severely injured. Although everyone cursed the increasing number of ordinances, fines, and punishments, these were nevertheless accepted, since accidents were inevitably the other person's fault, and even when the punishments became more and more draconian and drivers guilty of the most flagrant traffic violations were sentenced to death (if they had survived on the road) by being flattened in their cars with metal compactors, the public at large still did not protest. Strangely, now that the quest for freedom entailed the danger of becoming a victim of the traffic police, the temptation to violate the traffic code grew, and the most dangerous traffic desperados were celebrated as heroes of freedom. The chasm between the traffic users and the Traffic Bureau and its police deepened. A plebiscite prevented the introduction of a forty miles per hour speed limit, even though the enormous increase of automobiles did not permit anyone to drive faster than twenty miles per hour. Traffic jams, once an exception, were now the rule. In addition, the smog occasionally stopped traffic altogether; dead men and women sat upright clutching their steering wheels, and only the happy circumstance that everyone had one or more cars—at least a Cadillac or a Rolls-Royce, a Mercedes and a Porsche, or an Opel Monza and an Opel Rekord, or just a VW or just an Impala, but one of the really old models, and so on— this alone could make up for the fact that pretty soon a driving permit was obtainable only on certain days, which were determined by the final digit on one's license plate. In the beginning it was once every ten days, then every ten weeks, then every ten months, and then never again. Traffic jams were now no longer the rule but a permanent condition. The interminable honking had died down. Only the howling of fire engines and police cars continued. They couldn't budge, and amid the packed rows of queued-up cars among towering automobile graveyards, survivors had set up house in their wrecked cars and had even planted little garden plots next to the clogged highways. These gardens, however, were endangered by the newest cars (now finally equipped with catalytic converters), which were steadily advancing as they were pushed forth from the fully automated factories, despite the fact that no one was buying them. For years, Parliament had been convening in an underground garage. In the center, inside a Rolls-Royce, sat the head of the Traffic Bureau, surrounded by the members of Parliament, officially called Traffic Users Representatives, each of them in a vintage automobile. There were three parties: one that was categorically opposed to any kind of traffic regulation whatsoever, a second one that was stubbornly trying to propose a speed limit of at least fifty miles per hour, sixty-five on the highways, and a third party, the smallest one, assembled in a minibus, the Pedestrians' Party, which was suspected of sympathizing with the railroad party that ran the government in the neighboring country, an utterly incomprehensible rumor, since pedestrian ways were not only tabooed in the neighboring country but also forbidden. But in reality, Parliament, which signaled its approval with blinking lights and its protest with tooting horns, had long since lost its influence; state power had long since passed to the head of the Traffic Bureau; the blinkings and tootings of Parliament were completely ineffectual. But the power of the head of the Traffic Bureau was illusory also. In reality, power rested with the Bureau itself, which gradually became the supreme authority for the entire country—not just for the traffic police, but also for the fire department, emergency hospitals, highway churches (including a highway mosque), rest stops, traffic education services in maternity wards, daycare centers, bordellos, erotica outlets, saunas, retirement homes, primary and secondary schools, high schools, and universities. The number of Traffic Bureau officials assumed an astronomical magnitude. The various functions and jurisdictions were so densely intertwined that no one had any idea who was actually in charge; even so, the Bureau somehow managed to govern itself. It was impossible to tell, for example, whether it was the Traffic Bureau or one of its subordinate departments, the Ministry of Defense, that arranged to have the overgrown railroad tracks cleared and restored. On the one hand, the civil service apparatus had to be flexible; on the other hand, freedom, though it was no longer practicable, had at least to be defended. Now the Ministry of Defense could count on the automobile plants, which would have been rendered useless by the saturated market had they not begun to produce cross-country vehicles and armored cars, which were not restricted to the street system. The Army, therefore, was well equipped, but the heavy nuclear rockets could only be transported by rail, since the roads were congested. Thus, suitable railroads were needed by the Traffic Bureau, for the transportation of civil servants, and for the transportation of the Army's nuclear bombs, and these railroads had to be imported from the railroad nation—and not just railroads, but also gasoline. The two rival nations complemented each other magnificently. The railroad nation built railroads, had gasoline, and did not produce tanks, while the automobile nation had a tank industry but no railroads and no gasoline. Its garages alongside the highways were useless, but at the border of the railroad nation, tanks could be exchanged for gasoline and railroad cars according to an exact code that guaranteed to both armies at all times precisely the same number of tanks and railroad cars and the same amount of gasoline: a balance of terror. Thus, both nations reached a political dead end. They were supported by nothing but slogans. Only the Traffic Bureau and the General Railroad Management sustained them in a kind of pseudo-existence. Their antagonism was purely ideological.

If the premise of the automobile nation was freedom, that of the railroad nation was justice, its doctrine being that only the railroad is just. Everyone must keep to the scheduled departures and arrivals, thus upholding the resolutions of the Railroad Management, without which there would be no railroad, for the railroad is the result of a revolution: indeed, it was the advent of the railroad that started the Industrial Age. The railroad system depends on tracks. Unlike the automobile system, it requires planning. The automobile is nothing but a reactionary development of the carriage, but the railroad is something fundamentally new. It cannot be bought, everyone can use it, it doesn't need steering, it is steered by tracks. It cannot be driven by its users; it does away with the inhumane division into licensed and unlicensed drivers, and establishes the humane division into passengers and railroad personnel. A steam-powered train needs only three functionaries: the conductor, the stoker, and the engineer; an electric train needs only two. This ratio is nothing short of ideal, for a train transports hundreds of passengers, while a car holds five or six at the most. Also, the Traffic Bureau's lack of organization and the abusive tactics of their police are well known; it is self-evident that a tight organization of railroad workers, gatemen, switchmen, signalmen, stationmasters and central stationmasters provides a security that bears no relationship to the insecurity of the road. Such was the ethos of the railroad nation. But of course this doctrine did not win the hearts and minds of the people right away. The neighboring nation with the freedom warranted by the automobile seemed at first to have the better argument. A Traffic Bureau was founded, roads were built, cars were introduced and even constructed. But the country's enormous expanse favored the railroad. The locomotive began to gain ground in its race with the automobile. Privately at first, and subject to the Traffic Bureau's jurisdiction. Travelers were assigned to different classes, depending on their material means—first class for the government, second class for the rich, third class for the middle class, and fourth class for the proletariat. Even so, the private railroad system didn't work. The schedules were too complicated, people missed their connections, one landowner would ask for a special time of departure, another would demand a different one. But a schedule has to be dependable. In order for the schedule to be dependable, the organization in charge of making the schedule dependable has to be dependable. Making the organization dependable is the task of the General Railroad

Management. If the latter is to be dependable, it must be infallible, omnipotent. The Traffic Bureau, an indecisive institution to begin with, was unable to prevent the General Railroad Management from fomenting a revolution with the help of the railroad workers. The Traffic Bureau was overthrown. The head of the Traffic Bureau fled to the neighboring country, and the General Director of Railroads assumed power. Private automobile traffic, pedestrianism, coaches, and cars were prohibited, every street was covered with tracks, and the country's industry was converted to the production of trains. In the name of justice, the classless railroad was introduced, and everyone had to travel fourth class. Not everyone, of course. After all, the General Railroad Management had to use the train once in a while: you can't have management without inspections. It wasn't an easy problem to solve. The "Railroads for All" principle was sacrosanct; on the other hand, the General Railroad Management could not be expected to travel together with the people, for its task was to manage the people's railroad, not to mingle with the people. Fortunately there were still a few railroad cars, dating back to the days of the old Traffic Bureau, that were of a suitable class for the General Railroad Management. Thus, since the General Railroad Management consisted of the General Director of Railroads, the General Vice Director of Railroads, and seven Railroad Directors as well as seven Railroad Director Trainees, it was possible to equip every train with a first-class car, a first-class sleeping car, and a first-class dining car for the General Director of Railroads; a first-class conference car for the General Railroad Management; a first-class car with a second-class sleeping car and a second-class dining car for the General Vice Director of Railroads; and in addition seven second-class cars plus two second-class sleeping cars for the seven Railroad Directors, as well as a second-class car with a third-class dining car for the Railroad Director Trainees, to which were added a third-class car and a fourth-class dining car for the railroad engineers. Since the locomotives were incapable of pulling more than twenty cars, there wouldn't have been any cars for the people, but since the General Director of Railroads absolutely never, and the General Vice Director of Railroads practically never, and the Railroad Directors almost never, and only one Railroad Director Trainee occasionally, even if rarely, rode in a train, it was possible to attach two or even three additional cars, all of them fourth-class cars whose benches had been removed. They were so heavily booked that it would have been impossible to sit. And so everyone stood pressed belly to belly, backside to backside, backside to belly, without having any choice in the matter, since no one was able to move. But because justice demanded that every municipality must be accessible by train, the railroad net had to be constantly expanded. This, however, made it impossible to acquire tanks, which, as we know, were so urgently needed for the defense of the country; and there were other problems, too, which the national plan had never foreseen since they were inherent in the plan itself. The passengers of the two or three over-crowded fourth-class cars at the end of the trains had a tendency to wonder why there had to be twenty usually empty railroad cars rolling ahead of them. When the crowding got excessive, they would move into the roomier cars. Once a passenger had even been seen in the first class car of the General Vice Director of Railroads. The General Management was forced to call in the secret police, for the conductors proved to be all but powerless. The impertinent passengers were arrested, the prisons and labor camps began to fill up, taking some of the pressure off the railroads. It was in the cities that the principle of justice was most difficult to enforce, since one of its fundamental tenets was that there was an inherent injustice in walking. Walking to work, to the supermarket, to the theater, or to the movies took longer for some than for others; therefore the use of streetcars was made obligatory, the idea being that this was the only way to overcome injustice. The ultimate effect of this thesis was that, while there wasn't a street without a streetcar, the streetcars had to stop at every door, which made them extremely slow, so that taking a streetcar took much longer than walking, especially as the streets before long were so full of streetcars that city people were forced to walk, not next to the streetcars, which was strictly forbidden, but inside the streetcars from one car to the next. Justice put the whole country to a halt, for after a while all railroad traffic had to be suspended; since the country was producing nothing but railroad cars and streetcars, the railroad lines, too, were soon crammed full of trains that were standing around motion-less, puffing steam, so that people were forced to walk from train to train. But since no one was allowed to walk alongside the trains or through the twenty cars of the General Railroad Management, people walked on the roofs of the railroad cars, sometimes for hours, until they would reach a train that could actually run for a few miles. Thus, eventually people stopped traveling altogether. The country came to depend on illegal trade, on farmers who smuggled groceries in wheelbarrows to the black market, which was only accessible by an arduous trek along the roofs of the trains or by working one's way through the overcrowded streetcars. The theaters and movie theaters remained empty: they were too inaccessible. On television one could see trains racing across wide plains, through winding tunnels and over viaducts, and cheerfully dining workers in the dining cars. These images were interrupted by traffic reports about accidents on the streets of the neighboring country. But in reality, a turning point had long since been reached. A General Railroad Management that wants to maintain control of a country must be capable of locomotion; a motionless army of railroad officials is powerless. At first they drove around in the cross-country vehicles they had bought from the automobile nation; they certainly had enough gasoline. Then special roads were built for the General Railroad Management, strictly off-limits to the general population. The first luxury limousines appeared, then more and more chauffeured limos, a development that led to the first summit meeting, motivated less by political necessity than by a kind of political nostalgia. The General Director of Railroads longed to ride in a train again, and the head of the Traffic Bureau longed for a drive in a car, and because the tracks of the railroad nation were crammed full of trains and the roads of the automobile nation were stuffed full of cars, the General Director of Railroads and the head of the Traffic Bureau agreed to a trade of privileges that would permit the latter to drive a car in the railroad country for a week and the former to ride in a train in the automobile country, also for a week. They both met at the border, exchanged a few polite words; then the General Director of Railroads rode in a train in the automobile country and the head of the Traffic Bureau drove a car in the railroad country, and when they met again, the General Director of Railroads playfully called the head of the Traffic Bureau a General Director of Railroads and the head of the Traffic Bureau adroitly returned the compliment by calling the General Manager of Railroads a Traffic Bureau Director. The railroad and automobile rides were repeated, pretty soon the General Vice Director of Railroads and the Vice Director of the Traffic Bureau participated, and then the Railroad Director and the office managers of the Traffic Bureau, followed by further civil servants. Eventually half the Railroad officials resided in the automobile country, while half the Traffic Bureau officials lived in the railroad country; furthermore, the railroad lines needed by both countries for the transportation of nuclear bombs were connected, whereupon each country kept its bombs in the other's territory, thus maintaining the balance of terror. Gradually the population, too, got attuned to the new way of thinking. While there were mounting demands for a return to the purely automobile-related or the original railroad-oriented way of thinking, a strangely lackadaisical mood befell the two countries. In the railroad country, black market dealers rented third-class and even second-class cars, someone even succeeded in opening a first-class dining car restaurant, while among the automobile graveyards in the automobile country the first horse-drawn trams were beginning to flourish. Freedom and justice are complementary concepts; freedom is no more feasible without justice than justice is possible without freedom.

The Brain

If modern cosmology imagines that this world was born of nothingness, as the explosion of a dimensionless point within which not only all the matter and all the energy of the cosmos but also its time and space were compressed, a construction that is only mathematically possible, then we can also, instead of this purely hypothetical point, imagine a pure brain. A brain without any idea of an external world, because none exists; and just as the cosmos took sixteen billion years to reach its present condition, this brain has sixteen billion years to go on thinking, and more than that, it has all the time it will take the cosmos to vanish into the void or reverse its course until, with a great, gradual shrinkage of space, it collapses back into that dimensionless point, one trillion years after its explosion, give or take a couple of months. At first the brain will only feel, and because there is nothing outside itself that it could feel, it will feel only itself, but since nothing is stored in it, it will not be able to feel anything other than emptiness—it will feel that it feels nothing. In the beginning there will be dread, pure horror. It is uncertain how long this condition might last, maybe millions of years, maybe just a fraction of a second, it is a living human brain we are imagining, the most mysterious and intricate configuration known to us, a galaxy of circuits, of interconnected neurons, divided into cerebellum, brainstem, midbrain, cerebrum, it will immediately or eventually feel the electric current, the ions flowing through it, and since it feels them as impulses, it will feel and then not feel and then feel again, with horrible regularity. But because the ions do not transport any information, because this brain is all there is and nothing exists beside it, no space and no time, the brain will begin to think, which of course should not be taken literally. It possesses neither language, nor images, nor sounds. Its thinking is more like a kind of feeling. It will explore feelings—of time, to begin with, a feeling arising from dread. It feels out the present, the impulses flowing through it, one after the other, on and on, rising out of nothingness; and then the past into which the impulses vanish after they have occurred. Memory begins to develop, the knowledge that impulses come and go, came and went. But the feeling of time adds to dread the fear that time might pass away and leave only naked terror. In panic fear of losing time, the brain will ceaselessly try to feel every nuance of time, chase it down again and again, and because it feels only impulses, it will feel out the series of binary numbers and keep on counting in order to elude the constant advance of time. With every number it counts, the brain will move away from fear, but each time it stops counting, the edifice of numbers collapses, and dread returns. At first the brain will start counting again from the beginning, over and over again, and then it will remember the number up to which it counted and go on counting from there, on and on. But since we are assuming a human brain, all feelings within it are preprogrammed. It will eventually feel boredom as it goes on counting, and so, in addition to the feelings of dread and fear, a third feeling, boredom, will come, and out of boredom a constant attempt to do something other than count. The brain separates numbers from impulses and feels out rhythms, until these culminate in a wild drum concerto, spurred on, at first, by fear of dread and then driven by curiosity, the desire to make something new. Feeling out tones in the rhythms, the fifths, the octaves, the various keys, music itself, it thinks music without knowing that it is thinking, for it lacks language and thus cannot know that in composing music it is thinking, it only feels an intoxication of felt sounds, into which it feels an order and a first feeling of joy at having established an order—for an infinite series of numbers was not yet an order—and so, in the measureless time it has at its disposal, the brain teeters from tonal to atonal music, composes without hearing what it is composing, but as soon as it stops, it falls back into dread, a plunge into hell. Dread is always present, and can only be endured as long as the brain thinks something against dread. But something new is added to the dread of nothingness. Because the feelings of boredom, curiosity, and joy keep collapsing into nothingness, the feeling of impotence arises. Impotence produces anger, then rage, and finally sadness. But one day—after millions of years, after a billion, two billion, many billions of years, or else right away, as an immediate response to anger, rage, and sorrow?—the brain will discover "itself," the "I" that thinks and thinks of itself as a Something that is confronted with dread, that is no longer dread but feels dread and that was able to feel out time and number and developed rhythm and music out of counting. But now that the brain has bumped into itself, now that it feels itself as an "I" into which time plunges and from which time glides away, the brain becomes pure feeling. All its awakened feelings are set in motion, start quarreling with each other, joy, impotence, anger, curiosity, sadness, a storm of feelings, emotions in search of their reason, for only thought can provide them with a reason, and so, to endure this assault of emotions, the brain clings to the first object it found, and in which was contained all the protection it has ever had against dread. The brain will cling to numbers. Curiosity will make it examine what numbers are, it will think the even and uneven binary numbers, and then the zero. Glad and proud of this discovery, it will find the negative numbers, its imagination catches fire in contemplating the series of binary numbers, an explosion of mathematics through logic, the brain comes upon the irrational numbers, prime numbers, powers of numbers, square roots, imaginary numbers, its thinking meets with difficulties, it feels despair when it fails to find a solution and boundless joy when it finds it, its imagination becomes more and more audacious, it feels out the plane, feels analytical geometry, analytical stereometry, and then, boldly, space as a pure mathematical object, the brain effortlessly feels out non-Euclidian geometry, because, unhampered by visual perception, it can construct freely, and now the brain's mathematical thinking advances further, unfolds with inexorable logic. But its flight is merely apparent. Wedded to quantity, to form, to structures, finally, to functions, and so on, in short to pure mathematical concepts, it has built an enormous mental edifice, but this edifice offers no genuine other, it is not detached from the brain's thinking but, rather, immanent in that thinking, merely the mirror of the brain's thought, and so the brain tries to conceive of something separate from itself, an otherness. Desperately, because, when it does not think, it stands again and again before the bottomless abyss, which it has tried and continues to try to fill with all the mathematical objects it has thought of, until, out of sheer despair at not finding a way out of the prison of its mental constructions, it thinks up matter along with space, no longer just as a mathematical construct, but also as a space outside itself, enclosing the brain as well as the matter conceived by the brain, from the first infinitesimal particles through the virtually endless series of ever larger particles up to the quarks, then the stable and unstable elementary particles, leptons, mesons, and baryons, protons and neutrons, the atom, the elements, the molecules, the carbon compounds, interstellar matter, the nebulae, their condensations into suns and planets, galaxies, quasars, universes, stable and disintegrating, infinitely expanding or collapsing universes, antimaterial universes, universes with particles that move faster than light. Worlds within worlds vanish without an echo. But just as everything seems doomed to be perpetually devoured by the abyss of dread, after several millions or after several billions of years, who can say for sure, there dawns in the brain, in that enigmatic "I," that which it has been seeking: not just something it can conceive as being outside itself, but something outside itself that can feel and think, a second "I." But what does it consist of? With what does its "I" think? It has atoms consisting of a cloud of particles, and molecules consisting of atoms, its "I" must consist of a complicated arrangement of atoms and molecules, its "I" must be something spatial, a far more complicated formation than anything it has thought until now. Unbeknownst to the brain, new patterns flow from its stem and midbrain and blend into its deliberations. It peruses the thirty amino acids, by no means just mathematically—that would be impossible given the enormous number of possible variations (a figure with 190 zeros) and the limited time at its disposal, one trillion years, 10^{17} seconds, a 1 with 17 zeros—but in a selective fashion, playfully, piqued by the impossibility of the task, composing with molecules as if with musical notes. Improbably but actually the brain strikes upon the primitive cell and senses within it something it had felt at the beginning along with the primordial dread, the very feeling in which that dread resided, but of which the brain was unconscious until now, after this enormous detour: Being. And as the primitive cell divides and subdivides into two, four, eight, sixteen parts, and so forth, the brain thinks up life and the system that makes life possible, the sun and the planets, the earth with its moon, the original oceans, a soup of primitive cells. But the more the primitive cells divide, the more frequently imprecisions take place in their reproduction, and this imprecision also divides, and the brain thinks up evolution, and starts playing it through. Just as it once counted impulses in order not to lose its first concept, time, it now counts reproductions; and each time a reproduction fails so thoroughly that no further reproduction is possible, the brain suddenly pauses. The mightier the swell of the stream of life, the more frequent the interruption: nothingness. Feeling begins to count the intervals of life: death. It integrates nothingness into life, but in conceiving death, it conceives the murderer: Being is contradictory. The brain feels that it has a right to this Being, but mathematics also is, but only in the brain's thoughts, these are not outside the brain, are not, like the brain, part of Being, but the life conceived by the brain is within it, too, the protista and protozoa, fungi, microorganisms, worms, nematodes, articulates, molluscs, echinoderms, vertebrates, fish, reptiles, and birds, self-devouring evolution striding from death to death, from murder to murder, battening on its own ordure, all of it is within the brain, thought by the brain, not outside it. Who thinks life must think death, being and nothingness together. The brain is forced to think a doubly nonsensical world, an absurdity in thought and an absurdity in itself, a world that is not a right or a wrong, but a useful or a deadly, a hell. The mathematical world has become a world of values, the brain has thought up a world without comprehending it. Now the brain is gripped by a tremendous urge to play, insatiably and irrepressibly it plays and performs life as a monstrous grotesque unfolding within the brain. Now the brain is confused. It has the impression that there is a second brain within it, a brain within the brain, an intricate mutuality of brains, an "I" within the "I," and as it thinks that, the whole evolution comes plunging down upon it like an enormous torrent, all the mammals at once, hordes of trampling mammoths, mastodons, elephants, rhinoceroses, swarms of wild cats, herds of buffalo, packs of wolves, antelopes speeding across the prairie, bats and vampires darkening the sky, spectre-lemurs and orangutans clambering through the jungles, roaring baboons, screeching chimpanzees, gorillas thumping their chests, a neighing and bleating, mooing, howling, barking, bellowing, trumpeting, hissing, and spitting fills the air, until the torrent suddenly halts. After playing through the whole evolution of mammals in an almost absentminded manner and with unbelievable facility, the brain has stopped short right after designing the primates. It is not quite sure where it made the mistake, it happened in one of the apes, a mutation, an ape without fur, something an elephant can afford, its physical volume being greater than the extent of its surface, so that the sun cannot burn it, but this naked ape, driven out of the trees by the giant apes, has no choice but to throw itself into the lakes bordering on the savannas by the edge of the rain forests. For hundreds of thousands of years—a second for the brain—the ape scarcely survives, for the lakes are full of crocodiles, but then, as the lakes dry out, the new creature hops into the savanna. Its long back and powerful legs, developed by all that swimming, enable it to stand upright, and upright it peers across the plain, and though it was once a gatherer of nuts and fruit, and then lived off fish and frogs in the lakes, now it must become a hunter. But it is ill equipped for that, never before has the brain thought up a more pitiable being, and only an inexplicable curiosity on the brain's part sustains this mental abortion, this all too evident idiocy. But nevertheless: just as in the brain's beginning there was dread, this creature's beginning is haunted by fear, it is more threatened by the environment, and hence more fearful, than any other creature. But the brain can feel its way into this being more easily than into any of its other creatures, a most annoying fact. Yet the stubbornness with which this being tries to survive fascinates the brain, seduces it into sustaining the being in its thoughts and thinking it further. Naked, without fur, the being is drawn to fire, and by taming the fire and dragging it off to the caves, it overcomes its fear for the first time, for it has found the security of the womb, the cave, with the fire inside burning high, settling to a glimmer, and rising high again, a source of fear for the beasts of prey and a shelter for the being, but a shelter from which it bursts forth again and again, a dash into danger, for after taming the fire, the being has come to love danger as something alluring, seductive. It no longer goes hunting, it sets out for war, first with stones, then with clubs, stone axes, spears, then it invents the bow and arrow, war sharpens its thinking. The large beasts are its enemies, not just the beasts of prey, but also animals like the buffalo, the giant stag, or the mammoth. War has its rules—you don't hunt a deer if a saber-toothed tiger is nearby—the being is still inferior to most of the larger animals, but when there is a fight, the struggle claims victims on both sides, the animals' as well as the being's. If a member of its horde is trampled to death by a buffalo, the being will avenge him by killing a buffalo with its primitive spear, no matter whether it is the same buffalo or another. A herd of buffalo is fighting with a herd of beings. Just as the being thinks it has avenged its kind by killing a buffalo, it thinks that a buffalo hurtling another being into the air is avenging a buffalo stabbed to death by a being; and though this feeling with which it kills isn't really revenge yet (the brain, too, doesn't know what that is) but rather an intensification of rage (the brain, too, feels it): what the being feels toward the animal is greed, fear, enmity, hatred. All rights to the strongest is the only commandment: the strong kills the weak—openly if attacked, or from an ambush if his females are at risk—and if the weak kills the strong, he in turn is the stronger one. Thus, killing becomes the vehicle of evolution, the beings stalk one another in the cave, to sleep is to take a great risk. Nor is nature friendly toward the being, the lightning bolt threatens it personally, the rapids seek personally to destroy it, as does the rock that comes thundering down from the mountaintop. The being takes everything personally. But to see oneself surrounded on all sides by enemies and hostile forces is to live in perpetual fear, which the being can only overcome by opposing that fear with aggression. The being becomes the most aggressive of all the beasts of prey, because it is physically the weakest. But as its aggressiveness sharpens its mind and shapes its language, consisting of whistles and cries of warning and menace, and as its memory develops along with its thinking, and its associations along with its memory, and its imagination along with its associative range, gradually the being's feeling of "I" turns into the concept of "I," the first step away from the animal, for while animals possess consciousness, they have only a feeling of selfhood. They know danger and how to avoid it. They can distinguish between what is good for them and what is bad, what is dead or alive. But nothing is abstract for them, everything is concrete: danger, for the gazelle, is a lion, and for the lion, the gazelle is food. There is no death in this world, only dead animals, and an animal is quite capable of feeling that another animal is no longer alive—the corpse doesn't move, doesn't play, or participate—but no animal is able to comprehend death: the animal lives in a concrete world without concepts. In discovering its "I" as a concept, the being understands that the other members of its horde also possess an "I." And it sees this "I" not only in beings of its own kind but also in animals, in fact every thing becomes a person, an "I" distinct from the being's "I": beast, tree, water, rock, lightning, all of nature. But the being also understands that it must die—its first "scientific discovery," the first conscious logical inference about its own existence; for this realization of its own inevitable death is a generalization, a transposition into the realm of logic, an abstraction, a reasoning process. But the simpler a syllogism, the greater its impact. The being's consciousness is transformed by the discovery of its mortality. By coming upon the concept of death (without knowing that it is a concept), the being has excluded itself from the animal world (without knowing that it has done so). At first it loses the courage with which it fought within its own horde and waged war against the animals and against nature. Fear can be overcome by stealth and caution, but the fear of death is unconquerable. It strikes the being with overwhelming force. The being threatens to founder on this shattering discovery, to become an animal again, to return to the womb of its origins. But the brain, which is thinking this unhappy being, feels caught in the act by its own creation, for the brain itself has long been aware of that supreme paradox at the core of existence, its transience, which the being has now stumbled upon. This fear of transience was there for the brain from the beginning, the fear of the void, dread itself, and now the being knows it, too. The brain never overcame this first feeling of boundless emptiness. Now it finds itself staring fear in the face, the face of its own brain-child cowering by the wall of its cave. But as the brain thinks its way deeper into the being, it feels the being twice, as man and as woman. She experiences death more immediately than man, who experiences it in killing, as something immediate, as an event in which he is entangled, as something opposite to life, as an accident that threatens him always and will one day be inescapable. But woman gives birth to life that is destined to die. What comes out of her womb is part of her and is as mortal as she is. Death is a problem for man, not for woman. The fact that he is mortal puts man in a panic. Man rebels against death, woman accepts it, and because she is able to accept it, she becomes stronger than man. While man stands powerless before his first scientific discovery—the knowledge that he is mortal—woman conceals from him her own discovery, the second one: that the origin of life is not birth but procreation. That is her secret, and upon this secret rests the dominion of woman over man, which she establishes gradually: the matriarchate. Animals have no notion of the causal connection between procreation and birth, for to make such an inference requires far more complex reasoning than it does to conclude that the being is mortal. By withholding this knowledge from man, woman casts him back into the animal kingdom. And worse than that: man does not only become an animal that knows it must die, he also loses his biological function. For thousands of years he humiliated woman with his unrestrained sexuality; now the woman humiliates him. She leaves him in his ignorance, but lets him partake of her faith, for again and again she gives birth to new life. Embraced and caught in the cycles of nature, she "believes" the soul into existence. The weapons and traps invented by man were the products of experience. Not that he moved from the throwing of stones to the slingshot, the arrow, the hand-ax, and spear—let alone such a sophisticated weapon as the boomerang—without thought and without observation; but it was experience alone that guided him, not "scientific thinking," not "physics." Man's concepts, too, evolved with experience: ax, spear, animal, food, woman, man, child, life, death. But man will not be able to bear his existence—which has become finite with the discovery of his death, that empirical terminus—unless he finds a way of surviving, and to do so he must overcome the evidence of experience. But he can do that only through woman; it is she who knows how to hurl thought beyond experience. In the magical world she creates for man and that is her dominion, she makes nature double by infusing it with soul. Humanity now sees itself as made of mortal body and deathless soul. The human being becomes a metaphysician in order to survive. But the concept of immortality is still too abstract. When Odysseus goes to the entrance of Hades on Circe's counsel and slashes a lamb and a ewe,* letting their black blood stream into the votive pit, "the souls gathered, stirring out of Erebos, brides and young men, and men grown old in pain, and tender girls whose hearts were new to grief; many were there, too, torn by brazen lanceheads, battle-slain, bearing still their bloody gear. From every side they came and sought the pit with rustling cries." This description of the dead, which the brain will eventually make when it thinks up Homer and the *Odyssey* is probably close to the human being's first notions of the soul. It is a ghost, the world is full of ghosts, those of dead humans and those of dead animals.

---

*In book 11 of Homer's *Odyssey*.

From now on, the struggle of man against man and the war against the animals will be fought on two fronts: this world and the world beyond, although the "Beyond" is not quite beyond yet, but lies embedded in the here and now. If a human being kills a buffalo or a lion, he avenges the souls of his horde members who were once trampled by a buffalo or devoured by a lion; but if a human being is killed by an animal, that is revenge for the soul of an animal who was killed by a human. And if a man kills the chief of his horde to put himself in his place, the dead man's soul will take its revenge by killing the new chief. Hate has become revenge, and revenge becomes a metaphysical duty. For if a man fallen in a fight with another man or in the war against the animals is not avenged, his soul can cause harm, it can send diseases or misfortunes. Thus, humans are threatened not only by dead humans, but also by dead animals. The angry ghosts must be placated. The human being can surmount the fear produced by his first scientific discovery, but only by exposing himself to an even greater terror: the world of the ghosts "beyond," whose power reaches into the visible world. All of man's technical abilities are useless, stone axes and arrows are powerless against ghosts. The women know what to do. Still exposed to the insatiable lust of men, constantly pregnant, giving birth, and suckling their young, they invent art. Since the image has not yet been distinguished from what it represents, the first cave paintings are produced. The soul of a panther creeping into the cave to attack sleeping humans, or the soul of the ancient first mother of the horde, find the cave already occupied by their kind and are frightened away. He who possesses the image controls what the image depicts. Out of magic, art evolves, and not just painting: the hostile animal souls are invoked with dances in animal masks and dispelled by drumming. On the hither side of things, human beings have developed such effective weapons and traps that the animal world has been pushed back, the war between man and animal has become a hunt of animals by men, and the ice ages and other catastrophes have created an environment in which human beings can survive much better than the animals. When the glaciers recede, the humans are able to expand their territory. Gradually the first settlements develop, hamlets surrounded by thornbushes. While the men hunt, the women gather; while men invent weapons, women expand their knowledge of nature, of edible and inedible fruit, of poisons and medicines, and woman, too, learns how to kill. She creates the first culture, weaves the first patterns, applies the first ornaments, and now that the forests, marshes, jungles, and savannas are full of ghosts, full of souls that are hungry for blood and demand sacrifice, woman carries out the first ritual acts. She develops metaphysics beyond its rudimentary beginnings. To the imagination, once it has soared past the limits of experience, everything conceivable is real: the women imagine goddesses, deathless female beings. They imagine a cosmological dynasty, with a mother goddess presiding over all things; she makes women give birth and makes animals spawn, foal, and litter, it is from her womb that the waters gush forth and plants sprout and burgeon; she is Mother Earth, her daughters are the goddesses of the sun and the moon, perpetually reborn from her womb and perpetually returning to her. Beneath these principal goddesses reign the hosts of the animal goddesses, always lusting for blood, and the goddesses of revenge, who guide those souls whose bodies have not been avenged, appeasable only by ritual human and animal sacrifices performed by the priestesses of Mother Earth. But in the same degree to which the matriarchate extends into the beyond, it also arranges the hither world to its advantage. The chief of the horde has long since been deprived of his power, the eldest male receives the commands of the priestess of Mother Earth, sexuality is regulated with complicated taboos. Society becomes more complex. The first commandment is issued: thou shalt not kill a woman. Woman is necessary. She gives birth, she is holy, man has only one function: to protect her and to procure food; he is useful. Both must live. The mistress and her servant. The man learns to till the soil and tame animals. He becomes a farmer or herdsman. Cain and Abel. The herdsman is more important for woman than the farmer, for the herdsman protects the horde ruled by woman by protecting his animals from the wild beasts that still prowl around the kraal, he is herdsman and warrior in one. But man has found a new enemy. The old one, the animal, has been conquered, now the victor takes up arms against the victor. Cain kills Abel, man kills man. In the legend it is the enslaved farmer, dragging his plow, who kills the privileged herdsman—the first murder, for murder is only possible when there is a law. On the heels of the first murder comes the first treason. A woman reveals to a man the secret of paternity. Man recovers his biological meaning. Here begins the revolution of man against woman, possibly the bloodiest upheaval in human evolution: unspeakable atrocities, rapes; but the men do not kill the women, they kill each other over women, the law still holds sway. In the Beyond, a regrouping takes place: the mild, munificent, protective mother goddess is dislodged by the bloodthirsty, voracious father-god, the god of the horde who begat the horde with the mother goddess, for he lies as a rain cloud over the earth as a man lies on top of a woman; and where once there was a sun goddess, now there is a sun god; only the earth and the moon are permitted to remain goddesses, the earth as mother of all things and the moon as midwife, their priestess subordinate to the priest of the male gods. The second hierarchic dynasty of gods has been created. The Beyond mirrors this world, and this world reflects the Beyond. Man rules over woman in the name of the father-god, the chief rules over the horde, and in the name of the father-god the law is extended: no human may kill another, the chief wishes to be safe. The horde becomes a tribe. The brain thinks up an epoch of human evolution. The earth is still virtually uninhabited by humans, but there is more than one tribe, there are several, separated by distances that seem as insurmountable as the distances between stars. But inevitably there comes a day when one tribe meets another and their hunting grounds touch. One tribe meets another tribe and is astonished that another tribe exists; and because this other tribe worships a father-god who is not identical with the one worshiped by the first tribe, the two tribes stand opposed to each other; and because each father-god rules over gods and goddesses, each divine dynasty stands opposed to the other as well; and because each tribe respects the commandment, "Thou shalt not kill," they are faced with a dilemma. Is it an absolute commandment or does it only apply to the tribe? At first the two tribes retreat, advance, hesitate, withdraw, but eventually they attack. The gods demand it. The commandment only applies to the tribe. But no matter who conquers in this first war between two tribes, which is carried out simultaneously in this world and the world beyond, the victor can exterminate or enslave the conquered tribe, but not its divine dynasty. The victor has to subordinate the conquered tribe's divine dynasty to the dynasty of his own gods, and subordinate the alien gods' priest and priestess to his own priest and priestess. The larger a tribe becomes by conquering other tribes and their gods and goddesses until it becomes a people, the more divinities have to be included and the larger the priesthood becomes. Where there once was a single tribal and father-god, the imagination has created a Beyond full of hierarchically ordered gods and goddesses, and human beings begin to devise various connections between the deities. At times these embody certain qualities, at others certain human activities. But not all divinities are friendly; the gods of a formerly conquered tribe especially are not to be trusted. The priests and priestesses become more and more important. They believe they can tell who among the gods is friendly, and which goddess loves men and which murders them, which god dispenses Good and which Evil, which one gives life and which one death. The friendly god must be thanked with a sacrifice of one's dearest possession, the first-born son, a lamb, a ewe; to the hostile god, one gives prisoners taken from an enemy tribe. One metaphysical notion follows another, but millenia still separate one notion from the next, prehistory is far from over, the border between this world and the world beyond is still vague. A stone erected by human effort and smeared with blood does not represent the god, it is the god. A stake driven into the ground and surrounded with flowers and fruits is not an emblem of a goddess, it is the goddess. The human builds walls around the stone and the stake, lays boards across the walls, the first temples are built, habitations for the gods, the human laboriously chips and chisels the stone, a tenuous semblance of a face appears in it, the human carves the stake until it vaguely resembles a woman, humanity creates the gods in its own image. The first city grows around the house of the gods, and with it the first city-king: where once the chief ruled as deputy of the old tribal god, who as father-god held dominion over all the other conquered gods and goddesses, the nucleus of a comet-like whirl of divinities, now the city-king becomes a mortal god: smeared with the blood of his enemies he sits on his throne, eyes glaring, with the skulls of his foes heaped around him. He has made provision, many servants stand ready to satisfy his wishes in the Beyond, and when he dies, hundreds are sacrificed to increase the host of souls who will attend to the city-king's soul. He who obeys this mortal god and fights for him, partakes of his divinity. Man, who no longer fears the animal, now no longer needs to fear death; if he is pious, he accepts death, and if he is a hero, he holds death in contempt. Instead of death he now fears the immortal gods and the mortal god. What he commands, the immortal gods command through their priests and priestesses in the name of the city-king, and whoever opposes him, opposes the divine commandments. The city-king depends on the priesthood and the priesthood depends on the city-king, and both build a bulwark against the Beyond, behind which lurk the gods and the ghosts, and behind those, the primordial fear of the void. More and more cities spring up, one after the other, each with its own city-king, the brain invents names, and along with names it has humans invent writing. The names are the ones that come wafting across the ages to us with such a strange, alien sound, names of cities like Ur, Uruk, Lagash, Elam, names of city-kings like Urukagina, Lugalzaggesi, Urnammu, Naramsuen, Utuchengal, Sumuabun, Hammurabi finally.* The brain has begun to think history. Since it is a human brain we have contrived, it will contrive the history of our world, as bloody as it is random, as reasonable or senseless, depending on the point of view, which will in any case be subjective. Naturally. The brain will play through every possibility in the course of the millenia that are at its disposal. A slave revolt prevents the building of the pyramids,

---

Ur, Uruk, Lagash, Elam: Ancient Middle Eastern cities. Urukagina, Lugalzaggesi, Urnammu, Naramsuen, Utuchengal, Sumuabun, and Hammurabi were ancient Middle Eastern rulers.

a Persian spear pierces Alexander at Issos, Hannibal destroys Rome, Mohammed II conquers Europe, Montezuma casts Cortez back into the sea, Luther founds the cult of Wotan, the Mongols conquer Ivan the Terrible, World War One and Two are fought out between China and the American Inca Empire, but gradually, after countless further variations, the brain constructs our history. Again Cheops, Chephren, and Mykerinos force their slaves to erect pyramids, again Xerxes sees his fleet sink at Salamis and the Emperor Shih Huang Ti orders the building of the Great Wall of China, 1,522 miles long, again Brutus draws his dagger and a rebellious Jew dies on the cross, again the Orient is devastated by the Christians, Hus burns at the stake, and the last Greek Emperor dies in a street battle against the Turks in Constantinople, again Columbus tries to reach India and Pizarro has the Inca Atahualpa garrotted, again the executioner of the Lord High Steward of Waldburg boasts of having cut off the heads of twelve hundred peasants,* again the murderer of Henry IV is torn apart by four horses, Wallenstein is murdered at Eger, Frederick the Great is forced to watch the execution of his friend,† again Danton and Robespierre place their necks under the guillotine, Napoleon dies on St. Helena, Karl Marx writes *Das Kapital*, Bismarck stylizes the Ems telegram,‡ Hitler's application to the Vienna Art Academy is rejected, Wilhelm II didn't want it to happen, Stalin has Trotzky murdered, bombs fall on Hiroshima and Nagasaki, the jungles of Vietnam are defoliated and students are crushed by tanks in Beijing in the name of a little old man, again there are five billion people 160 generations after Lugalzaggisi.§ The same empires will rise and fall again, the same hot and cold wars, the same catastrophes, earthquakes, exploding volcanoes, thunderous collisions of giant airplanes, sinking oil tankers, millions of traffic casualties, the same economic development with its inflations and crises, exploitations and expansions will take place, the same revolutions and rebellions will succeed and fizzle again, the same religions and ideologies will be preached, will prevail and be corrupted, the same Buddha, the same Paul, hostile to women, asexual, and abstract, the same Mohammed shaken by

---

*Lord High Steward: Count Ludwig von Helfenstein, killed in the Weinsberg Act of Blood in April 1525 during the German Peasants' Revolt.

† Frederick, when Crown Prince of Prussia, plotted to escape to England with his friend Hans Hermann von Katte. Both were tried for treason. Katte was executed on November 6, 1730, and Frederick I forced his son to watch the execution.

‡ In 1870 Bismarck altered a telegram from the Kaiser to Bismarck to create the impression that each side (France and Prussia) had insulted the other. The publication of the Ems telegram led to the Franco-Prussian War (1870–1871).

§Lugalzaggisi: King of Umma in Sumer.

visions on Mount Hira,* again Grünewald will nail a giant to a cross so that the crossbeam bends, Isaac Newton will calculate Abraham's year of birth, and Bach, condemned to piety, will father twenty children, again Kant, with his small head, precise as a clock, will complain about the convicts singing psalms behind his house, Goethe will consider his *Theory of Color* to be his principal work, and Büchner, forgetting his *Woyzeck* fragment, will dissect frogs and toads, again Balzac marries Madame von Hanska, again Stifter cuts his own throat, Keller becomes town scribe, Verlaine shoots at Rimbaud, Joyce tinkers at *Finnegans Wake* for fifteen years, Ödön von Horvath is struck by lightning on the Champs-Elysées, world history sweeps over *The Man without Qualities*, Grass writes his recipes, Frisch builds his public bath, and quite by accident, an irrelevant detail in the flood of ideas, a flicker of an afterthought to an afterthought, I too will occur to the brain. It will start by considering me in various different possibilities. As a seven- or eight-year-old I will not survive the collision with a motorcycle or die of polio, I will become a painter, or go to rot as a student, until the brain finds me writing *The Brain*. That of course brings it into conflict with itself and me with myself. Is *The Brain* my fiction which I am writing, or am I the brain's fiction that is writing *The Brain*? But if I am merely a fiction, then *The Brain* I am writing is also fictive, but so is the reader of *The Brain* and the critic who reviews *The Brain*. Who has invented whom, do I even exist, isn't there really just a brain that dreams up a world to fend off dread, a dreamed world in which a man writes for the same reason that a brain dreams him? But the brain, too, is faced with the same questions and antinomies. The same Either-Or. What is real? It, thinking up someone who writes what it thinks, or someone writing that it thinks it is thinking him? This someone, is he real, is everything thought by this brain real, but who am I then, thinks the brain that thought it was thinking this someone who is writing about it? Could it be that only he who is writing *The Brain* is real and everything he is writing about me and my thoughts (thinks the brain) are his thoughts? Am I merely a thought? And I who have written *The Brain* ask myself, if I am a thought of the brain and this thought is writing *The Brain*, are not all things thoughts—*The Brain*, the hand that is writing it, the body this hand is a part of, the head that is thinking up *The Brain*, the I finally, my I? Doesn't everything revert to the brain that thinks me as its thought, and doesn't the brain become identical with the dimensionless point within which not only all the energy and matter of the universe but also its time and space, and therefore the possibility

---

*The site of Mohammed's vision in which he was told by God to go forth and preach.

of life, are compressed? But whether the brain thinks me writing *The Brain*, or whether I write *The Brain* that thinks me, is one of those matters that are thinkable but not determinable. It is either possible or real, though it's not possible to determine whether it is possible or real. And so everything around me is possible or real, the pencil I am writing with, the paper I am covering with my handwriting, the table I am writing on, the books on the table, six dictionaries, a dictionary of foreign words, the *Brockhaus* book of grammar, an old *Dictionary of General World History* published in 1882, a French, an English, and two philosophical dictionaries, half filled blank books, containers with pencils, a scissors and ballpoint pens, a telephone, a clock which I always forget to wind, presents from C.: a large quartz stone, a small silver tiger on a stone from the Sinai, a crystal pyramid, furthermore an eraser, glue, and a pencil sharpener, finished and unfinished manuscripts, the desk lamp (which is on during the day as well), the large blotting paper with the coffee stains, and the other blotting paper, the place where I draw, the records, the can of Nescafé, the thermos bottle, the big desk which is always too small, regardless of whether it's real or possible, existent or imagined, and just as real or possible are the windows opposite my desk, with the terraced garden behind them, which is gradually getting overgrown, because there are trees and bushes on every terrace, a garden which nevertheless I have or could have expanded again and again, making it more and more tiring to climb or have to climb uphill to my studio, from which I can or might just barely make out the lake and the Lower Alps; all this, whether it is in fact real or imagined, is conceivable, just as the world which the Alps raised out of the Sea of Thetys millions of years ago is conceivable, a world that is possible even if it were merely conceived by a brain that I had contrived in place of the dimensionless point that exploded twenty billion years ago, a brain that could belong to a god with a beard or to a diabetic god without a beard who sleeps on a beach somewhere, dressed only in an old pair of tuxedo trousers, lying on a mattress with horsehair spilling out of it, his face covered with a sombrero, near the water, drenched, porn magazines, *Stiering's Hand Atlas of Parts of the Earth and the World Edifice*, published by Justus Perthes in 1890, *Meyer's Conversational Lexicon in 18 Volumes 1893–1898,* the Marquis de Sade's *Philosophy in the Bedroom,* countless telephone books, the third volume of Karl Barth's *Church Dogmatics:* "The Doctrine of Creation: Concerning Divine Government," stacks of stock market reports, *Der Spiegel,* the *Biblia Hebraica ad optimas editiones imprimis Everardi Van der Hooght,* more pamphlets and tomes, and mountains of unopened letters, they cover the whole beach, flooded again and again by the surf, and everywhere among them, sparkling, lie countless wristwatches and pocket watches made of tin, silver, gold, and platinum. But even if this world were dreamed up by the brain of this metaphysical balderdash-god, it is still our world, be it real or merely possible, for the foundation of its being as it is or as it could be, lies or would lie within us, regardless of whether we are real or imagined, it lies in our evolution, which made or would have made us aggressive, because we were afraid of the animals and of our own kind, we who huddled together and loved each other and hated those who crowded around the fire that warmed us, and envied those who came home from the hunt with prey while our stomachs were empty. In the millenia that prepared or would have prepared us, we were conditioned or would have been conditioned, and thus conditioned we entered or would have entered history, equipped with the most complex organism known to us, our brain, which is or would be capable of reasoning out the universe, even if we never come or came to the end of this reasoning, so that it's irrelevant whether the brain represents a fiction or a singularity, in either case it will imagine other brains and hence other people, in either case it will, on the one hand, undertake the fantastic voyage into the realm of reason, and on the other cling to irrational supports, religions, cults, superstitions. Without emotions, without love, without faith, but also without fear, hate, and envy, the human being cannot live, regardless of whether he is real or a figment in the brain of a god who, somewhere near the South Pole, whirls the cosmos around with a coffee grinder; unless reason finds or could find that miracle in the human brain that is the object of man's love and awe: a rational reality. All this is thinkable, be it real or be it possible. But can or could reason be capable of this? The road from Cracow, too, was real or possible. We are or would be driving as if through a blooming chestnut forest, a convent on a hill where the strictest observances are kept, thirty miles through a fruitful land. Cars queuing up at the gas stations. Then a long red brick building with a restaurant, in front of it a kiosk, buses, people, a holiday mood. A housing development with parallel rows of houses, also of red brick, one's first impression is or would be that this is a working class housing project, above the gate a cast iron legend espousing the liberating effects of labor: "Arbeit macht frei."* The project is or would be surrounded by a barbed wire fence that was or could have been charged with high voltage electricity, and watch towers stand or could stand around it at regular intervals. Inside the identical red brick houses, in identical halls that were or

---

*"Work liberates"—the cynical inscription above the entrance to the Auschwitz concentration camp placed there by Rudolf Hess.

would have once been dormitories, are mountains of spectacles, shoes, and clothes behind glass, a chaotic assortment of crutches and prostheses, a room full of suitcases with their owners' addresses, then a heap of children's shoes, an exhibition that could have been assembled by Beuys. Everywhere tourists and teachers with their school classes are or would be hurrying through the rooms, corridors, and cellars, all of them curious and strangely hasty, and in front of the project surrounding the kiosk, children with ice cream cones. Then we drive or would drive from Auschwitz to Birkenau, also known as Auschwitz II.* A long building with a watchtower in the middle and railroad tracks leading through it. To its left and right, endless, the barbed wire fence, also set up for a high voltage current, and one watchtower after another, still intact, but fearsomely skeletal, ghostly wooden constructions. Behind the open gate for the train, the tracks divide. One pair of tracks turns to the right, the two others run parallel toward the back. We drive through an auxiliary gate, green meadows, tallish grass, far off in the back a leafy wood, on our right some barracks, evidently renovated. We reach a body of water and can drive no further. There is something eerie about this water. We walk across a narrow bridge. Through a meadow we reach a broad, paved square with a flight of low steps leading up to a ponderous abstract monument with a Polish inscription, which our guide translates for us. The inscription avoids mention of the essential thing that happened here. It also diminishes the horror exuded by the ruins on either side of the square, the ruins of the gas chambers and crematoriums to which the tracks lead. There are places where art has no business. We go to one of the ruins. A warning: danger of collapse. We look down into a long deep trench. We wander back toward the distant railway entrance on a road that is straight as a ruler. With the monument behind us, horror sets in again. Dark barracks right and left, barbed wire fences. More barbed wire strung from post to post on the endless plane to our left, taller than a man's height, each wire ending in a white porcelain insulator and leading on to the next post with its insulators. Behind that, a forest of red brick structures like cenotaphs of some alien religion, the chimneys of barracks that have long since decayed. Flowers are growing on both sides of the tracks. The landscape of death is green. This place was not contrived or dreamed up by my assumed brain, not by the brain of the god with beard

---

*The Nazi extermination camp known generally as Auschwitz (Auschwitz-Birkenau), located in Poland, was in fact three camps. Auschwitz I and Auschwitz II were extermination camps (the former mainly for Slavs, the latter for Jews), while Auschwitz III was a labor camp mainly for IG Farben workers.

nor that of the god without one, who lies on a bed in Jamaica dressed in a bathrobe listening to Gabriel's clattering typewriter, to the sound of the rain and the shuffling and sliding of palm leaves, nor did I think or dream it up. It is unthinkable, and what is unthinkable is also not possible, because it makes no sense. It's as if the place had conceived of itself. It just is. Meaningless, bottomless, incomprehensible as reality itself.

Vinter

Vinter had arrived in his country's capital. He was wanted all over the world. Everywhere rewards had been offered. He had only accepted the assignment because it was to be carried out in his own country. Perhaps it was a trap. But he wanted to go home and then give up his profession. The sum he had received for the assignment was a fantastic amount, an advance of a million was lying in a safe deposit box at the central train station. Afterward he wanted to drive inland, to a small village in the North. What he was planning to do was, for him, a business arrangement, and he had no idea what other purpose it served. All he knew was that in a shabby hotel in Cairo, a short, meticulously dressed man with a well-tended white goatee had given him the assignment along with a million in cash, and that this old man, who had addressed him in his native language and had looked strangely familiar to him, must have gotten his address from the Organization. But since he didn't know how the Organization had learned his address, and since the assignment could only be carried out if he became active again, it could also mean that the Organization had dropped him; in which case he was as good as dead. Nevertheless he had taken the trip. He had gotten himself a new false passport and had his face reconstructed, but he had barely set foot in Rome when he saw his face staring at him from an advertising pillar. But the passport control at the airport in his country's capital had been lax. He had counted on that. He needed two days to test the ground. He set out in the early evening. His raincoat was damp from the fog. He stopped on a bridge. He waited. The prime minister and a woman approached him. When they reached him, the prime minister lit a pipe. Vinter pulled a gun from his coat pocket and fired. Once. Vinter always fired one shot only. The woman screamed. The prime minister collapsed. Vinter fled across the bridge and past some people who were rushing toward him. After the bridge he ran across another bridge, then another one. He reached a square. A white palace loomed up between trees, surrounded by a three-foot wall with a thuja hedge behind it.* Vinter jumped over the wall and through the hedge and dropped face down on a gravel path. He remained lying there. People were running alongside the wall on the square. Shouts. Then the approaching howls of police sirens. A car stopped on the other side of the hedge. He heard a command: "Cordon off the square." He fell asleep. When he woke up later, he was still lying on the gravel path. The sun was burning down on him. He pushed himself up against the hedge. Behind him he could hear children screaming. A red ball flew over the hedge, rolled up next to him. He rolled the ball back onto the gravel path. A boy pushed through the hedge, took the ball, jumped back through the hedge. Something touched him. He carefully turned his head, stared at a fat rat that was staring at him. The rat scurried away. He looked around. Five steps away was the main entrance of the palace, with a stairway leading up to it. Across from the steps, the hedge was interrupted by a tall iron gate. It was obvious that the square with the trees had once been part of the palace grounds. Above him he saw a barred window. Again the red ball flew over the hedge. He ran in a stooped position along the hedge and around the corner of the palace. He threw himself onto the gravel path again. On this side, too, the palace bordered on the square, with only a thuja hedge between them. He was lying next to a basement window with a broken pane. He reached in, felt something furry slipping away. The fat rat. He managed to unlatch the window. It opened toward the inside. He squeezed his body through the frame, and as he lowered himself, feet first, the rat climbed up inside one of his trouser legs. After reaching the floor, he shook off the rat. Others attacked him. The basement was full of rats, he could see them in the light that fell through the window. He dealt out kicks. Boxes were piled up alongside the walls. They had burst, bunches of wood shavings stuck out between the slats. Slabs of ham and bacon hung from the ceiling, swinging back and forth, rats crawling all over them. Rats were squeaking inside the boxes too. Despite his kicks, they kept attacking him. He was bitten as he tore a slat out of a box. He used it to flail at the rats. He discovered an iron door in the background. He managed to open it, slammed it shut behind him. A rat was still clinging to him, its teeth sunk into his neck. Struggling, he managed to tear it loose and kicked it to death. It was as big as a cat. He was bleeding. He hurried through a corridor past iron doors, climbed a flight of stairs. A heavy oak door. Unlocked. He came to a modern kitchen, from the kitchen to a dining room, he wanted to go

*Thuja is a coniferous shrub.

back to the kitchen, arrived at a vestibule. Pictures everywhere. Matisse, Picasso, Braque. Through a large glass door he looked down a flight of steps at the closed door of the house. He walked through the vestibule past several glass doors, behind which lay a large drawing room. He went up a broad stairway. At the top was a gallery. He walked past a door and opened a second one. It was a bedroom with tall windows, through which he saw a lawn. A door on the right led into the bathroom. Towels and washcloths were lying about everywhere. He tossed away his raincoat, tore off his clothes. He washed, lay down naked on the broad bed, and went to sleep. He felt a sting. Someone was washing him. Someone was bandaging him. He slept. The little man with the white goatee from Cairo looked at him. The other two million, he said, putting two black attaché cases next to the bed. You have a fever, he added. The rats, Vinter replied, finding it difficult to talk. Again he felt a sting, and went to sleep. Someone was washing him again. Someone was feeding him some liquid. He fell asleep again. A rat ran across his chest. He wanted to scream. Woke up. Found himself lying in a silk pajama under a blanket. The door opened. A large muscular man came in, looking like a bodyguard in an old movie. He was carrying a tray with coffee, a poached egg, toast, butter, marmalade, ham, and croissants. The man swung a tray across the bed, filled the cup with coffee and cream, and introduced himself as Jean, the new butler, adding that he had always served in the very best houses. Vinter looked at his right hand. It was carefully bandaged, but his fingers were uncovered. He touched his neck. Another bandage. He asked who had bandaged him. We were concerned, the butler replied. Vinter drank. The rats, he said. The butler nodded. They're from the canal, he said. Vinter took a slice of toast and ate the poached egg. The butler waited. Then he cleared the table and left. Vinter left the bed. He felt refreshed. He opened the balcony door, looked down on a park. A lawn, flower beds, old trees, a garden house. He showered and shaved. His raincoat and his clothes were gone. Lots of suits in the bedroom's built-in closets. He was used to being neatly dressed. He put on some clothes. White suit, black shirt. Everything fit perfectly, as if tailored to his proportions. He took the two attaché cases that stood by the bedroom wall. He hadn't been dreaming. He went down the stairs. The doors to the drawing room were wide open. A concert piano, settees, armchairs, gaming tables, love seats, a door leading out to the lawn. He opened a door: the dining room. He opened the door opposite the dining room. A library. It was a spacious room, the walls lined with books from floor to ceiling, and more books filling the spaces above and below the large window looking out on the lawn. A fireplace set into the wall opposite the window, in front of the fireplace a leather couch, leather armchairs on either side of the fireplace. In front of the window a large old desk. On top of the desk, his passport, his briefcase, and the key to the safe deposit box. He took all these things. He left the palace with the two attaché cases. He scanned the length of the thuja hedge. On the path, on the spot where he had lain, a rat sat hunched on the gravel. Then it disappeared around the corner. He went to the cast iron garden gate and opened it. An iron grating had been added to the wall, higher than the hedge. He walked across the square with the trees toward the street. Some boys were playing soccer. On the street, cars passed him on their way from the bridge to the old town and from the old town to the bridge. In the middle of the street, a policeman was regulating traffic. He waited until a gap opened in the queue of cars and approached the policeman. A car braked abruptly. The policeman blew his whistle. He stepped up to him. Arrest me. I shot the prime minister. You want me to arrest you? The policeman laughed. And who's going to regulate traffic? The police station is on Jensen Street. Confess your murder to them. It'll make them happy. The station was in a rickety two-story building that interrupted the five-story buildings of Jensen Street with their luxury stores. As he walked in, a man with a bandaged head staggered past him onto the street. The room was divided in two by a barrier. To the left of the entrance stood a bench alongside the wall, and on the bench sat two prostitutes. On the wall, Vinter's portrait, and beneath it: "Reward: Ten Thousand." Above a door with a stained glass window hung the portrait of the king. In the background sat a sweating policeman with a coarse peasant's face, operating an old typewriter with two fingers. A brightly lit bulb with a shade was suspended from the ceiling by a long string. The room had only one window, which was situated next to the entrance and was open, but barred. The heat in the room was unbearable. Finally the policeman looked up at Vinter with a questioning look. Vinter said: I shot Prime Minister Erikson. The policeman did not understand: What did you do? The prime minister. I shot him. The policeman stared at him, ran his fingers through his blond hair. The prime minister—You . . . , he stammered, leapt to his feet, left the room through the door with the stained glass window. He was alone in the room with the two prostitutes, who were staring into space. The policeman returned, summoned him with his hand, opened the barrier and led him through the door with the stained glass window into another room. Air-conditioned, spick-and-span, high tech, full of gadgets, telephones, monitors, computers. On a black bulletin board, his portrait again, "Reward: Ten Thousand." Behind a desk sat an elderly policeman. He was not in uniform, but you could tell he was with the police. He had a broad, wrinkled face with a bulbous nose. What can I do for you, Prince Frobenius? he asked.

I am not Prince Frobenius, Vinter replied. The man behind the desk leaned back, played with his ballpoint pen: You're not? So who are you? Vinter pointed at his portrait: Him. The man behind the desk looked at the picture. The prime minister's widow identified him, he said. But you don't look like him at all. My passport, Vinter said, handing him the document across the table. It's fake. Made out to the name of Anderson. The man behind the desk leafed through the passport. It's genuine, he said, made out to the name Sven, Prince Frobenius, and gave him back the passport. Vinter put the two attaché cases on the desk and opened them. The cases were full of bills: The reward for assassinating the prime minister, he said. Two million. I killed him. He put the key to the safe deposit box on the desk: There's another million in the safe deposit box. My advance. The man behind the desk said: You are wounded. A rat, Vinter said. I know, a rat. It bit you in the neck. I am Chief Detective Axel. The butler called for me. He was afraid you might have been attacked. Five days ago. And you claim that on the previous night, you murdered the prime minister? the Chief detective asked, laying his ballpoint pen on the desk. Five days ago, Vinter said. Rat bites are dangerous, the Chief Detective nodded. It took us a whole morning to exterminate the rats. And you missed the prime minister's state funeral, too. Take back your two million, Prince Frobenius. Give them away, Vinter said. He left. The sweating policeman was still sitting behind his typewriter, the two prostitutes were still there, too. He stepped out onto Jensen Street. He walked through the city. Across the bridges, the squares, to the house of parliament, the shopping centers, the side streets, past the docks in the harbor, the workers' domiciles, the fashionable villas. He walked and walked. His portrait hung everywhere, "Reward: Ten Thousand." He stopped next to his picture on an advertising pillar. Men passed him, women. Some of them stopped. Looked at him, looked at the picture, at him again, and walked on. The fog returned. When darkness fell, he entered the palace. He heard the squeaking of rats coming up from the cellar. The drawing room was lit. A man in a dark blue suit was playing the grand piano. His shirt, too, was dark blue, and so was the scarf around his neck. He was darkly tanned, his face was long and bony. He shut the piano, looked at Vinter, and said he was the minister of the interior, Lindgren. Vinter said he was Vinter and had killed the prime minister. The minister of the interior replied that he knew that. You created quite a mess, Vinter, with your confession on Jensen Street. You almost got arrested. Fortunately the police were able to think on their feet. He pointed at three attaché cases standing by the wall, the promised amount. He had taken the liberty, he said, of sending a man to fetch Vinter's advance from the safe deposit box. But now I could use some coffee and a cognac, he said. They went to the library, sat down in the leather armchairs. A rat crossed the room, disappeared in the fireplace. The butler came, poured their drinks. One of my men, said the minister of the interior. What's the meaning of this game, asked Vinter. Everywhere I look I see my picture with a reward of ten thousand. True enough, the Minister of the Interior conceded. Your picture is posted everywhere. The people should know that you killed the prime minister, Vinter. After all, the people paid for it. The minister of the interior swirled the cognac in his glass. Man needs faith. Marxism was a faith in a more reasonable world order, it failed because of its own contradictions, a more reasonable world order calls for more reasonable people, and since man is unreasonable, the Marxist world order can only be introduced by force, which makes it unnatural, but since an unnatural world order is more unreasonable than a natural one, it stands to reason that the natural order will prevail over the rational one. In the natural world order, the more corrupt individuals are less conspicuous, they are in a sense more natural than those who are less corrupt. The minister of the interior began to orate, he was a parliamentarian. The natural philosophy of life lacks only one thing: one doesn't have to believe in it, it furnishes its own proof, just by being natural and therefore in keeping with human nature. But since man wants to be more than nature and since he can no longer trust his reason, due to the fact that the reasonable worldview has become the unreasonable one, Man becomes irrational, a prey to every emotion. He believes in Islam in the Islamic world, and in Christianity in the Christian world. The world has become conservative, if you're not a fundamentalist you wear your Christianity like a pinstripe suit, and so there is not a politician of the left or the right who does not avow his faith in Christianity. Our prime minister alone made the stupid mistake of declaring himself an atheist, said the minister of the interior, concluding his argument. It was for this, he said, that he was sentenced to death. All you did, Vinter, was carry out the sentence. He drank. Astonished, Vinter stared at the minister of the interior. Who passed the sentence? he asked. The people, declared the minister of the interior. A small northern sect decided to have the atheistic prime minister killed by you. A sect from the little village where you're planning to go to withdraw from the world. You are particularly popular there. What about the little old man with the goatee who brought me the assignment and the money? Vinter asked. The founder of the sect. The village pastor, replied the minister of the interior. Vinter rubbed his forehead. That's why he looked so familiar, Vinter said. He gave me my confirmation. The sect wanted to prove its Christian faith, the minister of the interior continued. They knew you were expensive. The sect started a collection. Three million for you, Vinter. I'm impressed. The minister of the interior poured himself another cognac and watched as another rat crossed the room and disappeared in the fireplace. We should light a fire in the fireplace, the Minister of the Interior said. There's just one thing I don't understand, he added, why did you want to return the three million? Out of pride, Vinter replied. He had fled into this villa full of rats, he said. But when he had regained consciousness, dressed in pajamas and bandaged, when the butler served him breakfast and he found the two attaché cases containing the rest of his payment, he realized he had walked into a trap. His professional honor could not accept this. His profession demanded absolute perfection. No fuzzy emotions. His desire to go home had prevented him from looking into the background of his assignment, he said. There was only one way to respond to such sloppiness: throw in the towel and turn yourself in. Nonsense, replied the minister of the interior. Vinter's assignment had been to kill Erikson for three million, and that's what he had done, business is business. The fact that the police commissioner had done his part in choosing the location for the assassination and preparing the palace as a possible hiding place was another matter, and besides that was his, the minister of the interior's, business. Why don't you have me arrested, Vinter asked, I beg you. My job is to arrest Vinter, not you, replied the minister of the interior. You are Prince Frobenius, take a look at your passport. Somebody forged it, Vinter interjected. It was already forged, the minister of the interior said. I'm in your power, Vinter concluded. You will have to put up with that, replied the minister of the interior, drained his cognac and stood up. Before you start practicing your new identity, the minister said, you will have to fulfill a promise I gave to Erikson's mother. She wants to speak to you. The minister of the interior left. By the edge of the street in front of the square with the trees a Rolls-Royce was waiting. Inspector Axel sat at the wheel. Dense white fog over the canal, brilliantly lit by a nearly full moon. The butler opened the back door of the car. Through the glass panel, Vinter could only see the driver's shoulders and the back of his head. The Rolls-Royce drove over bridges and squares, left the city, raced along a highway, crossed another long bridge, soundless, as if gliding along, veered into a forest, made another turn, drove uphill on a narrow road with many curves, stopped in front of a gate, which opened, drove through, a yard lit by moonlight, with trees and bushes, stopped in front of an old house covered with ivy. In the door stood a tall slender person whom he could only see as a silhouette. The figure beckoned him. He crossed a hall with ancient precious furniture, followed the tall, slender, old person up a stairway, and entered a bedroom that was lit only by a bed lamp. In a bed lay an old woman, almost hairless, small, girlish. The tall person announced him as Prince Frobenius. I am blind, said the old woman. Lina, leave, she commanded with a loud voice. The person left the room. Has she gone? the old woman asked. She's gone, Vinter said. She doesn't hear well, the old woman said. You are not Prince Frobenius, she declared then. I am not Prince Frobenius, he replied. You are the murderer of my son. I am the murderer of your son, Vinter said. Sit down. Close to me, give me your hand. He sat down next to her and took her hand. It was like a girl's hand. My son was a good person. I'm sure, he said. He only wanted the best. All politicians want that, he said. But he didn't believe in God. I don't either, he said. Why did you kill him? For three million, he said. The old woman lay there, her little face was as white as the pillow and the bedcover, the lace-trimmed nightgown, and the childish little hand in his hand. She kept her eyes shut. Money from the collection? From the collection, he said. I contributed too, she said. He looked at her hand in his hand and said nothing. It happened in God's name, she said. Go now. The Rolls-Royce drove down the hill and into the forest, reached the long bridge and with it the fog, white in the light of the no longer visible moon. The Rolls-Royce stopped. He crossed the square and approached the lighted palace. The butler was expecting him. He ate little and asked for his wine to be served in the library. The butler withdrew. He sat by the fireplace, stared at the burning logs. No more rats came. There were just some scrabbling sounds behind the books. A volume fell down. He finished the wine, went to bed. Fell asleep, dreamed, or took it for a dream. A woman had come to him. He felt her body against his in the dark, felt it through his sleep, without waking up. While he was still dreaming that they were making love, they made love, dream and reality and reality and dream intermingled, and he was unable to tell the difference between what was real and what he was dreaming, but when the woman cried out, he suddenly knew who he was making love to. He pressed down hard and squeezed. He turned on the light, jumped out of the bed, looked. A rat came scurrying along, climbed up the sheet, fell back. He got dressed, went to the library. A log was still burning in the fireplace. Several volumes had dropped to the floor. He sat down in a leather armchair. Smoked. The fire in the fireplace went out. More and more rats were flitting about. Day was breaking in the window. The butler came. The fire went out, Vinter said. The butler added new logs, set a fire, the rats were unconcerned. Go to the bedroom, Vinter said, and call the minister of the interior. The butler left. He waited. Rats ran across his shoes, sat on the backrest of the leather couch. It was bright daylight when the minister of the interior came and the butler chased out the rats. He sat down in the armchair facing Vinter. I was in the bedroom, he said. A beautiful woman. The prime minister's widow. I know, Vinter replied. A book tumbled off a shelf. It's the rats again, the minister said. There must be whole nests of them behind the book cases, Vinter said. Why did you kill her? the minister of the interior asked. Another rat climbed onto the back of the couch between them. Out of horror, Vinter said. Who let the woman into the house? Axel, the minister of the interior said. He thought she wanted to kill you. Would that have been a solution? Vinter asked. No, I fired Axel, said the minister of the interior, and rang for the butler. The rats are getting out of hand, he said. It's hopeless, the butler said, I'm afraid to go to the basement. And there've already been several in the bedroom. And the corpse? asked the minister. We secured it just in time, said the butler. I need another cognac, said the minister. The butler poured him a drink. The minister took a sip, said: another one, and then, after the butler had left, he gazed into his glass, swirling the cognac, and said: out of horror. Have you killed many people? he asked then. Many, Vinter replied. Two rats were licking each other on the armrest of the couch. Did you always kill with a feeling of horror? the minister asked. No, this was the first time, said Vinter. The others were executions, this was a murder. I demand to be arrested and sentenced. When? Now. If I arrest you now, the scandal will sweep away the government and make the people look like fools, said the minister. Be patient. You'll get your trial eventually, he continued, observing the rats with disgust. As Prince Frobenius, the man who murdered the prime minister. Once the people are ashamed of the assignment for which they raised the money. When they want a different killer. At that point, Prince Frobenius will be right up their alley. But for now, it's Vinter who will have to be considered the murderer, even though Vinter no longer exists. As for Erikson's wife, we'll put her body in her house and make it appear like a suicide. Hard to make that credible, Vinter objected. Let that be my concern, replied the minister of the interior. For the time being, go on living as Prince Frobenius. Until your trial. But even then people won't believe that you're not Prince Frobenius. You're to maintain that identity until your execution. Do not leave the country. In your own interest. I have come to terms with the Organization. Vinter was surprised. You got in touch with them? They got in touch with me, the minister corrected him. The Organization knows everything. I'm staying, said Vinter, I will wait for the trial, it's my right. And then, suddenly, he asked suspiciously who was the real Prince Frobenius: does such a person exist in reality? The minister of the interior looked at him thoughtfully. No one knows, he said, he disappeared. Long ago. Then the minister laughed: but now he's back! The minister stood up. Vinter accompanied the minister to the garden gate. Rats followed them. I'll call the Board of Health, the minister promised as he stepped out onto the square. As if the rats had understood him, they sped like arrows along the gravel path and disappeared around the corner. The exterminators worked for three days. They used poison gas, too. Then the palace was free of rats. Vinter lived as Prince Frobenius. He was invited and invited others. Society treated him with great respect. No one questioned him. Sometimes women visited him at night. More and more. Then he had his palace locked up at night. He no longer went out into society, and society left him in peace. The king wanted to speak to him. He met the king on the lawn as he was trimming his roses. The king was a tall haggard old bespectacled man who didn't look at him. I, too, made a contribution, the king said, occupied with his roses. Do you believe Vinter is the killer? Vinter is dead, Your Majesty. If you say so, I suppose you may be right, Prince Frobenius, replied the king, and went to the next rose tree without so much as glancing at Vinter. That same evening he arranged to have himself brought to the blind old woman and took her hand. I am awaiting my trial, he said. I am expecting my death, she said. Then we're expecting the same thing. At first she did not reply. Then she shook her head almost imperceptibly. Oh no, she said. Your trial will not take place. He dismissed the butler, locked up the palace, shut the windows, lay down in his bed. A rat slipped out of the closet. He waited. For the trial. When the real Prince Frobenius returned many years later, he found a skeleton in his bedroom. The policeman who came in response to his call found a passport under a heap of chewed up clothes. The policeman informed the police inspector, who in turn informed the minister of the interior. The minister of the interior asked his predecessor, who in turn asked *his* predecessor. The predecessor's predecessor said that his predecessor had unfortunately died. The minister of the interior had himself announced. Prince Frobenius received him in the library. The subject whose skeleton was found in Your Excellence's bed, said the minister, used a forged passport to pass himself off as Prince Frobenius. As your Excellence will have noticed, his passport photo does bear a certain resemblance. The police allowed themselves to be deceived. As minister of the interior I can do no more than express my regret, especially since there are grounds to suspect that the false Prince Frobenius was the murderer of Prime Minister Erikson, who was shot many years ago. Here, too, the police looked in the wrong direction.

The Traveler's Standpoint

And so I feel like a man who left his house going East and, stubbornly hold-ing to his direction, using every conceivable means of transportation, sud-denly finds himself approaching his house again from the West. Having left through the front door, he now finds himself at the back door faced with all those half-baked, barely begun or abandoned fragments, mere thoughts in some cases, which he tossed out the back door, thinking he would get rid of them that way: And now, if the traveler wants to complete his journey, he must clear a path into his house through all this rubbish. [. . .]

But if someone should ask me what is the point of this journey, my answer is: "The point is to travel"; and if he asks: "What is your standpoint?" I reply: "It is a traveler's standpoint." If, unrelenting, he asks: "I want to know where you stand politically," I reply: "That depends on where I happen to be. If I find myself in the Soviet Union I'm an anticommunist, if I should ever wind up in India or Chile, I'd be a communist, and so on. I'm opposed to the United States, but there are cases where I'm glad the United States exists, the case of Israel, for instance, even though I would be even happier if Israel did not need the United States"; and if he gets even more curious and asks: "Won't you at least tell me where you come from philosophically," I reply: "You guessed rightly, I started out from Kierkegaard and Kant, from what little I understood of their thought, though I'm not sure I understood any of it, which is why I don't know what regions my journey takes me through, except that it always takes me back"; and if he says: "Then why travel at all, it doesn't make sense," I reply: "That's why I tell stories"; and if he then reproaches me, saying: "But you just came back from a journey," I say: "That too was just one of my stories"; and if finally he gets impatient, seizes me by my lapels and asks: "So what is your faith?" I reply: "Among anti-Semites I am a Jew, among anti-Christians a Christian, among anti-Marxists a Marxist, among Marxists an anti-Marxist." If he then asks: "And when you're alone?" I reply: "I can't tell you. For what I believe depends on the moment. There are moments when I am able to believe, and there are moments when I am compelled to doubt. The worst thing, I believe, is wanting to believe whatever it is one wants to believe, be it Christianity or some ideology. Because a person who wants to believe has to suppress his doubts, and whoever suppresses his doubts has to lie to himself. And only he who does not suppress his doubts is able to doubt himself without despairing, for a person who wants to believe will despair when he is suddenly unable to believe. But he who doubts himself without despairing may be on the way to faith. Perhaps without ever getting there. But what sort of faith it is that such a person is walking toward—that is his own business. It is his secret, which he takes with him, for every profession of faith is impossible to prove, and what cannot be proved should be kept to oneself. Excuse me, I have to move on." "Wait!" he calls after me as I step out the front door. "What more do you want?" I reply, already leaving him behind. "You're confusing me!" he shouts. "You're confusing me, too," I reply, "you and your questions." "I have a right to ask questions," he yells after me, "I am your reader!" I stop: "That's not my fault," and then I walk on. "I bought your book!" he shouts, a mere silhouette in the front door if I were to look back, and because I don't turn back, he yells: "I could have seen five movies instead!" I look at the gathering dusk before me, at the steadily darkening strata advancing in my direction: "Next time go and see five movies." "Are you a Protestant?" His cry is just barely audible. "That's all I've done all my life, protest." His voice sounds clearer, he must have run after me: "Do you believe in anything at all?" I can hear him panting. "Are you starting again?" I ask in return, and keep walking: "I am allergic to this word, 'believe.'" "Give me another word," he begs, dropping back again. "Making sense," I say. "What makes sense to you?" he calls after me. "Lots of things," I reply, "the accuracy of mathematics or the possibility of metaphors." "Does God make sense to you?" he shouts from some place between me and the door from which I departed. "He didn't grant me the vision to make sense of him," I reply, striding into the steadily mounting, tremendous darkness. "So you don't believe in God," he shouts, "I finally pinned you down!" "Why do you have to get so damned theological," I yell, just before finally escaping into the night, always straight ahead, obstinately. "You're off on another journey!" I think I hear him shouting these words after me, mockingly, with all his might, even though by now he has lost sight of me, and I reply, though it is unlikely that he can still understand me through the infinite blackness between him and myself, between one human being and another, while I, in the vagueness, the vastness, begin to discern the first unearthly glimmer of light, a presage of the goal I am striving toward, my point of departure, which I left just a moment ago, the back door with the rubbish in front of it, and finally the questioner's back, visible through the front door where he stands in the night in which he hopes to espy me, in vain, since the nearer I come to him the further I depart from him: "All I did was tell another story." And as I walk on, further and further, someone suddenly asks, someone next to me, someone I have always passed by on my wanderings and always wanted to talk to, an actor: "Fine, but how should the whole thing be performed?" And I, already being swallowed by the night as it has swallowed my characters, Doc, Ann, Bill, Boss, Cop, Smithy, Oedipus, Tiresias, the Pythia, each and every one of them, reply: "With humor!"*

*Translator's note: The phrase "my characters" in the last sentence is my interpolation. Without it, the list of names would not make sense (since this piece is taken out of its context).